Quotes from readers:

You have beautifully described my family and the Indian ways of living…There are many things, which are really educational, especially when you compare various traditions and customs….You <u>must</u> publish it for the benefit of East and West and for the sake of the confluence of these two cultures, and for the betterment of this planet.
Prof. Budhi Godwal, BARC Bombay

This is not a travel report in the usual sense, but written with esprit, depth, a shot of poetry, philosophy and gaiety (serenity). How you describe the influence of different cultures on your soul, demonstrates not only high sensibility, but also openness and curiosity towards other peoples and cultures.
Prof. Bilal, Berlin

I really appreciate your excellent writing and your deep understanding of the Greek "psyche", that is, the essence of the Greek character. That is the proof for me to study deeper your reports on other cultures…
Prof. Gerasimos Kourouklis, Aristotle University, Thessaloniki

There is a brilliant idea of hope in the book…The idea states that happiness does not only refer to a state of feeling peace and light permanently, but also requires you to pass through difficulties and happenings…After reading the chapter (6) my faith and hope in human beings increased. The reading does not leave you indifferent.
Prof. Fernando Rodriguez, University of Cantabria, Santander, Spain

You have described your impression of Turkey and the life in Turkey…You noticed very small details, which often go unnoticed. Thank you for writing this script.
Prof. Kerim Allakhverdiev, Istanbul-Gebze

I oftentimes got so absorbed in reading your script that I forgot my editing job…
Ana Rocca, editor and student of University of Chicago

Your book should not end with the last page…
Kiran Doshi, former Ambassador of Austria and Superintendent of Atomic Energy Schools in India

Fascinating to read…
Dr. Jack E. Pendar, Superintendent, Colorado

EURINDIA

EURINDIA

✦

Inner Landscapes of a Traveling Teacher

*LiteraryTravelreport.rainbow.germany.greece.
turkey.india.italy.spain*

*Renate Hochheimer
with artwork by rainbow and poetry
by potawi*

iUniverse, Inc.
New York Lincoln Shanghai

EURINDIA
Inner Landscapes of a Traveling Teacher

iUniverse, Inc.

For information address:
iUniverse, Inc.
2021 Pine Lake Road, Suite 100
Lincoln, NE 68512
www.iuniverse.com

ISBN: 0-595-29194-5 (pbk)
ISBN: 0-595-75098-2 (cloth)

Printed in the United States of America

Contents

Part I   *Germany* *1*

Part II   *Greece, Turkey* *55*

Part III *India* *99*

Part IV *Alzheimer's, Italy* *171*

Part V   *Spain* *215*

Part VI *Alzheimer's, Germany, Homecoming* *367*

PART I
Germany

Dear Reader:

My editor asked me to create a stronger hook. So, I will reel out the line and explain some things in retrospect to get you hooked. Would I do it again: Travel through six cultures and countries in one year? Sleep in over twenty-six beds? Get seasick, stomach-sick, homesick, sick of my manuscript, sick of sightseeing?

You bet I would, because I am an adventurer and a Ambassador for Peace and Cultural Understanding, a title I have earned according to my "foreign" brothers and sisters. I did not want to create a regular travel book. I wanted to give birth to myself as a writer. And that's how the first chapter starts: with a birthing process, gently and slowly.

The birth of EURINDIA, the peace dove, who flies around the world, making connections and deep learning experiences: Learning to love and appreciate other peoples and cultures. POTAWI, "She Who Flies With Power", an Indian name she once received in a spirit quest in the hills of Santa Fe, jets to EURope and INDIA (=EUR-INDIA!) and back and forth to Germany to look after her family again and again.
It is not the outer journey, which sets this book apart from others. It is the inner journey, which will grip your heart and attention. So, let's start with the birthing process, together:

P.S.: The added STUDENT ACTIVITIES, which start appearing on p. 128 are examples that almost every chapter lends itself to a multicultural lesson, when "didak-tisiert" by an enthusiastic teacher. The book would have doubled in volume, had I consquently followed through with the student activities. I leave it up to my intelligent colleagues to invent their own questions and to create their own focus.

Birth of Eurindia

Permanent vacationing...Stillness...The old ways...Birth...

Vacationing, **permanent vacationing** ain't easy. Sometimes, I get homesick for my Baby son, sometimes for my workplace: for something real to do, something with a purpose, a calling, a challenge, and hopefully something useful and progressive.

Vacationing is a challenge; in that I need to set my own agenda everyday, my own learning program. I called Language schools, today. There is no need for a teacher for such a short time. Retirement will be a problem. I need to look for new avenues, when the time comes.

Am I looking for stress? Aye? Do I need that stress hormone that made my heart go backwards? NO, not really, I just need to settle in, relax more, live in the moment, and see the beauty and purpose in everything.

Being in **stillness** is a challenge. That's when you hear your insides the most. What is it that I really need out of life?

A colleague said at his retirement ceremony, "You'll find yourself, this year." But before I can find myself, I need to get lost, thoroughly...I need to lose myself. No, I am not ungrateful...who in the world gets a chance to travel through six languages and cultures in one year?! I just need to get out of my own way and enjoy.

What has been my way, so far? Goal setting, **set** goals, efficiency, no detours, results, schedules, more work in shorter time, time...not even any time for my dearest fellow-human-beings on some days. Roller coaster rides, frustrations, teaching against the grain, unwilling, unprepared students...on some days sun breaks through the clouds, satisfaction, great satisfaction, when a student's light goes on. On other days...deep darkness...where is my one, two, three, four-year harvest? Have I ever taught them anything? And another breakthrough: They start discussing in German with each other...it sounds native...it sounds real.

I pat myself on the back invisibly…**master teacher** that's who I wish to be. Is it that hard to keep them steady and motivated in their performance? It must be! There is no energy left on some days. I come home like a shriveled balloon where the air has evaporated through tiny pores of frustration.

Writing keeps me in balance—and art and music. I need to write everyday from now on! **EURINDIA,** Travel experiences of a frustrated US teacher, no, change that into: **Inner landscapes of a travelling teacher!** That's going to be the title of my private book, which I may share with some close friends and family. Eurindia, because I will travel to countries in Europe and India.

I will not write what you can read in any travel guide, not an abstract about anything, because I am not abstract, I am very real. I will take you to the mountains and valleys of my emotional landscapes during my one-year-travels through Germany, Greece, Turkey, India, Italy and Spain.

So, this script is born out of necessity:
>To generate a job for myself
>To keep myself happy
>To earn travel credits from the Colorado Department of Education (CDE)
>To make some friends happy, when I share
>To write an auto-biographical sketch for my grandkids
>To create a storybook for my students back home for a twenty-minute
Friday bonus
>To lay the foundation for a new multi-cultural course design

I will not use real names in this literary travel report, only nicknames. Although the places, dates and happenings are authentic, sometimes the narrative is arranged to accommodate the story line.

27. Juni

In my beloved Biotope

Energy conservation...Water conservation...Public Pool Pirna...

I am sitting outside of the Max-Planck-Institute[1] (MPI from now on!), on a huge wooden deck, in midst of a biotope. A variety of trees are whistling in the wind: Birches, cherry trees, willows. A little creek is flowing under the terrace, curving right into a goldfish pond.

I am waiting for my laundry to be done in guesthouse #2. It is obvious that many guest scientists are not using the dryer, because there are many visible stands with drying clothes. **Energy** is more expensive in Germany and people use it wisely. A washing machine costs € 1.50[2] at the MPI and double outside. A dryer costs € 1.00 here, and can add up to € 3.00 in commercial places. There are not many Laundromats in Germany, because people usually have their own washing machines. They take them along, when they move to a different location.

In Germany, it is very tedious to move, because the whole apartment or house is stripped bare of absolutely everything. When you newly arrive at a place, you must install the light fixtures fast, so that you can unpack the rest of the night. Everybody installs his/her own kitchen. Instead of walk-in closets most Europeans have cleverly designed cupboards. Some are built in, if you are lucky.

Water is also very expensive in Germany. You pay for the incoming and outgoing water to be regenerated in biological water plants. Many toilets have a double flush system: Short flushes for small business and long flushes for big business. Children are trained from early age to switch off the faucet in-between tasks and to not let it run continuously.

Germans enjoy water a lot: Here in Dresden, you find many huge plaza fountains, where kids cool down and lounge their little sea boats. The water in these fountains is constantly recycled, and whatever electricity is necessary for the pro-

---

1.   Max-Planck Institutes are all over Germany. They are highly prestigious research and training institutes, for everyone with a special focus in science. They were founded during the Kaiser-Wilhelm-Zeit, and are ruled by the Max-Planck-Gesellschaft (corporation), nowadays.
2.   Conversion: approximately 1:1

cess is provided by solar cells. You see these solar—cell plates everywhere: On vending machines, streetlights, public toilets, parking meters...

You could say that Germany is a nation of **recyclers and energy conservationists**. In our MPI apartment on top of the offices, we sort out six different categories of Müll= garbage: Plastic, glass, metal, biological, paper and cardboard, and rest-müll. Other environmentally dangerous waste is collected periodically, like oils, paints and batteries.

In stark contrast to this environmental concern stands the **smoking pollution** of the Germans. I haven't found a smoke free Café, yet, and it is very annoying having to breathe in polluted air while you eat your dinner. Under international pressure, I guess, the Frankfurt Airport is now smoke-free. Only in designated enclosed areas is smoking permitted.

A few days ago, I visited one of the huge **Public Swimming Pools** with indoor and outdoor Olympic sized pools. There was a kid's pool, a ten meter jumping tower with a separate pool, six different kinds of saunas with Kneipp[3] water applications, a huge outdoor park with playgrounds, and indoor and outdoor gastronomy. The facility in **Pirna**, circa forty minutes from Dresden on the S-Bahn, was spic and span. Whenever you moved into another zone, sanitary foot pools prevented the spread of fungus. The major building materials employed were glass, steel and Saxon sandstone, which is slip proof.

I spent a whole day there. It was a vacation within my vacation. My feet desperately needed a break from all that city trotting, side walking and sightseeing for six hours a day plus the one or two-hour evening power walks with my husband. My back was aching from hauling twenty kilos of mineral water into our apartment. I could have gone twice, but I thought some weight exercises along with the four-flight-of-stairs-aerobic exercise would be a good idea. Drinking lots of mineral water is a typical German characteristic, too. No German drinks tap water. It's supposedly safe, but it doesn't taste as good...too much chlorine and lime. In restaurants, mineral water is as expensive as wine and beer, but if you buy it at Aldi's[4] in a six-pack of 1, 5 liters each, it's fairly inexpensive.

Many water applications, underwater massages and the practical weightlessness, restored my aching back at the **Geipelts Bad in Pirna**. Fortunately, I arrived there on a Tuesday: women's sauna. Otherwise I would have suffered a

---

3.   Doctor in the 1800s who used the healing properties of water
4.   A German chain, which offers a selected amount of groceries and goods of high quality.

culture shock. After having lived in the US for fifteen years, I wasn't used to running around naked in a public place. It took me some time to drop that mid section cover. That whole day was a very sensual experience as I had forgotten how it feels, when the water floats around your body, the wind caresses your skin, and the sun warms up hidden spaces.

Every hour on the hour, a ceremony similar to an Indian sweat lodge took place. There was this anticipation in the air. All the women were getting ready and streaming towards the Finnish roundhouse sauna. I swam in the stream of sisterhood, not knowing yet what was coming. The **Bath Master** (Bademeister) arrived with a wooden bucket of water flavored with lime and a little bowl of ice. The chatting quieted down when he poured the fresh smelling limewater over the hot lava stones ladle by ladle. Then he heated up the ranks by swirling a big towel around. He folded his towel in half, and fanned a heat wave toward each of us women as to greet the goddess in each of us. Since the heat was pretty intense, now, he passed the bowl of ice-cubes around to cool us off, before he would start a second round. He wore those tiny European swimming slips; at least he wore something, so I stayed a second round.

After I had broken enough sweat, I ran under the cold shower, and then I hopped into the cold pool. I then decided to try the Turkish sauna. The tiles were beautifully ornamented, and an exotic scent filled the warm, humid air. I was the Queen of the Turkish Sultan's cabinet; nobody else was there. After that sensual experience, I tried the saltine inhalation room where I laid flat on my belly in order to feel my deep belly breathing as I learned in Yoga. Then I decided to cool off in the cold Kneipp creek, walking over the rough sandstone material for a foot massage.

The sun came out, so I layed down on my towel on an outside deck. I enjoyed the warm sunrays on my whole body, and the wind gently caressing my skin, drying off the sweat pearls. When I felt rested enough, I put on my bathing suit, and took a walk through the outdoor pool park area. Four large screens were broadcasting the **World Cup Soccer game**, Germany against Korea, entertaining the visitors. I had watched the game against the US a week ago, and my opinion, and the general opinion at the MPI was that the US team played better soccer, but Germany shot the goal. I felt for both teams.

My subconscious language is English now, I noticed after living for seventeen years[5] in the US, altogether, especially when it comes to feelings and emotions.

---

5.   1975-77 in Tempe, Arizona; 1986-88 in Los Alamos, New Mexico; 1988-now in Ft.Collins, Colorado

Sometimes, I don't even notice in which language I am talking. Sometimes people ask me for the time or the way and English comes up unconsciously. Onomatopoeias are so very different in each culture, even from dialect to dialect, that they must be experienced in context and sentence melody. The Saxon "Nö? Nö?" with a question intonation sounded to me like: "Isn't that so?" at first. I thought: "Why would they ask me? I have no idea, I'm not from here!" In reality it is an affirmation: Yes, indeed. That is so. Right on!

27. Juni

A Plea for Foreign Language Learning in the USA

Foreign Languages, a Global Necessity...

Languages and dialects are fascinating. At the MPI you hear different nationalities speaking their mother tongues: Japanese, Chinese, Russian, Indian, Croatian, German, Spanish, and English. The common denominator is English. But that doesn't mean American kids don't need to learn a language: They need to and preferably in the <u>core</u> subject area in schools, as in many European countries. Learning a **Foreign Language** improves the IQ and general test scores, widens one's horizon, provides better job opportunities, and educates students for tolerance and peace. It also makes your brain very flexible, because you constantly need to de-route, and search for other means of expression during communication. It is so very important that kids learn how to think outside the box and that there are many ways of doing things and ways of viewing the world. They need to learn that, although you are conditioned in a certain culture, you are not the navel of the world.

When the German carmaker Opel joined General Motors, they had enormous problems at first, because the American CEO didn't understand the German modus vivendi in the business world. We need to study each other's language and culture to find out what each culture has to contribute specifically to the development of the whole. Then we will produce a customer product, which will satisfy the needs of both cultures, and even be good enough to serve the world market. Even with a name a product can rise or sink. They tried to sell a car in Mexico, which had a bad name: NOVA, which means, "doesn't go". It didn't sell, of course. To the Spanish people coke tastes like medicine. So the industry had to add another flavor to adapt it to the Spanish taste. We need to cooperate and co-create. There is no other way to peace, harmony and productivity.

3. Juli

On a walk with an German Gymnasiast

Pisa Study[6]...Pay Moral...Television...Reflection on Languages...

That was the **Language ambassador** writing in me, in the previous chapter. In my American teenagers I notice a certain egocentricity which on one hand is normal for teenagers, but it goes way beyond that: "We are # 1!" "We are the super power!" "Football is <u>the</u> world game!" It all adds up to: The US is the navel of the world. Well, we are not: While we are a great nation of caring, optimistic doers, there are other nations in the world who contribute great culture and progress to this globe. We need to get away from this display of superiority and power, and become true partners in global awareness and finding solutions for peace. This is why Foreign Languages should belong to the core subject area, so that our students can view the world from a different perspective.

On one of my excursions to Luisenhof, outside of Dresden, I ran into a high school student (**German Gymnasiast**). He explained the way through the woods to this old castle to me. You could see that he came from a well-situated family by the way he carried himself and spoke High German. While walking together for twenty minutes, we discussed the German school system, and he informed me that he had been an exchange student in Georgia, last year, at a private school. Through this conversation and following many socio-cultural reports on the TV, it was obvious to me that Germany is facing the same problems as the US. During our stay in Dresden, there was a student-protest broadcasted on the TV. They were demonstrating for better facilities, more up-to-date equipment in the labs, and better trained teachers. The Georgian exchange student and I agreed that the weak Pisa Study-performance couldn't have anything to do with money and equipment, because the German standard of performance after WW II was much higher, in spite of destruction, run down buildings, minimal equipment and emergency teacher certifications.

The authority in regard to public education lies with the states (Länder). Certain states like Bavaria and Baden-Württemberg evidently performed much

---

6. Program of International Student Assessments, comparing student performances of 15 year olds around the world.

higher in the **Pisa Study**. These states are known to vote conservatively and family politics is given a lot of thought. Families are mostly intact there, and mothers and fathers function as teachers. For the rest of the country, teachers are taking or protesting against the beating, while parents are not doing their jobs, just like in America.

The Georgian exchange student and I came to the conclusion that the socio-economic changes must play a part in the underperformance of German students. With both parents working (2 out of 3!), there is no structure and support for learning anymore as it used to be. Also, there is a saturation of material goods instead of love, time for each other, and discipline.

Germans used to be known for their high **pay moral** and for their financial discipline. Now the average credit card debt is around € 5,000 versus $ 7,000 in the US. Goods are purchased <u>now</u>, above the means, without delay in gratification, which is a sign of immaturity and financial stupidity, because one pays up to 50 % more for an item with credit card's interest rates.

Watching **television** in another culture is extremely helpful in regaining a high level of proficiency, learning the trendy expressions, and about the changes and innovations in society. I wish our Hispanic kids in Johnstown could watch American channels. That would improve their English tremendously. I can watch CNN here, there is one Russian channel, but mostly I enjoy the socio-political debates, which are more frequent on the German channels. I can identify dubbed American programs from the bathroom, because they have this fast artificial sound. Hearing Colombo with a totally uncharacteristic, strange German voice is not an enjoyable experience.

Considering that English is a very **synthetic language**, it is obvious that they have to squeeze about one third more German words into a short English dialogue exchange. When you see German scientific abstracts versus English ones, the German version is about one fourth to one third longer, and the French piece is even more voluptuous, because of the way the syntax is constructed. Arabic languages are even more complex. They don't just say: "Sit down!" But something like: "Don't you see how this chair opens his arms for you to receive your charming behind."

During the computer age many expressions come from English and have been Germanized, just like my students would do in the classroom, when they miss the German word. This is a sign, by the way, that they have an acute sense of the German syntax. Expressions like: Papier geschreddet, ein Schreiben gefaxt, ge-emailed, ge-net-worked, and ge-dined are signs of language adaptations and globalization.

4. Juli
Happy Birthday, America!

On the Train to Saarbrücken

Signs of globalization...Aldi...ICE...Bahncard...Density... Homesick...Amortization...Dresden, old, new, in-between...Bombing...Dresden's economy...Phaetons... Darmstadt and Grandpa...

In Dresden on the Prager Str., one of the major shopping areas, there is an ice-cream stand "Ice cream the American way", which is quite frequented. It looks like Dairy Queen ice cream, dipped or parfait style. Also situated on Prager Str. is a Pizza Hut, a Burger King and further downtown, a Mc Donald's. At the "North Sea" (Nord See), a fast food fish place, you can now get Fish'nChips, salads to go, snack boxes for kids, everything with a German touch, of course. Using paper or styro-foam is being avoided whenever possible. Whole Stadtfests (city fests) are celebrated with real china, silverware, and glasses. You pay a deposit to borrow a set, and then bring it back to the dishwasher truck.

Always take a Euro along, when you go shopping. It releases the shopping cart chained to a whole row of carts. Since everybody wants his or her Euro back, people wheel it back and line it up nicely. It seems to me that within the last five years there has been a revolution in training cashiers at huge super markets the American way. They smile now and ask if you found everything all right.

A very economical way to shop is at **Aldi's**. They have basic high quality products. Just a few isles, no time wasted. I hate huge places like Sam's. I would rather go to Wild Oats all the time, if I could afford it. In consumer test magazines, Aldi consistently gets high marks on their products. When they have specials like flat-screen computers or luggage, they are gone in no time. There are Aldis in the US, too. Everything becomes more international. People seem to like the same things around the world, or it is suggested by advertising, but oftentimes adaptations to their cultures are necessary.

It is the 4th of July. I am missing one of my favorite American holidays. I am on a seven-hour **train ride from Dresden to Saarbrücken**, to the Far West of Germany in the Bundesstaat Saarland, which went back and forth between Germany and France after WWI. The **ICE** (InterCityExpress) is a very fast, comfortable means of transportation, that beats all the Staus (jams) on the Autobahn. I purchased a **Bahncard** plus for € 165, that entitles me to half price tickets on all my train rides, even in Greece and Spain. Gasoline is very expensive in Germany, € 1 for a liter, that's about $ 3, 60 per gallon. My train ride is cheaper and I have no delays. Reading, looking out of the window, dreaming, dining, walking up and down the isle, guarantees a leisurely trip. Trains are always punctual and very frequented. There is a dense net of public transportation all across Germany, but in spite of it, cars are lined up on each side of the street, so that two cars can barely pass in neighborhood streets.

Cities are very densely populated; there is virtually no sprawl anywhere. Wide-open lusciously forested landscapes give the impression that there is ample space, but the reality is that **81 Million** people are living in a country half the size of Texas.

Looking out the window into deep healing greens of forests my thoughts are drifting back home to my family and friends. It is a balming feeling having a son in charge, who is capable of conducting all the business at home and taking care of our house and a big yard.

I am riding in the dining car of the ICE, now, enjoying a delicious Ananas-Chili-soup (pineapple chili). I couldn't have cooked it any better. While traveling, I eat very lightly. Otherwise I get sick. The constant rocking lulls me to sleep frequently. This is one way my body deals with a hyper sensitive balancing organ. Mountainous serpentines I must drive myself, holding on to the steering wheel to stabilize myself. Otherwise I entrust my life to skillful drivers.

Riding now in the **West of Germany, leaving the East** around Eisenach, it is obvious that there is no destruction along the railroad tracks, while in the former East, before the fall of the wall in 1989, many buildings looked devastated and run down. The major arteries have been maintained, rebuilt or newly erected, but when you walk into neighborhoods like Plauen in our area of the MPI, every second villa is near breakdown and for sale. Many Wessies (Westerners) buy these villas for investment and tax-deferred purposes. They have to invest a million or two for restoration, but in ten years of tax deduction the money amortizes.

The train stops in Frankfurt. Everything looks familiar. This is the place where I was raised and attended the Johann-Wolfgang-Goethe-Universität.

Back to **Dresden**: It is a beautiful city, old buildings carefully restored, new buildings contrasting the old style. The old buildings have weathered hundreds of years, some dating back to 600, while buildings built cheaply during DDR times, are already falling apart. And in-between, destruction is still visible. It will take another ten years of reconstruction, depending on whether or not the economy holds its promises.

Dresden was **bombed** twice at the end of WWII by England and the US, to finally put an end to Hitler's madness. Actually, the bombing was an act of revenge and not really necessary to the surrender. Dresden lay in Schutt und Asche (debris and ashes). Considering the total destruction and the chore of having to rebuild the puzzle stone by stone, they did a remarkable job in half a century.

The unemployment rate is about 20% here in the East, and younger people tend to move to the West for better job opportunities and higher pay. The salaries in the former East are 85% of those in the West. Dresden has a huge VW-plant, and recently, when we visited the Moritzburg castle, there was a big parade of **Phaetons**, about a hundred driving up the castle with CEOs for a big promotion including a concert in the castle and a reception. Conveniently, there was a thunderstorm and supposedly a blackout, so they could get the regular folks (like us) quickly out of the castle for that special event. I had overheard a conversation earlier between the tour guide and the museum's clerk that the last tour had to be shortened, because of the Phaetons. The Phaetons are VW's luxury cars for about € 70.000 and up.

We are in **Darmstadt**, now, the city I spent many summer vacations in with my **Grandpa**. He owned pubs and hotels in different locations after WWII. He may have had a hot temper towards his own kids, but towards me he behaved very friendly. He wasn't exactly cuddly, but very protective and sponsoring of my own capabilities. He was divorced from my favorite Grandma, and lived with his girlfriend (scandalous in the olden days!), aunt Gretel, in an obvious harmonious relationship till they died.

By Darmstadt is the Odenwald, a German middle mountain region. Within the Odenwald is the Felsenmeer (sea of rocks), which I enjoyed immensely when I was on vacation at my Grandpa's pub. I would climb and jump from rock to rock, endlessly challenging my own jumping distance.

It was a great honor, accompanying Grandpa into the wine cellar, like a Holy Grail ceremony. He explained the fermentation to me, what role the oak barrels play, gave me a little sip of his favorite wines, petted me on the head, and I knew the world was in order. Alcohol is not a big deal in Europe. Kids get some in relation to their body weight for every major holiday and family events. Binge drinking doesn't occur as much as in the US under total restriction by law. Even when German students experiment with alcohol, they are safe for a while, because the driving age is eighteen.

Grandpa owned one of the first Opel-cars after WWI, the ones you had to crank on the outside front heck and hop in quickly. One time he ran after his car, running down the hill with two of his daughters in the vehicle. He must have been a heck of a driver. Later, he drove an Opel Kapitän (sort of like the PT cruiser). I trusted his driving style, but I got sick on a regular basis, puking at least once on every major trip, him holding my forehead, mumbling comforting words. It is a pity that most Grandpas and Grandmas are not there anymore, when you have these deep, probing questions about life. What I remember about Grandpa is that I felt very safe with him and free to explore and seek my own adventures. He was always encouraging. I think he did far better with me than with his own kids.

Graffiti art...everywhere on the noise-protection-walls along the railroad tracks.

11. Juli

Vacation in Saarland

Teachers are no Super-heroes...Reflections on Old Age...

My vacation in **Niederwürzbach/Saarland** with aunt Christel, Cousin Elisabeth and grand nephew Jean Pierre was very restoring to my health: Wholesome vegetarian meals, water applications, long walks, long talks, Reiki[7] and rest. Adapting to their life-style I noticed that I was still racing too fast inside, that I needed to breathe deeply to get more oxygen into my system.

The state of Saarland has beautiful, healthy middle mountain regions and vineyards along the river Saar. My uncle was a wine dealer, who taught me many things about quality wines. He died in 1989. I practically came home to my "father house", as he was my chosen #1 father, besides my adoptive father. It is called father house in Germany, not motherhouse as in matriarchal cultures. As a kid and teenager I had spent many weekends and short vacations with him and his family. After his death I developed an even closer bond to my aunt Christel. My cousin Elisabeth and I reminisced about her father (my uncle) and discovered that philosophically we were fine-tuned on the same wavelength. It was a delight to talk, joke and play with my grand nephew Jean Pierre, a kid who rests within himself, is active but not hyper, reflective and asks intelligent questions. After having experienced so many ADD[8] kids during my school career, I clearly saw that **superb parenting** and grand mothering makes all the difference.

No teacher can ever fill the emotional gaps and holes that parents missed to fill, because of egocentricity, materialism, irresponsibility, and unwillingness to set limits and rules.

Visiting my other cousin near the French border, who is also a teacher and whose husband is an assistant principal at a Gesamtschule (similar to an American High school), we came to the same conclusion: Parents need to do their job and send kids to school ready to learn. Teachers are not super heroes and can't do three jobs at the same time: Parents at home, teachers in school, and parents for un-parented kids.

I am sitting outside under the pergola behind my husband's father house in Flörsheim. It gets dark pretty late in Germany in the summer. Neighbors are in

---

7.   A healing method, removing energy blockages from the body
8.   Attention Deficit Disorder

close vicinity. You could shake hands across the fence; you can hear them talk on the veranda. In spite of the many planes, which frequent the air space, because of the near-by Rhein-Main-Flughafen, the biggest airport in Europe, birds are singing their late evening songs. It is 10:30 p.m. and I am still writing without artificial light.

My parents—in-law are already sleeping. Mother is getting up at 5 a.m. every morning in order to have some peaceful morning hours for herself, before her husband, hard of hearing and plagued with Alzheimer's gets up. Her greatest pain is that she practically lives in captivity, because she is his security blanket and he doesn't let her out of his sight.

Living with old folks for a while and doing chores for them, which they can't master anymore, makes you very reflective about your own life: We are born helplessly, and we will die in total surrender. All power, independence will be relinquished, before we can go into the Light. The more power, independence, and responsibility one has had in life, the more difficult it is to let go.

While trying to shave off my father-in-law's full beard, which he thought was a three-day beard, but in reality was fourteen days old, I was thinking: that could be my husband in twenty years, except he already has a trimmed stylish full beard. *In health and in sickness…in good and bad times…in the prime of your life and at the finish line…*Getting the old folks to the hair salon took all morning. I took a picture before and after the beauty treatment. They definitely looked ten years younger afterwards. When we finally bury our old folks, we have to deal with our own frailties unless they have already announced themselves. Then we wish to keep our independence as long as possible and finally let go with grace. Hopefully, we have some anchors along the way in form of partners, loving kids, and one or two friends who hold out the longest. Or we may have to master everything in solitude with guidance from above. We may have to suffer, before the soul matures, or we may transform effortlessly.

Love is the only yardstick, which measures the quality of life. How much love have you given and received? Are you ready to dissolve your Ego and reunite with the pool of Ultimate Love? All the money, possessions, titles are left behind. Only the effects one has had on different lives are valid and live on.

15. Juli

On the Train Ride Back to Dresden

Illness, a message from your body...

During my six-day stay in Flörsheim by Frankfurt I was again confronted with the meaning of illness in one's life. My friend, whom I have known since we were teenagers, is practically stiff from rheuma and has a hard time walking.

I was thinking about my own heart attacks at the beginning (Feb.) of this year and the message my body is trying to send me. I don't know if I will ever publish this chapter, but it is healthy to write about my heart pains, in order to shed some light on the **PrinzMetal heart spasms**. The official explanation is that the arteries are too sensitive to adrenaline, which is released plentifully in a teacher's career. The heart is the seat of love and compassion. When it spasms there is no regular flow or expansion. It is restricted; it is in pain and suffers from oxygen deprivation. What does that mean transferred to real life? Not living after my own heart? Not observing my own rhythm? Restricting and denying myself what I really want? All these questions I intend to solve during this sabbatical year!

Recalling my students' remarks, they sometimes say: "Take it easy! Chill! Slow down! Cool it! Lighten up!" when I push too hard. There is a saying: "Kids and jesters speak the truth!" Outside, I often appear cool, stoic, happy, jolly, but inside it looks different. On one hand, I enjoy my high sensitivity and psychic abilities, because I need it to express myself in art, poetry, music, to "read" people, to "feel" my class. On the other hand, I am deeply affected by insensitivity, impoliteness, rudeness, intrigues, unfairness and disrespect. I have to find out, this year, if my place is still in teaching, and if so, at what level and what kind of teaching.

In Los Alamos, in 1988, I got a clear command in my dream: "Go into teaching! Go into teaching!" I haven't heard a different message, yet. It was a calling, and I take it as seriously as a **priestess' vow**.

16. Juli

At the Biotope

Siberia...Necessity of Learning a Foreign Language...

Plenty of laundry has accumulated during our two weeks of traveling, so I am sitting in my biotope, again, waiting for the dryers. Last night, over dinner at a Greek neighborhood restaurant, my husband told me about his trip to **Jekaterinburg** behind the Ural in Siberia: The average monthly salary of a Russian professor is between $60 and $100. People live close together, three generations in two rooms. Space is very limited. Everybody has a garden in order to survive. People are very poor, but very giving and hospitable. The rich drive Mercedes and consume all the goods of the West. At the airport you are searched inside out. Russian travelers take these inconveniences stoically. My Egyptian friend said it's degrading. Passports are held onto for a long time and checked over and over again. But once you are accepted as a guest, they treat you like a king. Being an American of German descent, my husband noticed that Americans are not very sensitive towards other cultures. They mean well, but they just can't decode the cultural context.

It is very urgent that we get our kids ready for global awareness by making **Foreign-language learning mandatory**. Many states in Germany start English in first grade, now, since kids learn it very easily at an early age. Many things you do as a child, you can pick up again at a later age and become very skilled at it. Biking, skiing, swimming, playing an instrument, learning foreign languages are all life skills, which should be picked up around four years of age, playfully, without stress. The older you are the longer it takes to learn a FL. Your last chance to speak a language without any accent is as a teenager. Your speaking apparatus is set around the age of twenty, and if a FL is learned later, you'll always have that Kissinger or Arnold Schwarzenegger accent. There is nothing wrong with accents, as long as they don't interfere with communication. They are cute, add color and sharpen one's listening skills.

17. Juli

At the B'liebig

Packing for a whole year…Homesickness…Euro prices…

It has been pouring for two days now. In my little Stamm Café (regulars) the wooden tables are soaking wet. I am sitting outside trying to lure the sun out of the clouds. The humidity must be 90%. People are running around with jackets and sweaters. I am wearing shorts and my thin RHS nylon jacket. Typical Colorado girl, aye?

I brought some comfort clothing and keepsakes to prevent **homesickness**: My son's ankh[9], my Crabby Diem T-shirt, my RHS (Roosevelt High school=Renate Hochheimers School) Field and Track long sleeve shirt, my thick and thin RHS nylon jackets and a stack of pictures from home and work. I practically take those items on every trip, because they are very useful for most types of weather and don't take up much space. Plus they all carry my initials.

People asked me before the trip: "How do you **pack for a whole year?**" Well, it's easy. Having moved over ten times in my life so far, I consider myself an expert packer. You never take what you can't handle by yourself. That boils it down to two suitcases and a backpack. I like to have my hands free, so that I can knock out a thief or help an old lady. First, I took all my favorites out of the closet. Then I asked the following questions: Is it seasonal, practical, occasional, and situational and how can I coordinate the pieces to create a new look. I took two suitcases, but actually one and a half would have been sufficient. Things I don't want to miss, I hand-wash. I also hand-wash the dishes, because there are only four sets of everything. Only when we have guests, do I turn on the dishwasher with all the pots and pans, which I normally don't do at home, because of the waste of energy. Typical German, aye?

We have visitors every second weekend, because they all long to see us during our three-month stay in Dresden, and because Dresden is a very attractive city to visit. Although there is a 20% emigration movement to the West right now, they predict that with favorable economic development, **Dresden might be the Metropolis of the East in twenty years**. It once was under Albrecht von Sachsen in the 1700s.

---

9.   Greek cross with the omega loop

Let's compare **prices** now! Fortunately I have figured out the Euro sign by now, after having asked four of these smart scientists without any success. But since I hardly ever give up in using my own brain, here it is: Alt, Control, and E = €, that is on a German keyboard! With the introduction of the €uro at the beginning of the year, there has been a price hike in some areas like public service and gastronomy. People here call it the Teuro from "teuer"=expensive, and they still think in DM in order to compare prices before and after the reform. I do my bookkeeping in a one to one ratio; that's close enough. Actually, the €uro over-took the Dollar on Monday, the 15th. I draw money directly from my bank account in Ft. Collins with my debit card from any EC machine. For insured purchases I use my Denver Titanium. People here pay a lot more with cash than in the US.

Wine is very cheap in Germany. You can get excellent bottles of wine from € 2, 50 to € 4, 50, if you know the vineyards and grapes. And even if you don't, go to Aldi's! You'll get it for half price. Cheese is a lot cheaper here, too. I really enjoy the multitudes of hearty breads fresh from the baker. Specialty shops are everywhere in the neighborhood, within the vicinity of 300 to 400 meters. A cup of coffee costs around € 2, 00 in a premier café, which is fairly expensive, consid-ering the cups are half the size and there is no refill, but it is very strong. The average dinner meal is around € 10 to 15; lunches are in-between € 5 and 7, 50.

A Pension=Bed and Breakfast costs € 50, while a full service hotel during off-season in July and August charges around € 70 (normally € 90 to 110). In July and August, the Semper Opera has a summer break, the city is hot and humid and many parents with school age children leave town for vacation. Germany's favorite vacation spots are The Turkish Riviera, Hungary around the Plattensee, Southern Europe like Greece and Italy, and Germany itself. Teneriffa, once a favorite vacation spot, has become very expensive. Germans avoid it, because of the T€uro. There is a tendency to hold onto the money right now, because peo-ple don't trust the €uro, yet, although it exceeded the Dollar a few days ago. The German Mark remained the symbol of stability and German Economic Wonder-land (Deutsches Wirtschaftswunderland) for five decades after WWII.

1001 Nights in Yenidze

Honey-rub in Bath Pirna...

I am lunching in the **Yenidze**, a high-rise Islamic looking building, which was a former Salem cigarette factory, built around 1900. The light shines through the stained glass dome in brilliant colors. Originally, I just wanted to get tickets for one of the 1001 Night fairy tale events, especially for "The Little Prince" by Saint Exupéry, but the dome was closed. So instead I enjoyed the view looking upwards through the restaurant, and outside the tower windows, overlooking the Altstadt=Old City. I ordered Oma's Sülze (Grandma's lean meat in sour jelly, a favorite German summer dish) and a Clausthaler non-alcoholic beer. Maybe later, I will have some dessert: Warm Apfelstrudel and coffee. It's a day of celebration: Life with all its surprises, miracles, richness, opportunities, chances...

Yesterday, I returned to that marvelous **Bath in Pirna**. After having traveled through Germany from the far East to the far West, sitting in the train a long time and lifting suitcases, I needed a thorough under water massage for my aching muscles. Since the Turkish BathMaster wasn't there, I did the water applications by myself, moving from jet to jet. This time, it was a mixed sauna, but I didn't mind anymore. In the morning, mostly older couples were enjoying the peace and quiet of the sauna, and in the afternoon, some younger folks arrived.

All the people over fifty had bellies, even the ones who appeared slim from behind. Around fifty, hormonal changes occur in women as well as in men. Most look a little pregnant or a lot; very few keep the flat athletic belly of the youth. I saw only one perfect body, and that belonged to a man around thirty: Tall, athletic, well-rounded, strongly built, tanned smooth skin, some smiley dimples on his behind, smooth gate and perfect manners, too. He closed my necklace in the sauna, when the intense heat forced me to take the metal cross off my skin, since I couldn't see the closure without my glasses. The rest of the sauna folks had "imperfect" bodies, all beautiful expressions in their own way.

The younger folks were clearly less inhibited. This time, the BathMaster included a honey rub in the hot stone ceremony. He gave everybody a Dollar-sized scoop of crystallized honey in his/her palm to rub down the body. The crystals had a peeling and gentle massage effect, and the honey nourished the skin. It tasted good, too,—I couldn't resist. The whole sauna smelled like honey-melisse, since he also used that scent in his bucket to pour over the hot stones. During the honey rub ceremony a younger female said to her partner: "Didn't you forget a certain body part?" and gently rubbed some honey over his relaxed penis. The whole sauna laughed. There was nothing sexual about it. It was a totally natural, loving, sensual gesture.

21. Juli

A Saturday with Ana

Peaceful Sunday morning...Schloß Pillnitz...Elb-river walk...Students at CSU-MPI...German eating habits...

It is Sunday morning. I am sitting in my **biotope** again, in the shade with the warm summer wind caressing my skin. It is quiet and peaceful, only the solemn ring of the Sunday church bells is in the air. My husband is in his office trying to send the pictures from his recent conference back to Siberia via CD. It's the fastest, cheapest way to send pictures. With film development, they now offer a CD for € 3, 99. Picture development is more expensive in Germany: € 6 for 24 exposures, format 10x15 cm. You can't order doubles or triples, you have to reorder and it costs just as much as the first print. I guess it's that environmental consciousness, again, but it's much more convenient in the US, and it makes sense: If you order doubles or triples right away, you save labor costs, although some of the triples may end up in the waste basket at home.

Yesterday, we ran into our CSU student **Ana from Macedonia** by chance, and we spent the whole day together. My husband says Ana "unthaws" around me, otherwise she is very shy. No wonder, when men talk all the time. I just walk beside her listening. The art of listening brings many people out of their shell. Ana is here at the MPI for a four-week measurement research session. Eventually, she is going to get her Ph.D. in Physics. She started out as a ballerina and later switched over to Physics. What she said yesterday on the trip to Schloß Pillnitz was very interesting: Students here are more serious, focused, tense, pushy, and no-nonsense. Students in the US are more relaxed; they laugh a lot, and get their work done, too, even if it takes more time. I just fell into the typical trap of comparing two countries and generalizing. What one always compares is that specific place in time and space. So we are comparing the current situation at CSU to the MPI, in regard to graduate students. Ana would rather study at CSU than at the Max-Planck-Institute, because life is more fun. At the MPI there are students from all kinds of nationalities. The reason for this grim seriousness is, in my opinion, that they are only granted three years to get their Ph.D. with an occasional extension of a fourth year. That puts too much pressure on the student and would take the fun out of physics for Ana.

Together we went to **Castle Pillnitz** on the beautiful Saturday noon. First, we rode the tram, and then we set over to the other Elbe shore via ferry. The day started off cloudy, but turned sunnier in the course. Castle Pillnitz is one of the many castles Emperor August der Starke (the Strong) built for one of his Mätressen (mistresses). The symmetry and the wide-open spaces of the artistically arranged parks in-between the luxurious baroque buildings have a harmonizing effect on the soul. Parts of the castle have been restored and renovated; other parts are still under construction. It is funded with a Wiederaufbau tax (reconstruction tax) from the West, money from the Feds and state, and Lotteries from the general public, buying a Los=lottery ticket. We sat down in the castle's Biergarten for a luncheon snack, before we went on a three-hour walk along the Elbe-river.

Last week, when I was in Frankfurt, they showed pictures of the Elbe-River on the TV. The Elbe was once polluted from all the industrial waste of the East, and I bet of the West, too. In order to demonstrate that it was entirely clean now, swimmers all along the Elbe-river around Dresden jumped into the clean, cool water. At a little shore area I walked in, too, up to my knees and cooled off my arms from the summer heat. I would have loved to jump in naked, but I didn't want to shock the fish.

I counted seven Biergartens on our three-hour walk along the Elbe. So there really is no chance of dying from hunger or dehydration in Germany. The warm summer wind is fanning the aromatic scents of herbs towards me, so I get a free aroma theraphy session, too, on a peaceful Sunday morning in my biotope.

After our three-hour walk, we arrived at the ground station of the Schwebebahn=cogwheel train to Luisenhof. We took the ride up to another little castle for a **coffee break**, overlooking all of Dresden. Luisenhof has the freshest, most delicious tarts and excellent coffee, too. This is a German tradition, especially on the weekend, having tart and coffee, anytime between 2 p.m. and 5 p.m., usually around 3 p.m. Even bakeries are open during that time on Sundays, so that families can get their treats for a special get-to-gether. Family **meals** are more common in Germany than in America. Many families even sit down for breakfast together, but eating traditions have loosened up a lot since my childhood. Eating in your room was not an option; it was a punishment. Nobody wanted to miss that special family time around the dinner table, ever.

25. Juli

Writing at my little Corner Café

Craft of writing…Inner landscape…Kaffeepause…Personal atmosphere…

The weather is triste (French), today, 17°C, windy with lots of clouds. I have been working at the computer for about three hours a day. That's the most my shoulders can bare or they tense up achingly. My raw script is still flowing out of my pen. I need the **atmosphere for writing**, as well as the rhythmic flow of my thoughts into my hand. Many writers don't care for typing directly into the computer, because no inspiration comes through in that electronic environment.

There are only four more weeks left here in Dresden at the MPI. What has changed in my **inner landscape**, so far? I still haven't changed in setting a work agenda, but I give myself adequate breaks. I do not have to do it now; I can do it later with more enthusiasm and energy. Working is fun when it can be adjusted to your inner clock. I have regained more strength and sexual energy as my hormonal system has come into balance. The stress hormone thoroughly suppresses a woman's estrogen (a man's testosterone). As more life energy flows back, a stronger expression of the physical body is the result. I enjoy not being ruled by the belly, anymore as in my twenties, but by the heart. The physical expression is then the crowning of the heart's energy, and transformed into an artistic expression of human landscapes. That's what the Old Greeks called Eros.

My raw script allows me the freedom to spit out my ideas uncensored. The computer revision may throw out certain unofficial things later. It just depends how much insight I am willing to allow my readers. Or it depends on how courageous I am in standing by my whole self! Sensuality is part of my artistic nature. If I did not register things with my six senses, I would not be able to transform it into art, poetry, dynamic teaching, creative cooking, strong intuition etc.

More people are joining me now for **Kaffeepause** in this little Corner Café. It is almost 3 p.m. What is so intriguing about this little place is that it looks like Grandma's kitchen with four corner benches standing in each corner of the guestroom. An ambulance ta tü ta tü ta tü ta tü ta tü is passing by, giving me a flashback to February. That was the most expensive ride of my life, $ 1000 from Johnstown to Poudre Valley Hospital in Ft. Collins. You may have already realized that the onomatopoeia is different from an American ambulance, indeed.

And the emergency call is 110 here. German whipped cream from the baker is so delicious. My neighbor has a whole bowl full. I am not in danger of eating too many sweets, because I'd rather go for the hearty stuff.

That's also something I enjoy very much in Germany: The **personal atmosphere**. You always find the same clerks, they greet you, ask you about the latest news, know exactly what you want; they even know your little squirms, sometimes. Being a clerk or a sales person is not a quick job, like in America, it is a learned trade and it comes with a benefits package. Mc Donald's for example could only expand their franchises in Germany by observing this different social structure and following the Unions' guidelines. When a German asks you, "Wie geht's?" = How are you?, s/he really wants to know!!! It does not belong to the greeting formula like in the US where everybody answers "fine", although it's mostly a lie.

30. Juli

From Luisenhof overlooking Dresden

Trade schools...Exploitation scandals in both countries...Healing process...Manifestation of illnesses...

The **trade school system** is superb in Germany. Anybody who doesn't go to a University learns a trade or profession for three years with a Master teacher in a professional setting. One or two mornings out of the week are devoted to theoretical training. After three years of training you have to pass a board examination (Gesellenprüfung). It can't just happen that your roof flies off, like in America where "apprentices" are trained for about six weeks. German Handwerkers = handworkers, craftsmen have a lot of experience and would know that in the strong Colorado winds, one needs to nail down the shingles instead of stapling them with a staple gun. In Germany, my husband wouldn't have to suggest the working sequence to a plumber, and even help him out with the appropriate tools from his shop. No expensive Santa Fe tiles would loosen up in my kitchen in Germany, because of the cheaper grout. In Germany, they go for workmanship and durability. In America, they go for profit and short spans, not always, but often.

When we go to the upper ranks, it is the same in both countries. The **greed of the politicians and CEOs** has brought Enron and Telecom down. The stock market reacted like a psychological barometer. The shares plummeted, and small investors lost a big part of their retirement base. Retirement funds should be untouched, safe and totally reliable, like in Norway, Sweden, and Belgium, the top countries in social security, living and education standards. If you worked hard your whole life, you should not lose or have to delay your retirement, because of crooked CEOs or politicians.

This morning, I had a massage in the White Elk Sauna Club. The massage therapist made me aware of bumps and tenseness in the left half of my body. (The seat of the heart is mostly to the left!) My husband says, and my dentist, too, that I grind my teeth at night. There is still a lot of work to be done on my part, to dig out that buried aggression and smoothen out the tension. When I get impatient with the **healing process**, my Egyptian friend from Berlin who had the same break down, reminds me that it takes a whole year to recover, once the body was near breakdown. I always thought of myself as that not so lean, but strong and sturdy go-go-machine. That is another image I have to strip away to accept my vulnerability. Tauruses usually don't complain, unless it's almost too late. Their endurance level is higher than that of other signs. I have gotten into the habit, now, of letting out a moan and groan, when things get to be too much, to make my body audible to my brain, which wants to ignore such things.

Illnesses don't just happen to us. We have to work really hard towards them! (Double connotation!!!) They are manifestations of our e-motions. Motions get stuck at our weakest area, instead of being moved out=e-moted. They literally nag at your insides, until your body gives the red stop light to the soul in the form of pain. Even then, we tend not to listen, until we lay flat on our nose and there is no escape from the gurney.

5. August

Writing from Villa Maria at the Elbe-River

Villa Maria...Job=Play?...Blue Wonder (Blaues Wunder)...Colorado Club...Sophienkeller...Castle Königstein in Swiss Saxony...Oberschulrat (=Superintendent)...

Today, I am viewing Luisenhof from the Elbe shore. On the left side of the Elbe is **Villa Maria**, an Italian gourmet restaurant that serves only biologically sound nutrition. I should become a gourmet restaurant-tester, then I could combine my love for eating with my love for writing, Nay, I'd better leave that for a hobby; it's not challenging enough, no sweat or stress involved, it just doesn't sound like work. But who says work has to be strenuous? If playing were identical to work, one would hold the ideal job and never wear out. What other **play-jobs** would be attractive to me? A gallery-coffee house owner where I would combine my art with my craft of baking delicious cakes and tarts. My husband could contribute his unique soups, but I would need to be the boss. I need my own creative work-out-field, because I have my own ideas. I could become a Bed and Breakfast-owner, spoiling my guests with a wholesome breakfast and a relaxing homey atmosphere.

It is pouring, right now, but I am staying dry on the deck under the glass roof. The Elbe looks carbonated like Sprudelwasser (prickly water) with all the little raindrops dancing on the flowing river. I love this smell of high ozone in the air and the sound of splashing rain. Thick, dark clouds are drifting over Luisenhof. Canoe drivers are taking shelter under the **Blue Wonder** (Blaues Wunder), a huge Elbe bridge of steel construction whose green coat turned blue over time, hence the name the Blue Wonder! When was the last time I consciously and intensely listened to the rain? Our daily life in the US is too hectic. I read a proverb, recently, in a restaurant: "God gave you time, he didn't say anything about rush." White doves are flying through the blue steel construction. According to their laughter, they seem to enjoy the rain immensely. My Grandmother always said: "There is no wrong weather, there is only wrong clothing."

Last weekend, part of our **Colorado Club,** for whom we organize US trips, every three years, visited us in Dresden. They said they would have never imagined that Dresden was such a beautiful city and had so much to offer. The steamer Gräfin Cosel is passing by; she was the mistress of August der Starke, the Saxon King. He built all these little castles along the Elbe-river for his mistresses. Supposedly, he generated 200 boys and 100 girls during his lifetime. At the age of 50 he got diabetes and August the Strong wasn't so strong, anymore, so the child production stopped.

What you never want to miss when you visit Dresden is a reservation in the **Sophienkeller**. They serve authentic Saxon food, but the best parts are the impersonators of Gräfin Cosel, minstrels and knights of August der Starke who come to your table, playing out the history in costumes and language of the Baroque era, involving the spectators. Our Colorado Club from Flörsheim, Germany is a group who is always receptive to jokes and playing; they were totally fascinated by the historical event in the Sophienkeller=cellar (Sophie, wife of August the Strong).

On Saturday, we took them to **Swiss Saxony (Sächsische Schweiz)** to **Castle Königstein (Burg Königstein),** dating back to 1589. When you cross the Zugbrücke (drawbridge), you feel like you are back in the Middle Ages. It is unbelievable how they built the mighty stonewalls into the natural walls of rock. The whole castle area is a living museum with Lieutenant Quarters, supply rooms, weapon rooms, treasury, kitchen, Kasematten (bunkers), a church, and defense watchtowers. You can take a round walk on top of the defense wall (Verteidigungswall), constantly changing your perspective of the Elbe-river and of the surrounding middle mountain regions with high-rising rock formations. Within the castle area there are several Biergartens and an outdoor coffee place where they serve fresh cake from the wood stove (Holzofen). Sometimes, there are fairs and musical performances in the spacious gardens of the castle.

The food is indeed delicious, here, at Villa Maria. I had tuna stuffed tomatoes with green Princess beans, and for dessert apricot-streusel and one of those strong German coffees. The apricot-streusel is garnished with pistatio, a special touch and taste in combination with the butter-streusel. You might think I eat out all the time. Well, I don't! I cook everyday. It just happens that when I sit down in that special atmosphere, I get in the mood for writing.

School started again in Saxon, today. I'll give it another week, and then I intend to observe different schools around here. This week, I will make an appointment with the local **Superintendent (Oberschulrat),** to get his/her official permission, and try to prepare some contacts for RE-5J, our district in Colorado. These last weeks will fly by faster than I can write.

6. August

At Sophienkeller, Outdoors

Dresdner Zwinger concert…Back home…Little kids and foreign languages…

The weather is ideal, today, warm, but not too hot. I am sitting at a busy plaza in-between Sophienkeller and **Dresdner Zwinger**, a charming Baroque castle where I attended a classical outdoor concert, a week ago under a starry night sky. The Dresden Symphony orchestra played serenades from Mozart and Beethoven, and classical dances from Claude Debussy with a charming witty ballet choreography. I recognized the Cake-walk-dance from Debussy immediately, because I had instructed music in WCMS to a bunch of ADD Middle-schoolers after their third teacher had run out of the classroom. They had also danced on the tables and disappeared under the pastor's supervision. I got them to improvise the Cake-walk-dance; I always kept them in motion.

During the concert a white dove was circling above my head. I sent her **home** to say, "I dove you!" to all my family and friends. I miss cuddling with my youngest son, Manuel, who attends to our house, but he has something better to cuddle with, now: His future wife Vange. He went seamlessly from Mom's care into Vange's care. It is a good time to cut the umbellicord, right now. I felt the bond to my future daughter-in-law right away, knowing, sensing that she was the one—mother's instincts! I call Manuel my **B**iking **B**anker (Germanic alliteration!) now, since he works at a bank and lost his driver's license for too many speeding tickets. He should have it back by December.

Vange is of Puerto-Rican descent. Our family becomes very international: American, Mexican, German, and Puerto-Rican. Mixed races produce cute babies, indeed! I should know as a Grandma! I hope they manage to raise their kids **trilingual**: English, German, and Spanish. That would be a gift for life, because little kids pick up a language in about six to eight weeks. We went through this process twice with our three boys. Effortlessly they picked up English in Tempe, Arizona, in Kindergarten and first grade, and then as young teenagers they came back to Los Alamos, New Mexico, to perfect their English. Since my husband and I consequently spoke German with them, they are **fluent and accent-free in both languages**. Only the youngest has a cute American accent in his German, since he has lived in the US since he was three and a half.

It takes discipline and a conscious effort on the part of the parents to raise kids bi—or trilingual, but it is a priceless gift.

11. August

In the cooling shade of my Biotope

Ulmer friends...New perspectives of Dresden...Haute Couture...Frauenkirche...Kunsthof Passage...Luisenhof...Wildgulasch... The influence of architecture on the psyche...Back to school...

It is a peaceful Sunday morning. We are recuperating from our many visitors. Yes, we do enjoy each one of them thoroughly, but I need downtime for myself afterwards. Excessive talking, intense walking, elaborate cooking, all the excitement; everything needs to come back into balance, again. With every visitor we discover **new perspectives of Dresden**, because each of them has his/her special interest. Our **Ulmer friends** introduced me to the **haute couture of Dresden in Königsstraße**, yesterday. I gowned myself with sinfully expensive clothes, but I didn't buy any. I really liked one outfit in the Kunsthof Passage. It was an extravagant white hemp skirt with a red Spanish "el torro" shaped top. It looked very refreshing, but my husband convinced me that this material would be too hot for Greece and India and that we would get it for one tenth of the price there.

Two other scientists have discovered the serenity of the biotope, this morning. They are working on the sturdy wooden outdoor tables; papers scattered all over. Our Ulmer friends invited us to dinner, Friday night to **Villa Marie** at the Blue Wonder Bridge. (Remember?) The dinner was great, but very expensive. You pay for the ambiance of sitting in candle light by the Elbe-river. German gastronomy uses more salt in general than in the US. When we all came home to our MPI apartment, we gulped down liters of Sprudelwasser to quench our thirst.

Saturday, we had a light lunch at our place and went sightseeing. They had taken down the scaffold in front of the **Frauenkirche**[10]. The new white Saxon sandstone and the old blue grey black weathered stone reminded me of an Andalusian horse. Over time, traffic pollution will throw a coat over the cathedral and the appearance will look unified, again. Then we went browsing at the haute couture shops in Königsstraße and side Passagen. Our husbands were remarkably patient, because they could discuss Physics with each other. Every five minutes,

---

10.   Church of Our Lady

we would amuse them by modeling ridiculously looking gowns and we all would have a good laugh.

Afterwards we were steaming from all the dressing and undressing, so we went to the **Kunsthof Passage** in his Audi. They were former Dresdners, so they didn't mind chauffeuring us around by car. We always prefer public transportation in cities, since it is less unnerving. Only for grocery shopping and country-side outings do we take the Opel Corsa. Our friends had given us the tip to go to Kunsthof Passage at the beginning of our stay, here, but they had never seen it, since it is a recent project, and they have lived in the West since the erection of the wall. We enjoyed the ambiance of the artistic Hinterhöfe (back yards) and the unique shops.

Around 4 p.m. = 16 Uhr, we drove to **Luisenhof** for a mandatory German coffee break (Kaffeepause). The tarts were delicious: Black Forest, Cassis de Dijon, (Black current liquor) Poppyseed, Raspberry cream tarts, together with Eiscafé, Eisschokolade, and a Kännchen Café (small pot=2 cups). So far, I haven't gained any weight and I haven't lost any, either. My Ulmer friend who saw me a year ago on his sabbatical in Ft. Collins said I look so very content and relaxed now. He used stronger adjectives, but that's the most I can convey to you without blushing. The way he said it fed my female ego. I thought the same about him and expressed it later, after I had my "embarrassment" under control. He looked much younger and youthful after his sabbatical, too. The same holds true for retirees, by the way. Once they are away from the scene of the crime (job) for one year, they look ten years younger. We **must** all lead happy professional lives to add to our retirement years!

After the coffee break we stopped at a private gallery whose owner was from Ulm, but on vacation. Then we drove back to our MPI apartment where I had prepared an elaborate dinner, the night before and Saturday morning. For an appetizer we had tomatoes with fresh mozzarella, basilicum and a garlic baguette; as the main course, we had **Wildgulasch** with Semmelknödel, Serviettenknödel, and Rotkraut with Genever Cassis. For dessert, we indulged in Quarkstrudel and coffee. "Wild" is game and Gulasch is not mixed with anything, just generous pieces of meat in gravy. Semmelknödel are dumplings made from rolls, eggs and a little flour, Serviettenknödel are made from boiled potatoes. Rotkraut is red cabbage and tastes especially delicate with a black currant-liquor. Quark is something in-between cream cheese and cottage cheese, used for baking and desserts. My husband really doesn't like to eat out, because he says I can prepare it much better than any restaurant. He always cleans up afterwards, so the sweat is shared. After the clean-up my husband showed his friend his office and the laboratories;

while we women sat on the balcony in the cool evening breeze enjoying some more wine and sisterly talk. Later at night, they went back to their Bed and Breakfast where they always stay when they visit Dresden.

When the chatting calmed down in my brain and the nightgown fell over the institute I sat down for an evening meditation to inquire why I feel so great in this **environment.** The major factor is light. Everything is flooded with light, the offices, the apartment, the atrium, the seminar rooms, and the coffee corners. The building is made of glass and steel: very spacey and light. The second factor is nature. Nature is built in wherever possible; Terraria, biotopes, resting and chatting areas, planted rooftops, a pond and a fountain enliven and humanize the clear-line futuristic glass and steel structure. The architect even integrated two fully-grown trees into the building, instead of chopping them down. A poplar is surrounded by helium gas-tanks, and the path to the main entrance waves around a chestnut tree. The third factor is space: No clutter, only the most necessary things: Warm parquet floors, clean tiled bathroom, modern Bosch kitchen, cozy couch and love seat area which extends into a sleeping isle, a work area and an extra guest room. The fourth factor is art: Tasteful prints of Dresden, nicely arranged, stylish lamps, and esthetics everywhere.

When I visited **Einstein's house in Potsdam**, before the fall of the Wall, the same elements of the **Bauhaus style** fascinated me back then. Clear lines, futuristic designs, functionality and practicality. The MPI design corresponds with my soul's need for **light, nature, connection, space, order, art, and esthetics**. I already turn a little sad thinking I have to leave in three weeks. On the other hand I am curious how my soul will respond to the Greek Sirtaki and white beaches, the Indian 1001 nights, the stark contrast between poor and rich, life and death, and the Spanish corida and salsa.

But before we get to these exotic experiences, there is a lot of school—work to be done in Dresden. After finally breaking the phalanx of secretaries, I had the local Superintendent (Oberschuldirektor) on the other line. He immediately arranged a meeting, even with the Gymnasial—and Mittelschulreferenten. I must have sounded convincing, or persistent and tenacious, or all three of them.

13. August

From my desk, looking into endless threads of rain and ink-clouds

State of Emergency in Dresden…Gyno…Contrasting US and German culture…

We can't get out of Dresden to the embassy of Berlin for our visas to India. All bridges are closed. The **Elbe is flooded** and minor creeks like the **Weißeritz** have turned into roaring streams. Parts of the Old town have been **evacuated**; the hospital in Friedrichstadt is flooded. In Plauen, our area, the lower parts were totally flooded by the Weißeritz. She has separated the town, and people can't get to work. The main railroad station is eighty cm under water. The basement of the Landtag (House of Representatives), situated at the Elbe-river, is flooded. They tried to save the documents in the basement, this morning. **Sirens** are howling constantly and **helicopters** are surveying the city and **rescuing** people. Germany along the Elbe-river and the Donau (Danube) is **drowning**. The chancellor, Gerhard Schröder, has called a **state of emergency** and asked for donations for Saxony and Bavaria.

We are relatively safe at the MPI, however out of warm water. The laundry room is flooded and they have several pumps going into the basement. We had to move our car to the other side, because water was flowing into the Tiefgarage (underground garage). My appointment with the Oberschuldirektor (Superintendent) drowned in the floods, too. He was in a state of emergency. All school children were out of school, today, and during the two-hour rain break, around noon, many local families went sightseeing and took photographs of the critical points. Only one third of the MPI staff made it to work.

Instead of meeting the sup, I went to the **gyno**. I had to bring a towel to put my butt on. (Crazy Germans!) I had to chuckle. Well, why not, it saves paper and plastic. I was impressed with the professional goal-oriented treatment. But there was time for chatting, too. Compared to the West, the former eastern doctors are doing a much better custom friendlier job. They hold the opinion that 60% of the diagnosis consists of listening closely to the patients. WOW! The female gynecologist recommended another DNC, soon, but the problem is that the hospital in Friedrichstadt is flooded, too, and I am running out of time, because we are leaving on the 31st of August for Greece. She did a routine Pap smear with a rectal exam, a physical examination of the uterus and the bladder, a urine analysis, and an intravaginal ultra sound, all in one session. And best of all, she explained everything carefully, picturesquely and with a lot of humor.

Of course, I am always **contrasting the US and German culture**. In the US they hardly do a rectal exam at the Gyno, and for an ultra sound you would have to come in for another appointment. In Germany they don't cover up your body parts. Nakedness is no big deal in Europe. An American teenager would have a hard time dealing with that. During the exam I had to hold the upper stirrup. Nobody else was present. I don't know how they handle it here when the gyno is male; I suppose in the same fashion. I figured I would rather have the procedure done in Germany than in Greece, India or Spain where I can't handle the language. That must be a very frightening experience having to go to the hospital and not being able to communicate through language.

20. August

Back from Berlin

Calamities in Dresden…Unusual Weather patterns…Breathtaking Berlin…Linie 100 & 200…Sony Center…Buddy-Bears…

Four days ago, we drove to Berlin, leaving town across the only Weißeritz Bridge, which was open during that time, to get our visas for India and to spend the weekend with our Berlin friends. All the bridges in town were closed to traffic, except pedestrians and emergency vehicles, because they expected the highest Elbe level of 9, 66 meters, ever.

We followed the **calamities** on the morning and evening news: 20,000 people evacuated, billions (Milliarden) of damage in lost property, cultural attractions, public transportation networks; ghost towns at night, because the electricity had to be switched off. Water and electricity don't mix. The TV and radio networks made an appeal for donations: Over 22,000 000 € have been donated already for unbureaucratic direct-help. This was the only way I could help, too. If my health were in top condition, you would find me downtown helping with the cleanup. The town of Dresden is out of hepatitis and tetanus vaccines. They have asked America for help, and I am sure my beloved home country will respond immediately. In this extreme heat (32 °C) helpers are in danger of catching hepatitis in the polluted Elbe waters, a river that had been clean enough for swimming just a little while ago. Pictures on the TV don't capture the severity of the flooding.

Maybe it is a **wake-up call** to live in harmony with nature. The Elbe has been dammed and straightened out for decades to make sea ship traffic possible. Men disregarded the natural overflow (Auen) and built housing there. Geologists and meteorologists say, every century, there is a heavy flooding, but this time it has hit hardest.

In my opinion, through my five-decade observation, the **weather patterns** have changed drastically within the last five years: Extreme draught in the South west of America and high flooding in Germany. In former times when I was a kid, there was snow in Frankfurt every winter, but cars, airplanes and industrial CO_2 emissions have heated up the atmosphere. There are meteorologists who follow weather patterns all across the world on a big scale, but nobody listened to their warnings. Now they will get more and more platforms in public forums.

Berlin was breathtaking. Dresden is small scale, but Berlin is huge. All major streets have six lanes. In 1997, a student of mine who won the Daimler-Benz-Award said to me: "Berlin is one huge construction site." Now in 2002, I could see the results. We visited the **Reichstag** (seat of the Bundestag=parliament), the **Brandenburg Tor** (gate) which was clothed in a Telecom curtain for reconstruction, a **Buddy Bear exhibition**, and walked along the famous East street "**Unter den Linden**" to **Alexanderplatz**. We did most of the sightseeing on **bus 100 and 200**, the best-kept secret in town. In the 200-double Decker back to **Potsdamer Platz,** where the very impressive new **Sony Center** is located, I got seasick. Close to the Sony Center with its spacecraft-like dome, we took the fastest elevator in the world up to **Panorama** where we had a breathtaking view of Berlin.

On Sunday, we drove on the **Spree-river** on a water taxi. Berlin has more water streets and canals than Amsterdam. That was amazing to me. From the boat we viewed all the attractions from a different perspective, moving around the **Museums Insel.** (Isle of museums) We also went to the **Hack'sche Höfe**, former Handwerker (Handworkers) and Gilde[11] craftsmen quarters, which were turned into relaxing courtyards with restaurants and shops on the first floor and modernized apartment housing on top. We strolled through the old **Nikolai-Viertel** (Quarter) with the **Red Rathaus**[12] and its picturesque houses from the Jugendstilzeit. Our Egyptian friend who is married to a Berlin native, also named Renate, chauffeured us around Berlin to the suburbs to give us an impression of the dimensions: 1000 km^2 large is the city with 3, 5 million inhabitants. We also saw the **Bundeskanzleramt** (seat of the Chancellor, Gerhard Schröder), **Schloß Charlottenburg** and the **Tegel See.**

Berlin in two and a half days is just too much! I had been in West Berlin before the fall of the Wall and in 1993, but now, after the reconstruction of the former east, it is an even more grandiose pulsating city with huge green lungs (parks) like the **Tiergarten** with the **Englische Garten** and the **Wannsee** recreation area. We have to come back for another ten-day stay. My husband wants to spend one day solely in the **Pergamon-Museum,** which covers the antique cultures.

I liked the **Buddy Bear exhibition** a lot by the Brandenburg Gate. Bears of a two-meter height stood in a circle, all decorated by national artists around the world. The **US bear** represented the **Statue of Liberty**. Just picture the lady with a big bear butt and drapes around her voluptuous statue. Of course, I posed with

---

11.   Congregation of certain trades during the Middle Ages
12.   Color red, because of the red bricks, not because of the red Communist party!

her/him, and I photographed all the Buddy Bears from all the nations we have friends in. I shot a whole 36 mm-film in order to send the CD images back home to their respective countries. It is amazing what you can transmit via computer, nowadays, within seconds, but my freemail doesn't work right now, with the city under siege of water. We are a network of dependent human beings...one huge organic social structure. A philosopher once said: 'The slightest draft of a butter-fly's wing is not lost in the universe.'

21. August

After Wednesday-Women-Sauna

Sauna news...Ten-day count down...Health...

Since the flooding I found this little sauna nearby (**Sauna South**), because no trams could cross the Elbe-river. Everything here really is within walking distance: Two bakers, two butchers, two pharmacies, two houses with different doctors, including specialists, sauna, banks, flower shops, electronic shops, health food store, no need to travel anywhere.

Only ten more days in Dresden! I finally got into my freemail again, this morning, after the guest computers had crashed several times during the power outings. It is not a good feeling being cut off from the rest of the world. And as I am transferring my script onto the computer the freemail is not working again. Several handy networks (handy=cell phone) didn't work either here for a while, because of the flooding. My aunt from Saarland wrote on a postcard that she couldn't reach me by phone.

It is always interesting to get the latest Dresden news in the women's sauna. Today, I heard of an international school that mainly teaches kids from foreign countries who need to catch up on their German. Maybe it is still possible to arrange something, depending on whether the location is under water or not. I also heard that school children are back in school, today, wherever instruction is possible. They have praised Dresden's youth enthusiastically, for being engaged in the clean-ups and taking care of the stranded in the school gyms. **People do care** from wo/man to wo/man. It works faster than big politics where they quarrel back and forth about competencies.

In the women's sauna I also got information on how to get to certain places in town. Very few trams are going across the bridges. Engineers are being careful with static's. Buses, being lighter and flexible, have taken over mass transportation. I am getting a little sad, right now, thinking of my **ten-day countdown in Dresden.** The longer you live in a place, the more you get connected to it. Dresden will always stay in my heart as that special city where I spent the summer of 2002. My colleagues are returning to school, now, and I am continuing my nine-month sabbatical in Greece (Sept.), India (Oct./Nov.) and Spain (Dec.—May).

My **heart** has improved. It is relaxed most of the time. I have reduced my speed and I am afraid that I have to gear down even more in Greece, India and Spain. My husband is restless. Nothing goes quickly enough for him. He still has high blood pressure (guess why?), not extremely high, but over the limit. The MPI staff is either on vacation or busy with cleanup after the flooding. Maybe half of the personnel are here. I know how difficult it is to let go, step back, and go with the flow. It is just that we both have to "accomplish", not the usual professional goals. I call him my **High-pressure** man, since his specialization is High Pressure Physics. When he asked the doctor for a natural pressure-lowering medicine, after he had dealt with several side effects of allopathic medicine, she said: "Live a sane life-style!" Duuh!!!

Cooling off at the biotope

MPI helps with clean-up...Mexican Good Bye Party...

It was a hot summer day, today. So I am cooling off in the evening breeze up in the biotope. I can hear the rhythmic hacking of a computer-keyboard above the library. Somebody is still working at 7:30 p.m. The light of the sunset is reinforcing the bright orange of a field of wild sunflowers. The color reminds me of tigers, and my honey-covered skin in the White Elk sauna. This is my favorite time of the day: Dusk, when everything quiets down and retreats inside. I hear the sirens from far away. Young people from the **MPI** have spent their weekend helping to **clean up** the flooded areas in town. This afternoon, we invited them over for plum cake (Zwetschgenkuchen) and they were telling us that the mud is the worst. It dries up in the heat and sticks to everything. Officials have advised everyone to disinfect everything thoroughly, because of the swimming cadavers, possible chemicals and fecal matters in the water. I have seen many people break down in tears on the TV, because they have to start from ground zero. Thirty million Euros have been donated, so far. The shops are open Saturday and Sunday, right now to accommodate the situation; that has never been heard of in Germany in the past.

Today, I tried to make another appointment with the Oberschuldirektor (superintendent), but he is still too busy with the emergency situations in many schools. I just have to let go of school. There is only one week left and we will be busy with packing, cleaning up and a major **good-bye party**. We are cooking tacos for thirty people. We got the ingredients one day before the flood in the international department of Karstadt, a department store on Prager Straße. One day later, we would have lucked out, because the grocery department in the basement was under water. We'll start at 4 p.m. on Monday, but when Germans celebrate, it goes into the late evening hours. We are not used to marathon festivities, anymore, but I guess we have to condition ourselves, because in Greece and Spain dinner is usually served around 10 p.m.

The sky is baby blue with pink gray fluffy clouds. I feel chilly, now, so I shall return to our apartment at the other end of the building complex. I wonder why Weld[13] is not responding. Their server must be down.

---

13. My school district

23. August

At empty Luisenhof

Reflection…German teachers vs. American…DNC in India?

The flood receded, so I had to get out again to explore Dresden. All trams were going parallel to the Elbe across town, while mainly buses were going across the bridges. On my bus route 61 to Bühlau I saw "Bob's Corner": Pizza and American Foods and Else's Smoke free Coffee Corner. **Smoke free** is the exception for Germany. They are way behind Ft. Collins, here. I exited at Schillerplatz and crossed the Blue Wonder-bridge. (Blaues Wunder) My beloved Villa Marie was deserted. The flood had swamped the Biergarten and probably the kitchen, too. Where there was healing green three weeks ago there is brown beige mud up to the flood level, now.

On my way up to Luisenhof, on the cogwheel train, I talked to a group of teenagers. They had spent the whole morning down at the Elbe-river with their teachers, emptying and folding sandbags. Nobody is in the mood for fun. Luisenhof, a favorite excursion spot, is all empty, besides me and myself. It is 11:20 a.m. It is eerily quiet, a good time to **reflect** upon the last three months. I did not know how tired I was at the end of the school year. TV was putting me to sleep on a regular basis. I could not stay awake. After ten minutes of a program I was gone. Now, my sleeping pattern is from midnight to 7:30 or 8:00. In the US, I only get six hours of sleep, having to get up at 5 a.m. I just can't fall asleep before 11 p.m. Six hours are not enough, sleeping experts say, because the body cannot completely restore itself. So I robbed myself of one and a half hours of sleep each day for ten years, that adds up to about fifty waking days. I promise to take better care of myself in the future.

In **Germany, teachers** don't have to be in school all day. Teaching and babysitting (=Hort) is strictly separated in schools. As a High school teacher you have 26 hours per week to teach, each instructional hour is 45 minutes. You have to be in for a few conferences, and the rest of the time you can arrange according to your own rhythm in your home office. More preparation goes into each instructional hour than in the US. As I suggested so many times back home, academics needs to be reserved for the mornings and recreational activities for the afternoon. It should not be the teachers' job to keep the students in school all day. Communities need to organize AAA=After Academics Activities, so that the gimpy Mickey-mouse-things are separated from academics, again. Too many chores are loaded on the schools and the backs of the teachers in America, while it should be the responsibility of the communities and parents to keep their kids safe and entertained in the afternoons. Teacher burnout in the US is extremely high and I don't wonder why!

Cameramen with heavy equipment are taking pictures up here of flooded Dresden. It is a little hazy, but you can see into Swiss Saxony. The bouillabaisse was good here, at Luisenhof, fresh fish and baguette, but my husband's is much better. It has that zest...that well rounded fiery touch. It's not always easy to share the kitchen with a chef cook. We both have our specialties. But I guess it's even worse, when a man never enters the kitchen.

A worried friend of mine tried to convince my husband, yesterday on the phone, that I should not have my **DNC in India.** It is cute of her to be concerned, but the Bhabha Atomic Research Center in Bombay is a city in itself and has top scientists and medical personnel. I will go by my instincts and the advice of our local friends there. It is no fun running around with a "loaded" uterus, especially not in that heat. I want to be free to run and jump, but my uterus keeps me grounded. Here is a neat language joke: I am on the phone with my mother-in-law. Me: My uterus is troubling me, again. She: Who is that Mr. Uterus? (Gebärmutter in German= bearing mother, do you see the cognates?) For somebody who has been trained in Latin the expression "Uterus" is not a problem, but really, I wish I'd had three years of Spanish and three years of Latin, then I would have a solid foundation for Spain.

Why did I write about that uterus conversation? Because as a civilized country, we always assume that other cultures are not up-to-date, even behind the moon, in medicine, education, living standards etc.; a commonly made mistake by every industrial nation, especially in the west.

Luisenhof is semi-alive, now. I just heard a flooding joke: They are offering Zanderfilet today. It swam directly into the cook's pot, said a neighbor. Humor and laughter are the best stress relievers.

25. August

Peaceful Sunday morning in my beloved Biotope

Solemn Sunday mornings...Shocked at the Bahnhof...Man and nature...More to come

This is the last Sunday in my beloved biotope. The warm orange field of wild sunflowers blends right in with the orange balconies of the guest—houses. The complimentary color of the houses is royal blue. Two little girls are exploring the goldfish pond. They run around barefoot, humming and laughing.

There is something **solemn about Sunday mornings**. It is a whole bag of feelings that comes up: Being imbedded and connected to a church community as a kid and teenager...helping in the hospital on Sundays...listening to symphonies and arias in my uncle's wine cellar...my mother's festive Sunday morning breakfast table...sleeping in after a long Saturday party in my twenties...making Sundays special for my own family. I love Sunday mornings, because they connect me to my Higher Source and my memories of being content and connected.

Yesterday, I wanted to buy phone cards[14] **at the Central Railroad Station** (Bahnhof). I was **shocked!** Where there was international life a few weeks ago, now there was emptiness and odor. All the shops, but three on the outside had closed down. Everything was deserted; a few shop owners were busy cleaning-up.

The Weißeritz, normally a tiny river across town, had taken back what once belonged to her: Her original flood bed, where Dresdners built the Main Railroad Station on. Right beside the Bahnhof there were two basins with floodwater, about ten meters high where they had begun a construction site for underground garages. It is the stupidity and arrogance of mankind thinking they can manipulate and beat nature. The Native American Indians know exactly why man needs to live in harmony with nature, and why they don't pave the roads: Because Earth is a living, breathing organism! With less paved roads here, water would have had a chance to drain faster instead of being backed up by obstructed canalization systems. At the MPI all service roads are fortified with hollow stones where grass grows in between. The architect must have studied the Indian way-of-life, or was a very developed human being, who knew about mankind living in harmony with nature. The whole MPI design breathes this idea.

---

14.   Go Bananas and Go Spicy cards are the best, a tip from our students, here.

What once was a vibrant Downtown-Dresden, buzzing with tourists, are now empty plazas and deserted cafés. It will take at least three months to a year to get that city center back to life again. In the Prager Str.[15] some department stores had Schnäppchen tables (special deals) along the sidewalks. The odor of mud and mold was everywhere. Young enthusiastic kids passed out free[16] ice-cold cokes in those cute original glass bottles. **Self-contained units** like Italian ice cream stands, Bratwurst grills, and Döners (Turkish food) were the first up and running, again. The more self-contained and independent a unit is, the less it is affected by disasters. I suspect that **more calamities** will come upon us within the next years: More draughts and fires in the US and more floods in Europe, because we have to pay the consequences for how we have "housed" (Ger. gehaust) here on earth. Maybe, we need to think about how not to be so dependent on major networks of supplies, communication, transportation etc. Maybe, we need to be more self-contained in the future.

I will say Good-bye now from Dresden, Germany and will continue from Thessaloniki, Greece. I will walk barefoot back to our apartment on the other end to feel the living, breathing planet who sustains our lives. Thanks, Mother Earth!

---

15. Major shopping pedestrian zone
16. Coke campaign, advertisement

28. August

CODA:
From B'liebig (Stamm Café)

Hiob's News...Death at CSU...Reflection upon my Graduate studies...

This morning, my husband received the news via e-mail from CSU that my former mentor during my graduate studies had died. He was close to his retirement; actually he could have retired already. Slender and agile, never sick, athletic and a volunteer for Search and Rescue you would think that he would live into his hundreds. After my husband had called over from his office to our apartment, I sat down in an armchair, reflecting upon him and my graduate studies. First, I thanked him for all the support and care, and then I prayed that he might move onto the light as quickly as possible, if he wasn't already there.

I was the first graduate student ever in the foreign language department. By chance, I had my own light, spacey office, since one of the professors was on sabbatical. There was hardly a day when he didn't come in for a few minutes, always upbeat, usually with one of his dry jokes to tell. Sometimes, he sat down and we got involved in a serious discussion about politics, German culture, internal campus matters, etc. He was a tough professor. Through his prerequisite course 400something, he got me in gear for graduate studies. Every session, he posed three to five questions about the last reading assignment, usually 25-30 pages, which you had to answer in seconds on a little slip. You either knew the facts or you didn't. You could not circle around. He was a typical German professor. I knew that he couldn't tolerate hugs, so I never tried. Private sessions he would close with hearty handshakes. I had to address him formally, only later, when I was almost done with my graduate studies, he suggested that I could use his first name.

I knew he cared a lot about my graduate studies, and exchanging ideas about German culture, literature and politics. There was one topic we never agreed upon: That was the Holocaust. I think he was so ashamed of his country that he wanted to make that black mark in history go away through denial, and following the concepts of minorities who proclaimed that the Holocaust had never happened to that extent. In one of his seminars I gave a fiery, engaged talk about the Holocaust. As a visual aid I brought one of my art pieces where I had worked through the cycle of suppression and extinction for six weeks under a lot of tears. You could have heard a pin drop during that talk. He totally respected my opinion and emotions about it. He never tried to "convert" me, either.

When I celebrated my Masters at the Lake Sherwood Clubhouse with all my professors and their wives, with my family and friends, and with my fellow graduates and my students, he gave me a unique present which took my breath away. It was an oval shaped, golden key chain with my name engraved on it. He took me to a corner and showed me how the oval turned into a heart. I was speechless, because I'd never seen emotions on his part, before. I couldn't help but hug and thank him for all his support and challenge during my graduate studies. I never used his present as a key chain, because I didn't want any scratches on the gold. I wore it especially on those days in the loops of my jeans or as a piece of jewelry, when I consciously wanted to pass on his love and care to somebody who needed it that day in school. I saw him every now and then after my graduate studies at CSU and CCFLT[17] events, but my husband who had regular contact with him in the coffeeshop and in the faculty senate, kept me posted.

I got up from my armchair, fetched that golden heart with my name engraved from the loop of my jeans. I held it close to my heart, thanked him again and wished him a happy trail, a unification with and illumination about his Jewish brothers and sisters. Peace be with you, Klaus!

Just now, I heard from my husband that he had killed himself. He had had a coffee break with the chair of the department yesterday and she didn't notice anything unusual. Why, Klaus?

End of Part 1: Germany

---

17. CCFLT = Colorado Congress of Foreign Language Teachers

PART II
Greece, Turkey

From Thessaloniki, Greece
Thessaloniki= ΘΕΣΣΑΛΟΝΙΚΗ

Upper Town…Transitional Times…Analphabet…Baggage
University Apartment…Hospitality…

I am sitting on the deck of a little café in the **Upper Town** overlooking θεσσα←λονικη = **Thessaloniki.** Compared to the old town by the harbor, it is quiet up here. I desperately needed to get away from the hustle and buzz of this one-million-inhabitant city. I haven't written for almost two weeks, now, and I am trying to find my balance again. For the last two days I have been homesick, crying myself to sleep at night. During those **transitional times** from one country to another, from one climate into the next, adjusting to different times, beds, foods, customs, I have a hard time. Once I have found the "home" inside myself, my health starts to improve again.

We spent five days in Floersheim, by Frankfurt, in my husband's father house, repacking and helping out the old folks; like doing some major shopping, weeding the yard, getting them to the hairdresser, running errands, spending time with them, showing them pictures of Dresden, etc.

I am writing into a Greek spiral notebook. I specifically looked for a local pad, since most were in English. I am making it a point to buy native and local items, but oftentimes I am glad to find an international product in English, because I am too tired to decipher Greek. Now I know how it feels to be an **analphabet**. I can store bus destinations in my head using the whole-language method and trying to visualize the word.

After repacking in Floersheim, I am down to one small suitcase. I am tired of all this extra **baggage** that I don't really need. I boiled it down to the basics, since I noticed that I was using only 20% of my luggage in Dresden, anyhow. For India I will do the same thing: I will only take along the essentials. Since I like to wear whites a lot, I hand wash them at night and hang them up on the balcony of our apartment overlooking the sea. For the most part they are dry in the morning.

Our **University apartment** is spacey, but noisy. There is a major road going in-between our apartment complex and the seaside. A beautiful park is across the road parallel to the sea. On this side of the bay you cannot swim, because it is built for a harbor and it is polluted. We have to keep the windows shut at night, because it is too noisy. The only time this city quiets down, is between 3 a.m. and 5 a.m. I am definitely not a city girl. I like quiet places, especially at night.

The **hospitality** of our Greek host family was very homey and caring. They housed us for three days, before we could move into our apartment. They insisted that we sleep in their master bedroom and use the children's rooms for our luggage, since the rooms were very small and the children were on vacation with their grandparents in Athens. Our Greek professor and his wife live in a three-story townhouse in a quiet suburb on the eastside of the bay in Perea, where you can actually swim. There are marble floors everywhere, very clean and attractive. Marble balconies and verandas extend the indoor space to fulfill the Mediterranean need for living outdoors. For three days we were spoiled with food at home and in Tavernas=Greek eating establishments, and with introductions to culture and history. Our host professor is a walking ancient history book. It is fascinating listening to him and refreshing my own knowledge of the Greek, Roman and Byzantine eras.

I better take the bus back to the Lower City, now. One never knows how long that takes in the afternoon traffic. (Bus 23!) Don't count on it. It may change next week.

11. September

From Macedonia Palace Café...

International Trade Fair...Tight security in US Hall # 12...Greek frappé...Fashion dictates...Prime Minister of Greece...Traffic...Public transportation...Taxi...Small "c"culture...German versus Greek culture...

I am writing near the seaside. There is a cool breeze fanning inland. This outdoor café belongs to the Macedonia Palace, which is about 100 meters from here and where the Prime Minister of Greece stayed last weekend for the opening of the **International Trade Fair.** Last Friday, September 6, when we moved into our University apartment by the seaside (exact address: Megalou Alexandrou 29), we were greeted with a spectacular flight formation of military airplanes. They even generated the American colors out of their exhaust system, flew in loops upside-down, almost touched wings with each other, separated in precise angles like a fan, and gathered again in a different formation. This show went on for half an hour, and was performed mainly for the Prime Minister and the International Trade Fair guests, so it was meant for us, too. It was quite a homey welcome having been greeted with the American and also French colors.

In front of me, looking to the sea, there is a huge sculpture with about 35 open umbrellas constructed from steel mash. Maybe it's supposed to keep the rain away from Thessaloniki. It only rained once, so far, yesterday, when we visited the International Trade Fair. Since our hostess was a participant at the Fair as a government architect, she welcomed us at the gate, pinned official tags on us, and showed us around for a while.

The **American hall # 12** had tight security. We walked through a metal detector and my backpack was checked. In spite of these 'minor' inconveniences I felt like walking on **homeland** for a while being surrounded by English speaking people. Major universities were represented, General Electric, **Fulbright**[1], Chrysler, and even Starbucks, where we had a frappe and talked to some young folks about globalization and huge chains "killing" the small entrepreneurs. I think they can both exist, since there is a totally different atmosphere in a Greek café than in a

---

1. Humboldt Stiftung (foundation), promoting exchange and learning experiences in foreign countries for academic people

Starbucks. I can sit here for hours with one **ice-cream frappe** and water (it's free here!!!) and nobody will bother me. This frappe is quite interesting in taste: They foam Nescafé with sugar and a little water, add more water, ice and ice cream. The only pain is that I always have to ask for a spoon to scoop up my ice cream, while the Greek people just mix everything with a straw and suck it up. I like the ice cream first and followed by the strong coffee.

Most of the time, I talk with my hands and feet. (German saying) Not as many people speak English here as I had thought. Some of the older folks speak some German, because they have been guest workers in Germany. Greeks are all over the world, but they always like to come home and be buried here, they told me. I had a German student in RHS[2] who had been born in Thessaloniki. Tabitha was her name.

There are two ladies sitting down. They look like mother and daughter and they speak Greek. The mother is wearing a tanga under her tight pants and it looks quite naked. The tangas were supposed to make the old-fashioned panty lines go away, but I can tell by the little triangle at the sacrum, when somebody is wearing a tanga. So what's the advantage or esthetics of a tanga? I bought one in Karstadt, Germany and it is pretty uncomfortable, too. Women let themselves be **dictated by fashion** all the time, while men go for the comfortable, practical, timeless and classical clothes.

Next time, I will come to earth as a man for many reasons: I can go anywhere I want to; I don't need to be guarded by our host in Istanbul where we go to in ten days; I can walk around in the dark, and not worry about attacks; I don't have to carry three babies, be limited by a monthly period, discomforts during menopause, uterus problems, etc. I am sure men have to carry their load, too, so maybe I'll incarnate as an androgen.

Back to the Macedonian Palace and the opening of the International Trade Fair: Saturday night, when we were walking along the sea promenade, three military sea ships were illuminated like the roof of a house during Christmas time in America. The whole city was on its feet.

<Oh my God, a beautiful pelican is flying majestically close by. It has an enormous wingspan. In Native American philosophy, it is the bringer of peace and renewal. >

A Greek citizen summed up the whole spectacle quite well: "I didn't know, until today, that we had police in Greece!" Police were on alert everywhere, because there were some demonstrations against the **Prime Minister**'s agricul-

---

2.   Roosevelt High school

tural policies. The harbor around the White Tower[3] and the Macedonia Palace was especially fortified. Police had emptied the streets before, in order to escort the Prime Minister straight to his hotel. Greeks were quite annoyed about that, because it caused delays and traffic jams, but the main reason is that the officials never get to see and feel the real problems of the city, and **traffic** is one of them.

The cars are parked everywhere, even in curves and on the sidewalks. A pedestrian has to slalom across the street, especially along the Via Ignatia, a major road along the university. Overcrowded buses handle all public transportation. You literally have to stuff yourself in like a sardine, and squeeze yourself out like the last lemon drop, at least one stop in advance. It is difficult to get around for foreigners, since there are no printed bus plans, which would tell me where to go and with which bus. I could figure out everything by myself if I had one. The other day, I got a whole group of Greek bus drivers at an end terminal to discuss the "missing bus route plan". One of them spoke English. They discussed back and forth, and came up with the final statement that no printed plan existed, except on the bus stations themselves, and that I should ask people. Good for social interaction, but that doesn't help me, as a tourist, to make quick decisions and transitions in-between busses and sight seeing attractions.

The other day, on the way back from visiting the Upper Town, I waited for a bus for thirty minutes. Five buses had gone up, and none had come down. I figured there was an accident. So, I waved for a **taxi,** and had to explain with hand and feet and a city map where I wanted to go, namely to Aristotle University. I had my accent wrong on Aristotéles University, and I didn't know the word for university=panepistimio, so the taxi driver didn't understand me at first. When I heard him say the right destination I figured it out with my language background. It's a real handicap not being able to speak the language, but I always trust that I will run into the right people who will help me along in finding my way. So far, I have only encountered friendliness and helpfulness. Taxis are quite affordable, especially when you can share them with two other people. It's a custom here for taxi drivers to pick up other people along the road who are going in the same direction.

I am glad that Greece has the **Euro,** too, otherwise I would have to handle the different currency on top of the language and transportation problems. I am sure I would figure it all out, if I stayed here longer, at least the things, which are most important to me. I am getting a pretty good idea of how our Mexican students

---

3.   Landmark by the sea: Part of the fortification of the city walls, dating back to the Romans

feel when they first come to Johnstown. It takes about six years until you figure out the language and the culture, all the silent encoding of the so-called small **"c"culture**, like driving conventions. Nobody talks about it, but everybody knows what to expect, how to react and respond with body language.

Last night, we met a Greek student on the bus who had studied in Köln (Cologne), Germany, for six years and held a job as a graphic designer. She said that she couldn't put up with the Greek "chaos" anymore, but that she loves the relaxed life-style in Greece. Our Greek professor said: "The main difference between the **German culture and the Greek culture** is that the Germans need to have everything planned out and organized. Greeks on the other hand let life take care of itself, create from the chaos, take time, and live life as it comes along."

There is the majestic pelican again, flying right above the riffled sea, probably looking for his dinner. I shall go home now to our apartment, which is right across the street, prepare some Greek salad with tomatoes, cucumbers, peppers, olives, feta cheese, garlic, olive oil, balsamic vinegar, sea salt and freshly baked bread from the baker to dip into the marinade. I should buy some Retzina, too, Greek wine with the special taste of resin from a pine tree. You see, we live like the Greeks in Greece, only disguised as tourists.

12. September

From a Taverna by the Loutra Thermis…

German-American…Taxi driver…Thermi Center…Loutra Thermis…Official health pass…

This is hard to swallow for a **German-American**. I am one person with two hearts beating inside, but I was treated as two different people. Well, let me explain everything step by step. Since nerve pain was shooting down my legs at night, I thought it would be a good idea to do something for my health. I had seen a brown street sign "Thermi" during another outing, so I asked for the bus number to get there. "It has no number. It is the bus to Basilika", they said. I waited at the bus station for half an hour, and no bus showed up. I finally waved for a taxi. The **taxi driver** was a well-nourished Greek who spoke with a lot of body language like me, but we communicated quite well, and had a few good laughs. He said Germans are always serious and grim in Germany, but when they come to Greece into the sunshine they start smiling. He was laughing so hard that his belly was shaking. He pointed to my well-nourished thighs and stated that I must love food, too. He recommended some Tavernas to me. We drove about 20 km, passing IKEA following the sign to Thermis. He asked "Thermi Center?" and I said yes, figuring it was the main entrance to a thermal bath. He dropped me off in the center of the suburb Thermi and there I stood. So the Thermis don't exist, I thought for a minute, it is the name of a town. Then I saw two young ladies sitting on a bench whom I suspected to speak English. I asked for the Hot Springs or the Thermal Bath and which bus would go there. "No bus from here", they said, "Take a taxi!"

So off I went again another 10 km to the middle of nowhere and there was indeed a sign **Loutra Thermis**. I went into what looked like the main entrance, and asked if somebody spoke German or English. There was one good-looking, very friendly bath employee who spoke some English. She brought me over to another building where a nurse measured my blood pressure. I said, "It's perfect!" in advance and she started laughing when it was perfecto in deed. Then they filled out an official looking pass, asked for my name, telephone, Greek address, age, etc. Thank God I had written down my name in Greek the day before, and had it checked over by our host professor, so they had no problem reading it off my map of Thessaloniki. They sent me over to the ticket booth. The pool was already closed for the ladies. It was the men's turn, now, but I could take an individual bath, they said. So I purchased a ticket for three €uro. They entered more official data into my pass, stamped it three times, and brought me over to the bathhouse. I got a ticket with the number four on a little wooden plate, indicating when it would be my turn. While waiting for an individual bath tub...

13. September

From the Thermis...

Greeks are...Hotel...Physio...Sulfur...F-word and others...Feldenkreis...Buddha...Philosopher...Free treatment...Greek health pass...

While waiting for an individual bathtub, I chatted with other clients in English, German and French. **Greeks** are very **social** and **communicative.** They will never die of loneliness like old people in other cultures. They always leave their house at night to meet up with other Greeks in the park, in the Tavernas, or at the sea promenade.

When it was my turn, I walked into a spacious bathroom, freshly cleaned and disinfected. The bath employee let the bath water in, told me that she would knock on the door in half an hour, and that I should unplug the closure. The temperature of the water felt exactly right. It smelled and tasted sulfuric. After my bath meditation I asked for a massage therapist. They said I should go over to the "hotel", last door on the first floor. Since they weren't sure I had understood, they sent an escort with me. I would have never found it, since the hotel didn't look like a hotel. My escort knocked on the physiotherapist's door. That day I wore a camouflage T-shirt from my boys, khaki pants which zip into shorts, white tennis shoes, and I spoke English. The therapist said he was booked for two weeks.

Next day, I went again to the Thermis; this time, I purchased a ticket to the pool, so that I could talk to other women and ask questions about Greek culture. There was only one woman who spoke a little English. She explained that the Thermis were good for the bones and the neck, and that they were theos. I figured they were holy deriving from Theology, but when I checked in with our Greek professor at night, he said it means sulfur. Cognates are very helpful in languages, since the brain always needs something to connect with, but sometimes, you can go very wrong. (For example: gift in German is poison.)

I learned the F-word, today. It's the most important word in any culture:
ef caristo = thank you!
calimera = good morning!
panepistimio = university
theo = sulfur

catálogo = menu
jassas = good bye
jamas = cheers
So far with my Greek. Don't hold me to my spelling. That's how it sounds.

Latest village news is announced over loud speakers here. Just like in the olden days: The town crier or the African drums, but with more of a modern technique. A little ant is dragging a breadcrumb over the table. It is bigger than her. So why am I complaining about my load? (Whatever package I have to carry, metaphorically speaking)

After my bath in the large pool I figured I would try again to get a massage, since people might have cancelled. Passing by the manager she asked me how my physiotherapia had been yesterday. I said that the ΦΥΣΙΟΘΕΡΑΝΕΥΤΗΡΙΟ was booked for two weeks, but I would ask again. She guided me across the street like a child and I said "Ef caristo, Mama!" and she started laughing. She brought me to the Physiotherapist. Check this: Today, I wore a white pants, white keds, an elegant beige T-shirt from my mother-in-law, and I spoke German. Guess what? "Wait around till 1.p.m., till I am done with the Grandma, here, then I will treat you", said the therapist.

I didn't do any of this consciously, and maybe it has nothing to do with nationalities, maybe he just had a bad day yesterday and wasn't in the mood for more work. Anyhow, I was quite impressed with his treatment. He worked with the **Feldenkreis** method, balancing and integrating the meridians through physical impulses. He had studied in Berlin and spoke German quite well. "You look calm like a Buddha from the outside, but inside you are a boiling volcano!" he threw right at my head. He inquired about my aches and pains, my professional life, and started the treatment. After half an hour of remapping the body, I felt much better. Back at the desk he asked me: "What is your **truth**?" A little bit stunned and hesitating I said: "Well, we are all God heads, tiny spark plugs of the creator and there is an interchange. *Pars pro totum* as Socrates said. *The part stands for the whole.* We are one large organism."

"What is your truth", I asked. "To live your own life experience authentically", he answered. "True!" I said. Greeks are **philosophers.** They always were, and they always will be. I also noticed that many men have butts like women, and when you look at the old Greek sculptures nothing has changed. Different cultures have different physiognomies. American men are mostly slender in their hips, even when they have a belly.

When I wanted to pay for the treatment he said: "It's free! It comes with the pool pass." I assume it is supported by the government. This is unbelievable. I, as a foreigner, receive **free treatment** in Greece. He wants to see me for six to eight sessions. "You'll see a miracle happen in five to six months", he said. "I've had great success with the Feldenkreis method, combined with intuition." "Ef caristo! Tschüss!" I said, thinking we'll see what happens in half a year. "Bis morgen"(till tomorrow), I said. It's hilarious: With my Greek health pass I am an officially adopted Greek-German-American world inhabitant.

16. September

From Harry's Spot...

Home...Greek students...Excursions to Virgina, Pella and Dion

I am writing from a typical student establishment. Greek disco music is playing at a reasonable volume outdoors. After two days of rain, everybody is longing for the sunshine again, meeting up with other people, and playing all kind of games. I hear a lot of laughter around me. It feels like High school. The rhythm of the music is speeding up my pen. Every now and then a romantic song slows down my pen and makes me daydream of home. What exactly **is home?** It may be a place, people you love, the feeling of sitting in Abraham's lap, but most of all, I think, it is being content within yourself wherever you are, wherever you go.

My banana shake is being served with cookies and candies. Greeks never cut down on foods. They'd rather not have a new TV or more clothes. The scent of Armani is in the air. It is coming from the young man on my right, playing chess with his friend. He is getting ready for a long Greek night. Life, real life, starts around 10 p.m., and students often go to bed in the early morning hours. Only 2 % of the enrolled students work for their life-style. For the majority, the state and the parents are paying for education. They only have to pay for housing, not even for food. Everything else is provided by the state: Tuition, cantina food, books, health care, and bus transportation. There are about 70,000 students in Thessaloniki. Rich Greeks send their kids to Athens, Rome, England, Germany, and the USA. It is hilarious: I am the only "professora" among these young folks. There are only two tables of female students, and about ten tables with male students. Does that mean female students study harder? (That is so indeed, said our Greek professor, later)

On the weekend, we undertook two excursions with our two Greek brothers. Yesterday, we visited the tomb of **Philip II in Virgina = BEPΓINA**, two hours west of Thessaloniki (on the Gulf of Thess.). Philip II was the father of **Alexander the Great** (reigned from 336-323 B.C.), who conquered half of the world, North Africa, Minor Asia, (American Pie is playing!) up to the Indus, practically all of the civilized world. Alexander the Great was educated by **Aristotle**, and so were other twelve disciples. This is how Alexander built this great emporium, with his co-eds in charge of his conquered provinces, promoting Hellenistic civilization.

There is a story about Alexander the Great that shows the strength of his leadership, and the solidarity among his soldiers. When he was stricken with a high fever, one of his soldiers found water for him in the desert, and brought it to him in his helmet. Alexander refused to drink a drop, since there was not enough for all of his soldiers. He often fought in the front row during battles. The name of my oldest son is Alexander. He was always very tall for his age, so we named him Alexander the Great. Alexander der Grosse hat beschissene Hose. It only rhymes in German: Alex the Great has his diapers full.—

In **Pella** = Πελλα, we visited an excavation site of a Greek city. You could clearly see the water pipelines and the heating system in the floors. The bath areas were ornamented with elaborate mosaics depicting Greek mythology. Pella was Alexander's capital at that time. Twenty kilometers from there, he prepared himself for the big battles in Dion, where he sacrificed to the Gods.

Dion = Διον is a huge excavation site where you can observe the Greek building styles (~ 600-50 B.C.), overlaid by the West Romans (~250 B.C.-400 A.D.), then the early Christians around 100 A.D., and finally the Byzantine era from about 400 A.D.-1400 A.D. The huge communal bath (~1000 square meters) depicted elegant mosaics. Again, there was central heating and flowing water. The narrow clay pipes in-between measured the water supply of each family. In the communal toilets they sat thigh by thigh, probably discussing daily politics. The holes in the stone toilets were awfully small. They had to aim closely. I wondered why all these well-rounded stones were lying around. Our walking ancient history book (our dear Greek professor!) said that that was the way the emperor collected taxes. Since everybody had to clean their backsides, the stones were sold right there. I can imagine how the cleaning procedure would work in combination with water, but in dry condition, they'd have to have callused bottoms. Since the stone seats were very cold in the winter, they sent their slaves to warm up the toilet.

In Dion it was drizzling all day. The place was full of mystery and history. A beautiful crane landed elegantly on a lush poplar. A water—saturated jungle covered up more of the ancient sites, but there is no money for this undertaking right now. I fell into a meditative state while walking on the soft ground, reflecting on the human chain. Our Greek professor must have picked up on my brain waves: "Those who don't know history are ignorant and arrogant. They think they are the center of the world. When you come here to reflect, you know your place in history, in the long chain of mankind, in the waves of civilizations."(Indirect quote!) "You'll be very tired, afterwards." And sure enough, as soon as he started the motor of his Toyota, I fell into a deep ancient sleep, carried away by antique gods and myths. It felt as if the dead had drained my energy to come alive once more in my memory.

17. September

At the Thermis...

Western time...Greek rhythm...Goethe Institute...

I just took my sulfur bath, and I am waiting for the Physiotherapist, right now, who is taking a little break after treating <u>one</u> client. (Later I heard that it was the birthday of the director and they had a little celebration going on in the back.) It is really funny how I still operate on the **Western time** schedule. (That's especially the US and the German) Originally, I had an appointment at 2:30 p.m. Trying to make the appointment on time I took a taxi for the last stretch, since no bus arrived. I was here at 2:15 p.m. and guess who wasn't? I went over to the Taverna to enjoy an ice café in 15 minutes, which was nuts in the first place for me to order, because it arrived at 2:30 p.m. So I came over to the "Hotel" at 2:40 to check if he was there. A lady who spoke some German told me that she had an appointment at 2 p.m. "Well", I said, "Tell the Physio that Renate is here, but she'll go over to take a bath, first.

When I came out of the sulfur bath, he crossed the street to take a break. That's the **Greek rhythm.** Nothing is ever sure. You just sit or stand back, let time take over, and live in the moment. So I found a half-shady bench in front of the "Hotel", which is actually something like a sanatorium, to use the time to write. "For doing nothing takes all I got!" (Quote from a poster where a cat lies on her belly stretching out on all fours) In the bathtub I sang two Ave Maria, one from Bach-Gounoud, and the other from Brahms, and then a lullaby that I had always sung to my kids. The acoustic was superior. They did not knock on the door after 30 minutes. They wanted me to continue singing, I heard later. With my internal clock, however, I drained the bathtub after 35 minutes, and got dressed.

I hope my Physio is coming back on time, because I have a bus to catch. Tonight is the birthday of the Goethe Institute of Thessaloniki, where they celebrate with beer, pretzels, Kuchen (cake), and music. The Goethe Institute is quite near us where I can use the Bibliothek (German word derived from Greek) and the Internet. But it is awfully slow, so I prefer to use the guest computer in the University (=panepistimio). The ground, the Goethe Institute is built on, belongs to the German government. Hurray, he is coming!

I did catch the bus on time. The Physio pulled the devil out of me. This shoulder pain that I had carried around for a whole year seems to be gone. It started when I was cutting the hedges for six hours straight with a heavy hedge trimmer. I had heart spasms back then, but I didn't recognize them as such. The Physio did other weird pulls and adjustments. The pain went back and forth between my uterus and the sacrum. At least the nerve pain is diminishing at night. The fest at the Goethe Institute was great, because we got to talk half of the night with two young Greek mothers who had grown up in Germany, comparing the Greek and the German cultures.

18. September

At the Thermis (cont.)…

Cultural conditioning…Greek schools…German health care…Greek teachers…Prices in Greece…Temptation…World community…Olive oil…Another stamp…Chalkidike…The Greek way…

It is interesting to observe how humans are **conditioned by specific cultures** within their Umfeld (social milieu). These two young women were more German than Greek in their behavior and philosophies. **Greek schools** are too lax, they said, teachers are not professionally dressed, and children don't learn how to study systematically. Now keep in mind, as a reader, that these opinions are always formed through specific experiences and cannot be generalized. The one beautiful looking woman with olive skin and turquoise eye shadow was a language teacher, teaching German in a private school, and the other nice looking lady was an engineer. She had two gorgeous looking sons with Greek profiles, ages eight and twelve, and her friend had two attractive girls, ages ten and thirteen. The older son wanted to become a chef cook. Ever since he was a little boy, he expressed that passion, and now he was waiting for his "examina" results to be allowed to enter cooking school after 7th grade.

The women found the **German health care** system, especially for mothers, much more attractive than the Greek. Mothers in Germany get eight weeks off from work before and ten weeks after the birth of a child. The state pays an allowance of ca. 300 € each month to the mother, when she stays home to raise her kid by herself. Greek men are spoiled. Women do everything for them on top of working their jobs. These two women were married to the "old" kind, but they said that the scene is changing slowly, that men are getting more involved in child rearing, since more and more mothers are working. They will start raising their children <u>right</u>, they said.

Greek kids are in school from 8–2 p.m. They go home, eat and rest, and then around 5 p.m., they go to private schools, learning more languages, and being tutored on the morning session to keep up their grades. **Teachers** in the Gymnasion (Middle school) and the Lyceum (High school) teach 15–19 hours per week. Since their salary is around 1500 €, they teach the financially very attractive private evening lessons.

Prices in Greece are pretty hefty. A family can't manage with one salary. A second car is very expensive and is taxed progressively. Housing is as expensive as in Germany or Ft. Collins, but the salaries are 1/3 to ½ lower here. Food in a Taverna is pretty reasonable, except in those tourist places, like the tomb of Philip II in Virgina. They even charged us for bread and olives there, which are usually free. It is always a good idea to ask for the catálogo first, to get a general idea about the prices, but since we had our other Greek professor with us, we didn't especially pay attention that day.

Tonight, we are invited to his house for a Greek family dinner. **Both Greek professors** are practically like brothers. They always show up together at conferences and I know them from way back (1984). They have been to our house in Ft. Collins, too. When I check into our host professor's office on some mornings, and I find him busy on the computer, I tend to retreat, but he always takes time to find out how I am experiencing the Greek culture and if I am still happy.

The **temptation** is great on some days to retreat inside, hang out by the sea, read, dream, cry, write, but then I wouldn't learn anything new and wouldn't give life a chance to surprise me and people to spoil me. This Thermis community out here has taken me in like a little kid. They model words for me, pat me on the head when I get it right, laugh about my TPR[4] approach playing everything out, until I get my point across. It is really one large **world community**, if you can trust like a kid, and be faithful that only good things will happen to you.

I took my sulfur bath, already. I had a Greek salad in my Taverna and a Retzina. Because of the **olive oil,** I have no problems here with digestion. Usually, I stuff up while traveling, not here, though. Food adaptation is a big part of your health and well-being every day. From our Greek hostess we learned that the best olive oil has less than 0, 5% acid. I always had an aversion towards olive oil in the States, since it was always overpowering the salad. Not here: It must taste light and sweet, then it is pressed right, and has the most value for your organism. I hear cowbells. My goodness, there is a whole cowherd across the street. I just took a picture (as if I had never seen one). They have those cowbells that they have in the Alps. The sound was totally familiar to me.

I am waiting for my physio to show up. I don't see his colorful motorcycle, yet. After the treatment I have to go over to this other building with a Red Cross to get a **stamp** from the doctor into my pass. I have no idea what it is all about, but I will ask our Greek host families, tonight. It's not to say that they know

---

4.   TPR=Total Physical Response, method often used in Foreign language classes to speak within context while playing out the words or the meaning.

<u>everything.</u> Some things they learned from me, because I am making my own experiences in this culture. I paid exactly 5 € for an elaborate Greek salad, bread, one glass of Retzina, and a coffee. That's adequate, right?!

I haven't had time to write about our outing to **Chalkidike**, yet, two weeks ago. Our Greek professor drove us down to **Moudania**, SE of Thessaloniki, then further to Kassandra beach where we took a refreshing swim in the ocean at **Kalithea**. It is situated on the first finger of these three finger islands. At first, it was quite chilly, because the sky was cloudy, but when you swam in the water for a while, it was ok. Afterwards, we had a Greek lunch in a Taverna overlooking the ocean. For all three of us, with wine and everything, we paid 15 €. When the restaurant owner likes you, he brings a dessert for free. We always got one, except in that touristy place in Virgina. My strategy to look for good Tavernas when I am by myself is to look for Greek natives. They always know where to get the best food for the best price.

"Never drink your coffee in the same place where you eat. That's the **Greek way**", says our Greek professor. "Why?" I asked. "Is it so that you can enjoy another scenery and sit down philosophizing twice?" "You got it!" he said. I learned the "dipping thing" from him, too. They call me the Big Dipper, now. "Never waste any precious olive oil. Always dip your bread in it." OK, Herr Professor! In Greece I do like the Greek, and I'll take some customs back home, too! My health is improving through those treatments; therefore, I have a more positive outlook on life.

19. September

At a Bus Station: ΗΜΟΣ ΚΑΛΑΜΑΡ, waiting for the bus to Basilika...

Greek Gala Dinner...Greek Coffee...Sirtaki...Shared taxi...Birthday...Greek Potato Salad...History of Thessaloniki...Icons...

Last night, the **dinner** at the other Greek Professor's house—let's call him Dionysos here—was great (absolute Spitze! Top of the line!). His wife, Athena, had cooked about ten different dishes: A Greek salad, a spicy feta cheese dip, stuffed eggplants, garlic eggplant dip, a white cabbage-carrot salad, meatballs, tsaziki, Spätzle with gravy and a master rooster...That's a free running cock. It's very lean and tough; therefore, it must cook in red wine for about two hours before it is roasted with different spices in the oven. After the main course a fruit plate was served, and then the meal was topped off with a crockant tart and a **Greek coffee**. It is cooked in a tiny pot with very fine coffee flour and must come to a boil three times to unfold its full flavor. It is similar to Arabian coffee, which is spiced with cardamom. The old fashioned way is to move the tiny coffee pot around in hot sand or ashes, as they showed us at the International Trade Fair, so that the liquid is heated evenly.

At the Thermis= ΛΥΤΡΑ ΘΕΡΜΗΣ...

That was so funny just now: I went over to the Physio to leave him a note on the door if I could have the very first appointment, today, because it's my husband's birthday, when a pair of old Greek citizens danced the **Sirtaki** in the hallways, accompanied by loud rhythms coming from the Grandpa's room. They didn't notice me. I just stood there and enjoyed the performance. I applauded when they were finished, and they reacted as if I had caught them stealing cherries. Then they giggled like teenagers and the woman disappeared into her room. The Grandpa conveyed to me with <u>one</u> German word "Nacht=night" and the rest with body language that they meet for dances every night in the forum.

I missed the bus to Basilika again, since I was writing and not paying attention. You have to stand, wave and be very alert; otherwise they pass right by you. The bus was supposed to come at half past the hour, but it already passed by at twenty past the hour, so I waved for a **taxi**. I **shared** it with an English speaking young woman who was dropped off by a brand new hospital right across from IKEA: **International Balkan Studies for Medicine**, it said on the front entrance. A little later, a Greek businessman joined the ride. From the conversation with the taxi driver I understood that he was intending to do business with the **Coca Cola Company**, which was on my way to the Thermis.

Tonight, the same party with our two Greek professors and their wives will be meeting again in the Upper Town in a very romantic Taverna right by the illuminated city walls, dating back to the Galerius times around 300 A.D., for my **husband's birthday**. I wanted to hire a Greek Bouzouki player for an hour, but our Greek professor (let's call him Sokrates from now on) said: "It's not like in America. They come by chance. You can't call an agency and hire them." Maybe I can initiate a last minute surprise. I already got him pralines, yesterday with a little <u>private</u> gift certificate, but I am up for something hilarious, spontaneous, extraordinary...

"Mansaria" I just learned a new Greek word (or so I thought) from the Sirtaki Grandpa who ordered a take-out meal in the Taverna. Have a good meal! Mansaria! Mahlzeit! I had **potato salad** for lunch: Hot potato pieces swimming in olive oil, sprinkled with fresh parsley and pepper, with lots of onions and two lemon wedges. As my Greek professor said, it's boring to eat alone, because you can't share the many different dishes to taste, and you don't have a friend to talk to. The social aspect of a meal in Greece takes precedence over just eating or filling up. Fast food is not for Greeks, although the **Goody's chains** offer Greek **Fast Food**, but they still take their time to eat on real plates with knives and forks.

Some **history** about **Thessaloniki**, since I am spending the night between ancient walls: Thessaloniki was founded in 316 B.C. The city is named after the sister of Alexander the Great. Four historical figures are dominant in the city all the time: **Aristoteles, Alexander the Great, Galerius and Dimitrios**.

The university is named **Aristotéles panepistimio**. Aristoteles was the teacher of Alexander the Great. Teachers always have the power to unfold the greatness within a student: e-ducere (lat.) to draw out, to draw out the best in a student, but there is also another proverb: When the student is **ready**, the right teacher will appear. Education is a two-way street. It is nearly fruitless to teach unwilling students, and we US teachers waste so much energy with motivating the "unmotivated" that we drain our energy like a well drying up in the desert oasis.

There is a monument of **Alexander the Great** by the sea promenade: Alex with his sword on his horse. Kids like to skateboard there. Since I already wrote about him, we'll move on to Galerius who was the Roman emperor around 300

A.D. The mighty Galerius gate is still giving testimony about the triomphous Einmarsch (entry) of Galerius into the city, overpowered by the Romans.

Dimitrios was an early Christian martyr who was stoned to death. The Agios-Dimitrios Cathedral was reconstructed in 1948, and is a prototype of **Byzantine Greek Orthodox churches**. The **Icons** play an important role in Greek orthodox denomination: Greeks kiss them and light candles by them, and when they pass a church, they make three holy crosses across their chests. Bus and taxi drivers have built whole altars above their driver's seat along with family photos. They surely need all the protection they can get in this insane traffic. Bus drivers and taxi drivers drive like the "Henker" (executioner) as we say in Germany, but nothing usually happens. They are master drivers, especially the bus drivers, who maneuver their busses by the centimeter around ancient city walls and other obstacles. Greeks love to honk their horns, policemen love to whistle their whistles; nobody follows the rules, yet the traffic is flowing most of the time. As a pedestrian you are not even safe on the crosswalk. The other night, a lady drove right into a swarm of pedestrians, ignoring the red light. There you could see some very angry Greeks. Usually nothing can shake them that quickly.

I will go look for my Physio now, since I wish to catch the earlier bus back to Thessaloniki. My Physio said that mansaria was an Italian word. His Greek fellow men wanted to communicate so badly with "Germania" (that's my nickname here) that they use whichever language they think I might understand.

20. September

Writing from my bed…

Before the trip to Istanbul…Reflection about the Physio…Poetry…Teaching…Learning…Books…

It is around 10 p.m. The **music festival** is blasting in the park across from our apartment. We have three hours before we have to get up for the trip to Istanbul. Maybe I won't sleep at all. The music is really good, a variety of styles.

I am **reflecting** on the last conversation I had with the **Physio**. I should have been quiet during the treatment, so that he could have concentrated better, but I thought this is my last chance to explore deeper about the Greek soul. And sure enough, we got into philosophizing again. One time when he was in a meditative alpha state, he experienced himself as a poet. "**Poetry** is truth" he said, "From right to left, upside down, reversed, it holds true from all angles. Where do you get your strength from?" he asked. "Through teaching sometimes, meditating, praying, creating art, through music, writing, writing poetry", I said. "Write down a poem for me and I will know who you are." I could only recall one, because my son Sven had inquired recently if that was a quote or an "original Mom", at the end of my letter. These are actually the closing lines of a longer poem:

Educator's Prayer

For what I teach I learn
And what I learn I master
And what I master I become.

Original Mom!

Then we talked about **teaching**. He does physiotherapy for eight months and teaching for four months out of the year at the College level. "So, which do you like better?" "Teaching oftentimes leaves a hole in my solar plexus. So much energy goes out." "I know what you mean", I said, "Those days when no energy is flowing back, when you teach against the grain." "What I like most", he said, "Is continuous professional development. **Learning**, that's my passion and **books**! When I read Wolfgang Borchert[5], I started to accept myself, because I could totally identify with the loneliness inside of the main character when I was a young lad." "Yes, books are very important for me, too. They literally fall out of the shelf on my head when I need to learn something new, or specific book titles are recommended by total strangers to me." To carry on a philosophically educated discussion like this, you need a high level of language skills. His words were tempered and forged. Before, I had heard him speak in Greek to another patient explosively. He could not apply that same passion and temperament to the German language, but he retrieved amazingly complex words from his student times in Berlin. I thanked him for his treatments with an envelope of a little monetary gift, and promised to write when a major shift in my health would occur. **Healer...teacher...poet...eternal student**...Many aspects of mine were reflected right back to me. I am always guided to where I have to go and whom I have to meet.

---

5.   German author, known for his short stories and other works: "Draußen vor der Tür"

29. September

Back from Istanbul and Athens...

*V*iew to the sea...Birthday in Perea...Byzantine museum...Greek "Greyhound"...To be an American...Free Eagle...Xenophobia...Istanbul: Western city...Turkish men...

I am writing from our communal living room of our spacious university apartment, overlooking Thessaloniki towards the umbrella sculpture, the Macedonian Palace and the White Tower. Far out in the sea, an illuminated ship anchors for the night. The traffic of the six-lane Megalou Alexandrou is roaring as usual, but we are up in the 4th floor now with an unobstructed **view to the sea**. From my bed I could watch the waves, boats and the sunset, but today the weather was cloudy in the morning and it is raining tonight.

We celebrated our Greek hostess' **birthday in Perea** today. From our balcony I could flash signals across the bay to their house in the East. The poor birthday kid cooked an elaborate Greek meal for the usual party: Our two Greek professors, their wives, three kids and us. We promised her a US style birthday, if she'd fly to Colorado, next year.

After the birthday party around 5 p.m. we went to the **Byzantine museum**. It was one of the free days today. Pleasant surprise! The Byzantine phase started about when Emperor Constantine founded Constantinople (now Istanbul) in 338 A.D. and lasted till around 1400. It incorporated Greek, Roman and Early Christian elements. The museum was well organized. Most of the artifacts were within reach, not behind glass vitrines, which get you more involved as a spectator. The music corner with ancient music felt like a sanctuary. They broadcasted the ancient fortification of Thessaloniki on three screens, positioned in a U-shape, drawing you into ancient history as a participant. I'd love to have a meditation room like this.

In 1453 Konstantinopel (Ger. sp.!) was conquered by the Turks, a nomadic tribe, and you can still feel and hear the resentments of the Greeks: "They came into an already made nest (sich ins gemachte Nest setzen), never created their own culture and declare it their own now."

So much has happened since we left Thessaloniki, last Saturday when the music festival started right in front of our house. I always wanted to travel on a

Greyhound in America to experience the real world, not just my protected, privileged academic environment. You get what you pray (and pay!!!) for: We rode in a Greek bus for 12 hours experiencing the real world. The toilet was conveniently locked, presumably out of order. You never knew when the next pit stop came. When a fellow American who sat across the isle from us complained, the bus driver said something in Greek that didn't sound like an invitation to me. Later it was translated to us by a German-Turkish guest worker as "Suck it up". The Turkish-German traveler who had worked at Opel in Germany for many years took care of us during the whole trip, translating back and forth and informing us about the rules. We in return translated back to our fellow American keeping him informed. There was also a Greek student, going to Ankara, who spoke English very well and contributed a lot with his cheery nature creating a good atmosphere.

At first, it felt very strange and lonely on the bus, but after we had formed coalitions and translated back and forth between the parties, we could even joke about that moody pascha[6]-bus driver. For the first half of the trip, the bus stopped in every little fisher town picking up people who were standing 50 meters apart. We did not understand why there wasn't a central pick-up station along the highway. It is not for me to judge. They probably have their reasons. Every pit stop cost me between 30 and 50 cents. You had to pick up toilet paper before you went squatting on a floor toilet. It's actually pretty comfortable and hygienic, because you don't have to touch anything, but you better jump out fast after flushing or you might get your feet washed.

At the Greek-Turkish border, we had to get out twice, and again I experienced that **Americans** have a harder time standing in this world than Germans. With my American passport I had to pay $ 65 for my entry visa; while, my husband got through with his German passport, although Turkey is not in the European Union, yet. He discussed so hard with the Turkish official about that injustice that he forgot to stamp my visa (But we didn't know it at that time). During the discussion, I overheard a Spanish traveler say: "It's only fair that the Americans pay. They use up over 50% of the resources of the whole world."

Our American fellow traveler, who was a laid-back and well-informed guy in his thirties, said to me jokingly: "You look very militant in your army shirt. I hope they don't stop the bus again." "They better not mess with me", I replied, "I am a **Free Eagle!**"

---

6.   Ger.: Male dominant ignorant person

When we stopped for a forty-minute lunch break on the Turkish side I didn't feel like eating at all, because of all the rumbling in my stomach. The food looked really good, though, but I only ordered some yoghurt and rice. I was the last to come out of the bathroom when I saw the bus rolling and my husband knocking at the bus door and shouting: "Stop, stop!" in panic. I knew it was a joke and didn't speed up at all. After all, this grumpy bus driver had a sense of humor, and if I had spoken Greek I would have broken down his fear of strangers (**xenophobia**).

On the Turkish side the domineering landmarks were the high-rising minarets of the mosques. When we approached Istanbul, I was surprised to see a city landscape of a modern **Western city** with high rising buildings made from glass and steel. Around 3 p.m. we reached the bus station and were picked up by a good old friend from Azerbaijan, who is a Turkish professor now, and by his Turkish professor friend from Ankara. Being a little seasick and dizzy from driving in that rocky bus without any sleep for two days (remember that music festival), our Turkish friend from Ankara took care of me immediately. He accompanied me to the bathroom, paid 500.000 T Lira, and waited for me to come out. "When was the last time a man accompanied me to the bathroom? Probably my father"—I thought. It felt so protective and caring that I could have cried on the spot, but I swallowed my tears and played tough. Both of our Turkish professors applied that same care and attention during my whole stay in Istanbul.

"**Turkish men** are so very aware, caring and attentive. They think ahead and notice everything." I said to my husband. "If I would 'father' you like that you would start a revolution for independence and freedom!" he replied. Maybe he is right[7], but it felt so good for the time being, especially so far away from home on foreign soil.

---

7.   He probably is!

30. September

From a Taverna in Ano-polis (Upper Town)...

Retzina...The wounded Greek soul...Gebze...Fresh figs...Turkish toilet...Cultural intelligence...Belly dancing...7th Sultan Baroque castle...Sultan's harem...Cultural traps...

Before I have to leave a place, I usually try to get an overview. So I went on the overcrowded bus #23 to the Upper City (Ano-polis), overlooking all of Thessaloniki. You can even detect Mt. Olymp in the South as a hazy silhouette. I had just had baked beans and half a liter of Retzina, which I probably won't finish. The baked white beans in tomato sauce are huge and delicious. It's not the Greek way to eat, but that's all I need for lunch. For dessert I had bread and wine. My favorite **Retzina** is the **Georgiadis**. The taste of resin is not as predominant as in the other wines. Only two days are left in Thessaloniki. When you come back to a place it already feels homey, so it is a matter of getting to know and connecting with people and places.

This morning, I had an interesting conversation with our apartment manager. She asked me: "How was Constantinople?" Note that she didn't ask me: "How was Istanbul?" Oh, oh, the **wounded Greek soul**, I thought. "I am enchanted by that city", I said. "You have to go there and see for yourself. They are running specials for € 99 for five days, incl. everything. "I couldn't go to Constantinople", she said. "Because your heart would bleed seeing all the conquered Greek culture", I empathized. I helped her out with her English, since she spoke on a second year level. "That's right!" she said. "I do understand your pain", I said, "but we must build a new world of brother and sisterhood and bury the old axes."

"Maybe some day!" she replied.

Back to my Istanbul=Constantinople experiences: We lived in **Gebze**, 40 km outside of Istanbul, with our friend from Azerbaijan and his wife. Again, they insisted that we sleep in the Master bedroom. You were not allowed to do any work as a guest, not even to take a plate to the kitchen. That's against their hospitality rules. They read every wish from our eyes. They lived in a modern three-story-apartment house, because our Turkish professor had had bad experiences with earthquakes in that region in the past. Around us were eight to ten-story buildings.

Modern and ancient worlds lived side by side: In between the apartment houses I saw free ranging chickens, goats and sheep. Fresh bread was brought straight to their apartment door around 7:30 a.m. every day, also on Sundays. For the first time I ate fresh figs. They cost a fortune in Ft. Collins, if you can get them at all. Turkish food is delicious, but they use less olive oil, so I had problems again going to the bathroom. The **Turkish toilet** is the best in the world, because according to Islam traditions, you must clean yourself with water. So after flushing, you open a little valve and clean your bottom. It also works like a French bidet for women, if you sit backwards. It's a great feeling to step fresh into the world every time you went to the bathroom. In public toilets, however, I have had problems. "How do you get the watering can behind you and pour it straightly, so that you don't get your clothes wet?" I asked our Turkish professor. He was laughing hard and said jokingly: "Decades of experience! You have to take a class in that."

He is not a strict Moslem, very Western educated and familiar with the US. He is a travel genius and can survive in many languages and cultures. He always gets what he wants, because of his **cultural intelligence**, his child like openness, his humor and his education. He had spent Christmas with us in 1984 in Germany, and it sure felt like Xmas to me in Istanbul, especially in the Bazaar. The Bazaar beats all Western shopping malls. It is like a fairy tale in 1001 Nights.

At the Bazaar I bought an aubergine (eggplant) leather jacket, which I saw later in Athens for seven times the price. I always wanted to practice **belly dancing,** and when I saw that blue and golden outfit, I was intrigued. Since I knew that the professor's wife was a dancer by nature, I bought one for her, too, and we decided to dance for our husbands at night while they would smoke an expensive Cuban cigar. (Women's fantasies!) We did dance indeed for our husbands, with clothes underneath, of course, since it was not a private☺ dance. And since I didn't know what to shake to make these metal coins ring, I shook it all. Our Prof from Azerberdschan said that he had only seen ONE belly dancer who could do that, and that I was a natural. "Thanks", I said, "but I don't know what I am doing. The art lies in the controlled movements!" I bought other little presents for friends, family and my class, like Turkish CDs, traditional and the latest hits, an Uzbekistan head cover, three shawls, and two carpet-cushion covers (for sofa pillows). I would have bought more, but transportation is a problem. I wish to travel lightly.

On the first day in Istanbul=Konstantinopel, we visited the Castle of the Seventh Sultan (The Dolmabace Sarayi), right by the seaside, built around 1850. The Sultan was so intrigued by the German Baroque castles that he wanted to build the ultimate **Baroque castle,** and he succeeded. Combined with Islamic elements, it was even more ornamented than any Baroque castle I have ever seen. A Turkish soldier was standing motionless on guard in front of the main entrance. "Turkish soldiers are the most disciplined." said our Turkish-Azerbaijan Prof. Passing the hall of ceremonies, going towards the **Sultan's harem,** I imagined what it would be like watching the dignitaries from foreign countries through those deep blue rosette windows and sharing one man with how many other women? I liked the idea of sisterhood, but not the restriction and the possessive aspect.

I could have walked alone in Istanbul, but our Turkish friends always took turns in protecting me from crazy drivers, street solicitors, beggars and other **cultural traps** I could have fallen into. I thoroughly enjoyed their company, because we were all feeding off each other's humor and different cultural experiences. I felt the muscles of my belly at night, because we laughed so hard together about so many things I can't recall now. The Retzina is getting a bit to my head. I shall take a walk along the old city walls and continue later over a coffee. Nobody has bothered me for two hours.

Later at a coffee place in Ano-polis...

Greek life...Agia Sophia...Blue Mosque...Spice rack...Bosporus cruise...Condoms...Bloody toilets...Tübitak...Grand Bazaar...Shirkan...Palm reader...Prayer call...

It is around 4 p.m., now. "Never eat and have your coffee in the same place." says our Greek professor. I am at a coffee place by the Upper Tower, which was connected to the White Tower by the sea with a thick city wall during Roman times and thereafter. It is peaceful up here, away from the city traffic. Opposite from me there are four tiny townhouses. I could imagine living there as an artist if I were a bachelorette. I wonder how much it would cost. (180 000 Euro, I inquired later!) You hardly get any property up here. Space is precious, and property is rather inherited than sold for profit. I moved inside, since my brain started to fry. It looks very Greek in here, and the Greek music is penetrating my soul. I must have had a **Greek life**. People here say, I have a Greek nose, and I recognized the Greek bathhouse immediately at the Temple of Zeus in Athens, although other spectators doubted.

Let's stay with my Istanbul experience during this coffee break in Ano-polis: After our visit to the 7th Sultan's baroque castle, we went to the Agia Sophia, a mighty basilica structure which had been built during different phases of the Byzantine era. The entry fee was $12 for the lower level, and another $12 for the upper level, which we didn't invest, because we thought it was outrageous. After the occupation of the Turks the Sultan had to build an even bigger place of worship than the Agia Sophia. So we went over to the **Blue Mosque**, the Sultan Ahmet Camii, situated at the Golden Horn, the smallest pass way at the Bosporus, put our shoes in plastic bags—I draped my head in a shawl—and we walked the precious carpets barefoot. It felt great relaxing my feet on the cool silky material after a hot summer trot on cobblestones. But there was a slight smell of cheese in the air, and my husband was worried about fungus; I could read it off his face.

There is a holy atmosphere in every sacred place, and I have no problems praying wherever it feels right to me, so I prayed for a good school year back home in my district, and other different things. In the Agia Sophia there was a wishing stone, polished from all these human thumbs and hands, which had made a 3600 radius to get their wishes fulfilled. There I prayed for wisdom in leadership.

On the second day in Istanbul in the morning, we visited the Castle hotel where the former German chancellor Helmut Kohl had married his son to a Turkish daughter-in-law. Everything in the Castle hotel was made from gold and marble. I was drawn to a "**spice rack**", all in gold, but it felt a little out of place in the lobby. Our Turkish friends laughed their hearts out, because it was shoe polish equipment. Every time we saw a similar facility, they teased me with my "spice rack".

In the afternoon, we took a **Bosporus cruise** with our two Turkish professors, over to the Southwest towards the Marmara Sea. The Bosporus is relatively clean. (Shirkan, it really IS, after I have seen other places, now!!!) It has that deep turquoise-blue color. Together with the white, it invokes the ultimate vacation feeling in me. Our friends pointed out different landmarks, like the two hanging bridges, master works of engineering, connecting the Asian and the European part of the city. They desperately need a third pass way, since the toll bridges are congested during rush hour. They are discussing an undersea tunnel. We got to see the Blue Mosque, the Agia Sophia, the Baroque castle, the Castle hotel, the Military school, and the city fortifications from a different angle.

Looking over the railing my husband said: "Why are all those **condoms** swimming in the Bosporus?" Our two Turkish Profs laughed their hearts out and said: "These are jelly fish! And by the way how would you explain that huge one over there?" We left the ship at a little fisher town and walked around in the fish market. I didn't care for the smell, but the stands had beautiful arrangements of all kinds of fresh fish. The Greek and Turkish especially like the tiny fish deep-fried, and it is eaten whole. So I got my calcium doses every day.

On the way back, my husband used the ship toilet. "Don't fall into the Bosporus!" I said jokingly. When he came back, his legs were wet up to his knees, and he was cursing about those **bloody toilets**. As I said, you better jump out fast. There was always something to laugh about, all day with our Turkish friends.

The third day, we spent in **Tübitak**, a heavily guarded research institute in Gebze, the work place of our host couple. Checking my passport the official noticed that my visa wasn't stamped. Since our friend has a good standing with the Turkish government, they let me in anyhow. We had to wear badges for identification. While my husband talked to other researchers, visited labs and gave a talk, I had time to work on the computer, and take a walk with the prof's wife through the gardens. While we were walking, she taught me some Turkish:

Raki-Anisschnaps=Anis liquor
Shereffe-Prost=cheers

Condoms~Jellyfish?
Tschoc merci-Vielen Dank=Lots of Thanks
Arslan-Tiger (also: Caplan)
Şinasi~Shirkan
Teschekürs-Thank you
Teschekülasch-Thank you all
Teschküler-Bitte schön=You are welcome
Meraba-HI
Hosch'gel din-welcome
Affiat olsun-Guten Appetit! Have a good appetite!
Nassel san?—How are you?
I em-I am good
Seşak-hot
Sojuk-cold
Kartal-eagle
Dolmusch-dolmuschis (pl.?) Small Turkish busses

The Tübitak property is a huge area reaching down to the Marmara Sea where we ate at night in the Institute's Taverna. Before the dinner I took a swim in the Marmara Sea. Although it was cold, my back felt better after the swim.

On the fourth day, we looked at some shops in Gebze to get a general idea about the prices, and to get us ready for the **Grand Bazaar** in Istanbul=Constantinople. In a leather shop, close by the bazaar entrance, I tried on about ten leather jackets. One aubergine blazer type jacket caught my attention. Since I am not an impulse buyer, I said, I would look around first and then come back. While I was playing uninterested, he went down and down with the price, and said he could shorten the sleeves in 15 minutes. "Look", I said, "If you have the best style and the best price, I will be back."

When we entered the underground bazaar it felt like 1001nights in the fairy tales: Gold, silver, carpets, silk, ceramic, leather, shiny belly dancer outfits, everything you can imagine. Never accept the price. You need to bargain. That's part of the seller's joy and the buyer's satisfaction of getting a good price. When you walk away, and they shout a price after you, that's about the right amount you should pay. The Bazaar Mafia determines the price of gold, every day. Many presidents and dignitaries have shopped here. (Hillary, too!) I tried on more leather jackets, but none came close to the aubergine. So we went back and got it. While we had the sleeves shortened we were offered apple tea and…

2. Oktober

From the Thessaloniki Airport back to Frankfurt...

Shirkan...Palm reader...Muezzin...

I just said Good-bye to our beloved Greek professor (Sokrates) who taught me so much about Greek culture and history.

...we were offered apple tea and our Azerbaijan hosts talked to the Russian sales lady. Then we headed back to the car, since rush hour was approaching. It took us three hours for the 40 km to get back home to Gebze. Waiting in the toll lane we got a call from our professor from Ankara. "**Shirkan**, hassle san?" I asked in Turkish, and we all had a good laugh. Since I couldn't store his name in my head, at first, which is a mixture of Sinaii and Onassis, I gave him a nickname, secretly: Shirkan, the Tiger from the Jungle Book. When we were all out for dinner, Tuesday night in a romantic Taverna by the Marmara Sea, I confessed at the round table that I had given him a nickname. He seemed to like it and wrote down the title of the film. A Turkish gipsy wanted to read my **palm** over dinner, but Shirkan motioned her away with his eyebrows. That's a Turkish NO and added "later" with the blink of his eyes. My husband was relieved that she wasn't there anymore after our two-hour dinner. Reading the palm is like reading the map in an atlas. Every human hand is different. Responsible readers don't give out negative self-fulfilling prophecies. Shirkan did not go to the Bazaar with us, since he had to head back to Ankara after dinner to teach the next day.

On the fifth day early in the morning around 4:30, I listened one last time to the **Muezzin**'s early prayer call. They do this five times a day, and I really enjoy their resonant voices and the five-minute spiritual reflection. After a delicious breakfast we headed out early to the airport for Athens, since our Turkish professor wanted to get a head start before the rush hour.

2. Oktober, same day

On the plane from Thessaloniki to Frankfurt...

Athens...Amphitheater of Dionysos...Plaka...Taxi in Athens...Metro system...National Archeological Museum...World Tourism Day...Acropolis...

I haven't had time to write about my **Athens experience**, yet. As in any capital of the world, life is more hectic than in the rest of the country. I saw it reflected in the eyes of the professor who picked us up from the airport to bring us to the Golden Age hotel, somewhat in between the university and the Akropolis. It was a fine hotel and very quiet, too. Since we were very tired, we took a late-afternoon nap first, before heading to the Akropolis with a taxi. He charged a reasonable price of € 2, 50. The Akropolis (Ger. sp.) was going to close at 6:30, so we stayed down at the **Amphitheater of Dionysus.**

The late evening sun was shining on the white marble, and you had to imagine the ancient actors playing out the Greek tragedies. Some seats were reserved for ancient VIPs with inscriptions on mighty marble benches. Yanni had broadcasted a televised live concert from the Acropolis some years ago, so I was familiar with the setting under the sky. We purchased a ticket for the next day to walk up to the very top. Then we strolled down through the **Plaka, the old town.** All the old facades were covered with very expensive touristy "schnickschnack" as the Germans say, so I didn't have the feeling of actually being in Old Town. To be fair there was only one day to discover Athens, so I probably didn't see some of the original parts. They are serving supper now on this spacious Olympic aircraft, so I shall continue later...

After a nice relaxing dinner in the Plaka we were trying to get home with a **taxi**. We were thrown out twice; that is illegal! The first guy wanted in between 12 and 15 € (for a 3 € trip plus one €uro night charge at the most), and the second guy made his meter jump by 70 cents every time he came near it. When my husband who sat in front protested, he pulled over at a bus station and said: "Take the bus!" My husband wanted to get away from these cheaters. He wouldn't spend one minute longer beside a guy whom he couldn't trust. I understand that. Me traveling alone, I would have sat there like a Buddha, observantly and awake, given exactly 4 €uros to the taxi driver at the hotel. Upon his protest I would have taken down the number of the license plate and called the tourist police. You don't mess with an American eagle! Taxi drivers in Athens have to shape up for the Olympics in 2004. They already have a bad reputation in the world.

After my bad experiences with Athens' taxi drivers, I decided to explore the **Metro-system**, the next day to get to the National Archeological museum. The Metro is the finest I have ever ridden in: Run by a private company it is very clean, esthetic and relaxing. They play classical and meditation music underground to relax the stressed citizens of the capital. Excavation sites and sculptures are behind glass to add an artistic atmosphere. It is my kind of subway. Until the Olympics, they intend to expand the subway. They have to go 40 meters below or the building process would constantly come to a halt discovering new ancient sites. The archeologists always have the first and last say in Greece.

The **Archeological museum** was not clearly organized, more like a warehouse of many sculptures. Our Greek professor verified my impression a few days later. I am glad I could help out a lady who took down notes (for a class?) to sort out the Greek and Roman phases. For me the most impressive sculptures were Poseidon, the God of the Sea, Zeus, the Father of the Gods, Athena, and the school of Diogenes. I returned home to my hotel with the subway easily to meet up with my husband after his talk at the university for an early afternoon excursion to the Acropolis.

There was quite a festive atmosphere since it was **World Tourism Day.** They offered free samples of Greek coffee, ice cream, wine, cheese, posters and played original Greek music and performed dances. After a short snack we walked up to the Acropolis in the hot summer heat, blended by the white marble, reflecting the sunlight. Only crazy tourists walk around in Greece between two and five. I had been on my feet, all day, my heart was piercing and my feet were burning, but I kept going. "Live today and die tomorrow." I thought. After hydrating myself on the top (They had flowing water up there 2600 years ago) and cooling off in the breeze under an olive tree, I started to appreciate the holy sites and different temples where the ancient Greeks connected to their Gods right under the sky.

On the flight from Frankfurt to Bahrain…

Trash…Look up…Arabic…Agora…Temple of Zeus…His/story-her/story…Travel as long (poem)…Eastern men…Walk together (poem)…

Coming down from the Acropolis we stood in line for this delicious Greek ice cream with nuts and candied fruit. When I saw all the **trash** lying around on these ancient holy sites, my heart started to revolt. "Would you please pass on a recommendation to the organizers of World-Tourism day?" I said to the young man who passed me the ice cream. "Ask them to put up big trash cans in the middle of the pass ways, so that these ancient sites stay clean." "I will", he said, "but they throw it down anyhow." "Modern civilization", I said with disgust shaking my head, "It's sad!" I was turning around to enjoy my ice cream, but before I could taste a bite, somebody tapped me on my left shoulder: "Don't be sad", he said. "Don't look down on the ground. **Look up towards the sky** and look at the beautiful Acropolis!" I have heard these words twice, this year!!! He said it with such charm and compassion that I had problems finding the right words: "Ef caristo", I said, "You must have been a student of Aristoteles up there in former times." For seconds our souls resonated as one. 'Another Greek philosopher', I thought. 'It's in their blood.'

We are flying Gulf Air. The announcements of the pilot in **Arabic** sound to me like an old forgotten song. The soft guttural sounds resonated in me like the hush of a lullaby. On this flight I have to conquer my fear of Arabic men (except the one in Berlin!), because I am surrounded by many. I suspect it is some residue (Karma?) from a former life, and I will have an eye opening experience, some day. The Gulf Air napkin with a falcon and Arabic signs are very appealing with their ornamental script, but I can't decipher anything. In Greece I could at least read like a first grader. We'll have a four-hour layover in Bahrain before we can continue to Bombay. The flight from Frankfurt to Bahrain takes six hours, and then another three and a half to Bombay. It's like a trip from Frankfurt to Denver, even longer. They are serving lunch now. I shall continue later…

After our hot summer outing to the Acropolis, we went down to find the ancient Agora, marching another three miles. I estimate that I easily accumulate about seven miles per day. The ancient trading place was fenced in, because of a nearby-subway construction site. Then we went over to the **Temple of Zeus** opposite the Plaka (Old Town). Zeus was the father of all Gods. In the Roman Catholic Church, there is a father principle, too. The yearning for the ultimate father and mother is in all of our hearts. In this lifetime the father principle is dominant within me. Sisters are my quiet support, but my sons, brothers, mentors, and grandpas are the driving force. It is simply the male (yang) principle within me that is thrusting for a stronger expression to get things done in this world.

Immediately, I recognized the baths and the Corinthian columns, which rose at least 20 meters high into the sky. Some had fallen down and lay like cold cut in the mellow evening sun. These ancient holy places radiate peace and instill a deep respect for ancient civilizations into my heart, although I couldn't have cared less about history in High school. But now it is not **his(s)tory** anymore, it is **herstory;** it is coming alive as **my** story as an active participant and traveler in and through this world.

Back in our gorgeous hotel at night, we had about one hour to rest up and get ready before the university people would pick us up for an elaborate Greek dinner in a Taverna around 9 p.m. Since I was wrestling with my health all day, I wrote down a poem that had condensed in my mind:

Travel as long...

Travel as long
As your heart
Is strong like a lion's
Your feet can carry you
Up and down Mt. Olymp
Your bladder can hold three liters
Your body can store water
Like a camel
Your back can sleep
On fakir mattresses
Or sagging sailor nets
Your stomach is tough
Like a cow's
Your intestines
Don't move too fast
Or too slow
Your shoulders can carry
Backpacks like a mule
Your eyes are sharp
Like an eagle's!
If not, just stay at home
And enjoy the small world
Or travel anyhow
And don't complain!

Potawi, that's ME

I just walked up and down the isle: Western men are napping with their legs stretched out diagonally, or they are lying flat on their bellies across four middle seats. **Eastern men** are rolled up in fetal positions. There is one gorgeous looking "Sultan" dressed in all white with a turban, sitting lotus style with a laptop on his lap.

Before starting my third travel phase, I talked to my sons extensively. My youngest is getting engaged on Saturday. He asked for my blessings. I am sure he met his soul mate. She wrote a beautiful letter to me, The Goddess[8], describing my son's traits, which he "inherited" from both of us, and how they enhance and compliment each other as a couple.

Walk together...

The heart of a mother is content,
when she feels the happiness of her children.
Walk together into the sunset, my children,
and start each morning with a quiet smile
For you have found the reflection
of your bright and ancient souls.

MOM (Goddess)

---

8.   I forgot how that nickname came about and some things are just too private!

4. Oktober

At the Bahrain airport...

One Human family...

We arrived in Bahrain around 6 p.m. and it was already dark. Prices here are like in the US: For two large cappuccinos and one orange-chocolate croissant I paid € 8.50. The airport is very clean. The toilets have a cleaning system with a hose attached right by. You can use it either way. That's an excellent feature for travelers when you have to do without a shower for 24 hours.

An Arabic family is sitting left of me. The "Sultan" is wearing a long silky white dress (actually like a Western shirt reaching to his ankles), and a white turban with black cords. The two women traveling with him (wives?) are wearing the traditional Moslem outfit (Burka) with only the eyes visible. One of the women turned to me earlier to offer me some French fries, which her husband had brought for the children. Just when I was thinking, "That smells like MC Donald's", she turned to me.

Many races, many outfits! All humans waiting for their planes! A truly international airport! **One Human family**! Why is it so difficult to live in peace side by side without prejudice? When will all these wars and conflicts stop? When will we be able to share and cooperate as a human family? It is supposedly 30 Celsius outside, but I am freezing in this air—conditioned climate. I will put on my RHS wind jacket and be content.

4. Oktober, same day

On the way from Bahrain to Bombay...

Moving from the shuttle into the airplane the air felt tropically hot. (30 Celsius) It is just 3 degrees lower in Bombay=Mumbai. The Indian Traditionalists call it Mumbai, since they do not want to be reminded of the British occupiers. The Indian vegetarian meal was delicious and I shall take a nap now. The driver from the Bhabha Atomic Research Center will pick us up at the airport.

End of Part Two!

PART III
India

From the coolest place in the apartment...

New climate...Backwards Visa...Bombay waking up...Driver and a car...Great hospitality...Crazy Europeans...Chutney with sugar...Napkins and sinks...

Welcome to India! This is my third travel phase. In every place, I start writing in a local pad, spiral, or booklet. I am sitting in the coolest place in the room: On my bed with white cool linens; the air conditioner is right behind me and two fans are running. It is 7:15 p.m.; pitch dark, and still 30 degrees Celsius that is 86 Fahrenheit with 80 % humidity. My body is working hard getting adjusted to the **new climate**.

"It will be cooler in two weeks", said our Indian professor who picked us up himself from the airport this morning at 4 a.m. He had three drivers posted at different ends of the airport. We came out last from the passport control, because at the Indian embassy in Berlin, they had issued me a visa from October 2002 to February 2002. My passport went from one official to the next one higher up, six steps high, until finally, somebody in charge made a decision. Our Indian host must have gotten up at 3 a.m. just for us.

Our driver, a fine looking young man with slacks and a dress shirt, loaded our suitcases into a spacey caddy, reserved for the VIPS of the **Bhabha Atomic Research Center** (**BARC**, from now on). They drive on the left side of the street here (just like the British, of course!), and the driver's seat is on the right.

While my husband was talking politics and research with our Indian professor, I was watching **Bombay wake up**. Along the airport road people were sleeping everywhere: On the sidewalks, on the trunks of their cars, on wagons, wherever there was space to lay down their tired bones. Wild dogs and cats roamed through the garbage. A little guy, about four years old, was squatting in the gully doing his business. People were waiting at bus stops or hanging around tea stands for their early morning tea.

As we got closer to the institute the shacks turned into concrete buildings. After a forty-minute drive from the airport we passed the security guards entering into the green and spacious privileged world of scientists. "The **driver and the**

car are at your disposal whenever you need it", said our host. They brought our luggage into our apartment, showed us around and how to operate different appliances. It smelled like mothballs. Compared to the people in the streets we live like kings. The standard of our apartment compares to the US in the thirties.

When I was about to fall asleep it sounded as if a bird was flying in the room. It was the doorbell. Tea was being served and they wanted to know what we would like for breakfast. They checked up on us about ten times, today, bringing bottled mineral water, breakfast, serving the 5 o'clock tea with biscuits, getting rid of the mothballs (actually my husband collected them all, or so we thought…). The "Boss" showed up twice and telephoned twice: **Great hospitality,** but we didn't get much sleep after our 24-hour trip.

We should have listened and taken the driver to the shop in the midday heat, but us **crazy Europeans** wanted to walk. Not a good idea! Tonight, we walked again to the market place to get some Camilla oranges, thinking it would be cooler, but it wasn't. My heart was pumping hard on the way back. Indian friends in the US had warned us to eat only cooked food and use boiled water for brushing our teeth. Did you know that our Mexican kids also get sick when they first come to the USA when getting adjusted to the new bacterial environment? It is not necessarily a matter of cleanliness, but how the body is trained to handle the environment. Our Indian brothers didn't sweat at dinner at all. We were drenched after the meal in the non-air-conditioned mess hall. As our host said: "It's better to eat in your room", but we didn't know why. Now we know!

I took very small portions, but I wasted chutney, which I thought was a meat dish, and sprinkled it with coconut flakes, which was actually coarsely granulated sugar. In my mind I had combined a rice-curry-coconut dish, while I really had rice with a load of salty **chutney** sprinkled **with sugar.** Tomorrow, I'll do better, I hope! I was content with the yoghurt, the pea soup, the chickpeas, and the Indian fried bread: Burri. "Tomorrow, we have to take napkins along", said my husband. "Imagine, if this whole mess hall full of people would use napkins", I said, "They'd produce three sacks of garbage." When we brought back our stainless steel trays with six compartments for food, there were five sinks to wash the hands before and after dinner, just like in Kindergarten. That's the Indian way!

6. Oktober

From the coolest place of the apartment...

The bird sound...Boy oh boy...Jungle waking up...Symbolic India...

The **bird sound** was going off at 6 a.m. on a Sunday morning. Half asleep I said to my husband: "It's that bird behind our air conditioner, again!" Wrong! It was communal wake-up time. They served tea, actually the **"Boy"** as they call it here. "Where is the Laundromat?" I asked yesterday. "Over there", they said, "but you don't go there. You just call, and a "Boy" will pick up your laundry and bring it back." The tea tasted great: Strong tea with <u>boiled</u> milk and sugar. It was still dark. I listened to the **jungle waking up**: Doves gurgling, exotic birds shrieking, monkeys crying, but I wasn't sure. I switched off the air conditioner and opened all the windows to be able to take in the sounds more acutely. Looking down on the Institute's roof of the commons area there was a whole monkey herd, playing hide and seek around the square blocks.

We live on the 13th floor. Everything is **symbolic in India,** even the highest floor. There is a 14th floor and the "Prince" rode with us in the elevator, yesterday. I call him the "Prince", because he has a round purple mark on the third eye on his forehead, meaning he belongs to a higher caste. With all the windows open the rooms filled up with humid air, but we wanted to get rid of the mothball smell. The Indian house manager was getting a kick out of my husband's mothball hunt, yesterday. He giggled like a teenager when Dieter made disgusted faces. When my head turned red and I broke out in a sweat it was time to turn on the air conditioner, again. I better order breakfast, now. It is 8 o'clock.

The **vegetarian breakfast** was wonderful: Flat bread filled with curry veggie and a coconut sauce on top, toast, butter, jelly and tea with milk. After breakfast, I brushed my teeth with <u>boiled</u> water and took a shower in the marble bath. A 200-liter tank is hanging above my head. I didn't switch on the heater, because the water is lukewarm at all times. On the marble floor there is simply a drainage hole. Simple and sufficient! Our "Boss" called already, inquiring how our sleep was, and if we were satisfied with the breakfast. Now he is waiting for the driver to show us around on BARC.

From the coolest place...

Town of BARC...Monsoon...Highly secured...Hottest month...Green lungs...Pollution...Anarchistic...Trash collection...Why Boys...Ayurvedic...Yoga...Meditation... Indian food...Poisonous snakes...Physics...Metaphysics...

We just got home from our excursion. The only part of my body that likes that climate is my hair. It is silky, shiny, and lush like the jungle. Our Indian professor had his (our) driver show us the whole town of **BARC**, except the restricted areas, of course. 15 000 employees work in the labs behind the hills, close by the sea. You need special clearance for that just like in Los Alamos or Livermore. My husband will have a two-hour clearance procedure, tomorrow, while they set up an internet-connection for me in the 14-story guesthouse. The employees live with their families in high-rise buildings, some twenty stories high, and some live in the "colony", which look like townhouses. The older houses look badly beat by the month long **monsoon**, very black and ugly. The newer ones still look clean. So all together, about 50 000 people live here in a **highly secured** area with watch posts all around and fenced in terrain. Since the conflict with Pakistan, they are even more on alert. The town has its own hospital, shops, post office, banks, dispensary=clinic for the small problems, etc. It's like living on Base. We shopped at the supermarket, and our professor insisted on paying. He said, he would also teach me some Indian cooking, combined with Western style, and how to make Chapatti, the Indian baked bread. I don't long for the kitchen, right now. Our apartment and I are just hot enough. October is the **hottest month** in India (daaah!) If I survive this month, I will be ready for the Sahara. Bill Gates has set up his trip for India, I read yesterday in the paper. He is coming mid November, when it is mild and nice. India is very important for his business, since Indian programmers are superb, and he can have them work for the highest salary here, which is around $ 500.

This city has **huge green lungs** of jungle around the apartment houses, shops and research labs. He hardly goes to Bombay because of the pollution, our Indian professor said. "Why can't the pollution be stopped?" we asked. "Because people are **anarchistic** here, they don't follow rules which make common sense. The unions are very strong. They do whatever they want. Maintaining your own car is very expensive. Drivers and those three-wheelers are much cheaper." We also saw some people throw garbage right out the window. You want to know how Indian **trash collection** looks like here: Women carrying huge plastic sacks on their heads to the extension of their arms in either direction. You want to know why they have **"Boys"** for everything? Because thousands wouldn't have a job in this community otherwise. Of course, the problem lies deeper: The stinking rich and the vegetating poor, and then the over reproduction of humans. And the cycle of poverty repeats itself again and again...

A sheet on the skin is already too much cover. Then the moisture can't evaporate as quickly, and cool down the body. Our Indian professor knows about **Ayurvedic Medicine**, Yoga, meditation, and healthy nutrition. How could he not? He is Indian. It all came from India and we Westerners have adopted it. "It's a matter of breathing to get that blood pressure down", he said to my husband, "I'll teach you some **meditation**." He'll arrange for **Yoga** classes for me in the mornings and get me to an Ayurvedic doctor to get that swelling of my uterus down. Judging by my lay studies of Ayurvedic medicine my Kapha dosha is going erratic in that heat, releasing too many estrogens, which are causing the swelling. A few more days of **Indian food and spices** will also help me in regaining my balance. A diet of a particular people is closely related to the climate and bacterial environment. Our Indian professor strongly agreed to that.

He does jogging in the early morning behind our guesthouse on the field and track area in midst of the jungle. I am not allowed to take short cuts there, because of **poisonous snakes**. "The body is like an engine. When it gets old you need to keep it running. A new engine runs by itself, but an old one needs a lot of oil." He is about my age. When sixty he wants to retire and do some real interesting research. "In what?" I asked. "In physics combined with philosophy, actually Metaphysics." "How interesting! I said that three decades ago: The time will come when physics will merge with metaphysics." I said enthusiastically. He'll also arrange contacts for me meeting teachers and students in BARC. I can't wait for the workweek to start.

ANNEX

The Bhabha Atomic Research Center=BARC is named after the famous scientist Bhabha from Persia, a highly educated Parson. He convinced Minister President Nehru in 1955 to found this institute. The British occupation had ended in 1947 with Mahatma Gandhi forcing the British out of the country with his peaceful resistance and hunger strikes. I remember President Nehru when I was a kid. His daughter, Indira Gandhi, who was not related to Mahatma, led the country after his death.

7. Oktober

From the coolest place...

Computers and gadgets...Downtown...Life and death...Shops...Lady High Tower...Eerie sounds...Rupees...3-Wheeler...

I had hoped I could have started a regular workweek, but the **computer** was set up in the <u>afternoon</u>. As I just found out, my work time will be from 10 a.m. to 2.p.m. After that the trainees need to use it. There are only two computers with Internet connection. I can receive calls in my room, but I cannot call out. I have to go down to a booth with a meter. There is an officer collecting money and keeping track of the calls.

Since I couldn't work in the morning I did Yoga first, and then I took a stroll **downtown** to look for an engagement card for my youngest son and his fiancée. Passing by a ditch at a certain point I always hold my breath and walk faster, since a run over dog is decaying in there. **Life and death** exist side by side in India. I haven't seen anything, yet.

The **shops** look like small quick stops, like German or Greek Kiosks, like booths with independent entrepreneurs. All I could find were birthday cards. Well, I thought, then we'll just celebrate the birthday of your engagement, kids, and I transferred the poem onto the card "Walk Together", which I had written on the flight to Bahrain.

It is 5:10 p.m. **Lady High Tower** (high=Hoch in Ger.) must order tea and biscuits, now, since she eats only fruit for lunch, and dinner is served at 8 p.m. These two love-doves scared me, just now, knocking against the window with their beacons. Until you can identify all the sounds around you, you don't feel safe in a place. Tropical birds live directly behind our air conditioner, singing their morning and evening songs. Doves are practically living with us in the bath-room, separated by a wooden screen. Beautiful falcons are sailing all day around the buildings. Paradise birds dive almost vertically into the air as if wanting to cool off in the draft. Monkeys play and groom each other in the early morning hours on the roof of the commons area. There are a lot more species living in the jungle judging by the concerts during dusk and dawn.

For the card and a gel pen I paid 30 rupees ~ 65 cents. The exchange rate is 44 rupees to a dollar. For quick calculations I double up the rupees, and I have the price in cents. I walked one more block to the post office, which looked like Germany after WWII, and purchased a stamp for 15 rupees ~ 30 cents for a heavy letter to the US (Airmail! I hope it arrives before Xmas!) Thank God, almost everybody speaks English here, let's say the educated, because of the British occupation, but the Indian accent is not always easy for me to understand, especially on the phone when one is deprived of body language, which comprises 60% of language transmission.

Since it was high noon and pearls of sweat were running down my face, I took a **3-wheeler** home. It is a motorized Rickshaw with the driver in front, and three guests maximum[1] in the back, open all around, but with a roof on top. Some of the good-looking younger drivers play loud rock music in their "Rickshaws". I could have called Hemant, our driver with the white government SUV, but I like to experience life from different angles. The ride cost 8 rupees ~ 20 c. for a mile. So, from Ft. Collins to the airport you would pay $ 12, given your back was fine, you had enough time, and your suitcase was small. But there are also taxis available which are double in price, if you need to go faster and further.

---

1.   We've seen as many as eight Indians in there!

From the coolest place...

Mothball hunt...Tea breaks...VIPS...Buzzing nightlife...Indian beauty...Garlands...The Seven Dwarfs...

Last night, we went **mothball hunting**, again. When my husband came home from work around 7 p.m., I had problems breathing. "It stinks like mothballs in here", he said, "Maybe we forgot some." We looked in every corner behind the furniture, and sure enough we had overlooked three, but they had also laid out new ones in the kitchen. My husband complained to the management, this morning, and they promised not to lay out new ones, again. I hope we'll not have a moth invasion, now. Hopefully all the birds around us will take care of them, and the salamander, which I saw climbing vertically up the wall, last night.

I worked at the computer for three hours straight without air conditioning, while the officer took two **tea breaks**. But maybe, he is the wise man, since I have an 80 over 50 blood pressure, now. Tomorrow, I will go to the cooling lounge in between and have a tea, also. The locals always know better!

They have the **VIPs** start rather late, here. The driver comes at 9:30 and work starts at 10 a.m. Then they send their visiting scientists home (or rather: It is suggested) that they have lunch with their wives (or they might die from loneliness, hahaha!) At 2:30, the driver picks my VIP up, again, and then he comes home around 7 p.m.

Life is **buzzing at night.** Couples shop at the market place; old folks sit around and talk; children are playing, lots and lots of people are walking: The women in their beautiful saris, and the good looking men either in traditional or Western style clothing. I find the Indian women very graceful, and the Indian men extremely good looking. In Greece my husband was enchanted by the Greek women. Beauty is in the eye of the beholder!

Last night, at the market place, my husband bought me a **garland** from fresh exotic smelling yellow and orange flowers, and put it around my neck. When they were in a group, all the men who passed by broke out in a smile or laughter. I wonder what the Indian meaning of this garland is. I asked my husband to ask Budhi, today, our Indian professor; I am not going to use real names in this travel report. He introduced himself that way on the phone this morning. So his name is Budhi. He is actually a Brahmin, one of the highest castes in India. I put the garland around the ashtray on the couch table and lit an incense to give this place a holy smell and to overpower the mothballs. The flowers are still fresh without any water, amazing. Last night, I ate a granite apple for the first time. You would never think it had so much juice inside judging from the rugged outside.

The light in the room is already changing. It is mellower than half an hour ago. (It is 4:35 p.m.) Lady Escort needs to order her 5 o'clock tea now. I really would like to watch them cleaning in here. It's a big social event. The "boys" show up like the **seven dwarfs**, and within 15 minutes there are fresh linens, the bathroom is cleaned, and the carpet looks vacuumed, while all they have is a little broom from dried branches. I couldn't watch, because they closed the sliding kitchen door while we had lunch: Lots of fruits, a coffee and some biscuits.

9. Oktober

From the coolest...

Patience...Otto...Department store...Cash machines...Manual labor force...Biogas...

You have to have **patience** here, lots of patience! This morning, the "computer lab" was closed, because the guy didn't show up. The house manager wanted to let me in, but after switching on the lights, all the fans, and booting up the computer, we couldn't find the keys to the locked keyboard and mouse.

Since I couldn't drown my energy in work, I went to the local department store with an **Otto**, a 3-wheeler. I suppose they call it Auto, but it comes out as Otto. So from now on, I will call my little two-stroke engine on three wheels Otto.

The local **department store** consists of a house ware-booth, an underwear and sock store, a pharmacy, a bakery and a supermarket the size of a small Seven Eleven. They even use a computer there. All the other shops write you an itemized bill by hand, and you have to pay it to <u>one</u> cash-officer, who is in charge of all the payments, and then pick up your shopping items. The most modern installations are the **cash machines** on base (on campus). There I will be able to draw rupees with my debit card directly from my US bank account. You really wonder why they are even there, when everything else is like in the olden days.

The major reason for all these service jobs, I think, is having a **manual labor force.** They want to make sure that everybody on base has a job. Today, I saw two beautiful women with colorful saris, plastic gloves and mouth covers sorting through garbage behind our guesthouse. "For heaven's sake", I thought to myself. "Stop it, never assume anything. It all makes sense in another culture!" I commanded myself. After my initial shock I posed a neutral question to the guys who were waiting with me in front of the elevator. "What is the women's job there?" "They are sorting out Biomuell (organic waste) for producing **biogas** for cooking." "Good use of natural resources!" I said aloud and to myself: "See, it all makes sense!"

10. Oktober

From the coolest...

Time...Ayurvedic doctor...Cultural conditioning... Ayurvedic treatment center...Holistic theory...Grand Central...Group Director...Divi...New World Order... Arrogance and Ignorance...India...Arranged marriages...

There is lots of **time** in the morning: From communal wake-up-tea-time at 6 a.m. until we leave the house at 9:30 a.m., Indians seem to love using their undisturbed mornings for exercise, yoga meditation, and personal toilette. This morning, while I had breakfast on the 13th floor, I was watching a guy on the 4th floor in the opposite apartment house oil his hair for 15 minutes. "No wonder they have such great hair!" I thought to myself. I do not need three and a half hours in the morning, but what I will take back home from this life-style is not hustling in the mornings, leaving enough time to focus and gather strength for the new day. A calm disposition will pay off for the whole day and divert many stressful situations.

Since I had pelvic pain the night before, they arranged for an **Ayurvedic doctor** to see me, last night. It was very odd, at first talking about my gynecological problems in front of three men. They had sent a coworker to take us to the doctor. The concept of privacy doesn't seem to exist, here. They were all invited in at the doctor's office, and I didn't want to throw them out being a guest in this country. "Just overcome your **cultural conditioning** and go with the flow." I told myself. I knew that Ayurvedic medicine did not involve a gyno-exam, but a pulse and tongue diagnosis, closely listening to and watching the patient. That's exactly what the doctor did. It was good that the coworker was there, too, because he spoke a more Standard English and mediated often between the doctor and me. He took down notes, arrived at a diagnosis, and prescribed internal and external medicine. I started the internal medicine, last night. The paste tastes extremely yaki, but who says that medicine has to taste like candy. He also prescribed fourteen treatments in a nearby **Ayurvedic treatment center.** In the US I would pay thousand of Dollars for this, here it costs a few hundred.

The doctor took me to the treatment center, this morning to show me around and to introduce me to the therapists. The medicine has to be prepared for a whole day according to my constitutional type, which is Kappa, primarily plus

Vata. The basic **Ayurvedic theory** is that the three doshas: Vata, Pitta, Kappa that control different functions in the body need to be in balance with each other. Vata is movement (air, breathing), Pitta is transformation (fire, digestion) and Kappa is cohesion and stability. Ayurvedic (=knowledge of life) is a 5000—year-old medical-system that treats the physical, emotional, mental and spiritual body of a patient. The doctor prescribed fourteen of these external treatments from 10 to 12 a.m., every day, which will leave me with very little computer time, but health is more important, right now. After a successful treatment another DNC should be superfluous, but I'll have it checked out in Spain, just in case. Our host's wife there is an M.D. I had no problems communicating with the doctor directly face to face. On the way to the treatment center he gave a lot of useful tips in the taxi, and on the way back in the Otto.

After the initial doctor's visit, last night, we were invited for dinner by the group director to an excellent Indian restaurant **"Grand Central"**. I noticed that the traffic makes room for the white government cars. The driver frequently honked his horn to get slower vehicles out of the way. He was very well aware of his superior status. When we arrived at the restaurant five Boys in neat uniforms opened the doors of the car. A "sultan" (in Sikh-clothing) invited us into to the air-conditioned restaurant. I noticed that it was even hotter in town than in BARC, which is situated right by the sea and breathes through vast green jungle-lungs.

The **group director** is a very influential man in BARC. This morning, everybody was informed where and with whom I had been dining, last night. News travels fast. During the very relaxing dinner with Budhi, my husband, the group director and me, my motto was: Listen and learn! The food was excellent, especially since we had gotten a little weary of the cantina food. I can't eat spicy, every day. It's a problem for my stomach. I have to have some mild food in between.

The group director (I will call him **Divi** from now on) had been involved in nuclear testing. Therefore, he was not allowed to see his kids and grandkids in the US for four years. (Poor grandpa!) Now, since he is close to retirement, he is allowed to visit again on a private visa. From him we learned that Budhi is a Brahmin, and Divi called himself a Warrior, which my husband confirmed with a reminiscing smile. He has a lot of respect for Divi (and so do all the people on the base), because Divi stood up for his country at a very important conference to state that this particular research had been done in India for years and that it did not originate from the US.

First I thought I would phrase it as diplomatically as I could, because my beloved America is my home country. Out of that love and compassion I decided to put it as bluntly as I could, because I have heard it from different nationalities, in different countries, from different angles now, over and over again: "The **arrogance and ignorance**, and that bossing around of the United States needs to stop in the world!" I have seen it myself on German TV after the reelection of Chancellor Gerhard Schroeder who is opposed to the Iraq war (as are many senators in the US). Bush said: "He better come talk to me in two days…" That is not the way foreign cultures (and Germany is rather close to the US) can be approached.

My personal opinion on this is that the United States does play a **leadership role** in the formation of a NEW World ORDER, but it must be done with respect for and knowledge of other cultures in the spirit of brotherhood, as stated earlier. The Big Brother cannot boss around the little siblings anymore, because the little siblings grow up and reject the dominance of the Big Brother. We will not create progress, understanding, and peace that way.

"Bombay is not the eye of India. People come here from everywhere", said the technology director and librarian to me, today. "I'll send for a philosophical book, for you in English where you can get into the mind of India." We philosophized about the brain and the mind, different religions, the state of former East Germany, etc. Divi must have done wonders, because two days ago, Libbi[2] wasn't very approachable, or maybe he was just stressed out.

India fits into the US three times, but has over a billion people. The US has one quarter billion (~250 Millions), but three times the space. In Bombay=Mumbai 14 Million people reside here, like in Istanbul=Constantinople. Although the salaries are low (around $ 500 max.), life is cheap. So, India has the fifth highest buying power in the world behind Japan, the US, Germany and China, meaning, you get the most for your rupees. When we drove to the restaurant, last night, I saw European type shops; American brand-name-stores, a coffee place, and Divi said that there are also Mc Donald's and Pizza Huts. New India and old India are living side by side.

Divi is the boss of the 400 most gifted scientists in the country. He has fine women scientists, too. They are excellent before they get married, and three years after childbirth. So, the institute (cuts them a slack) allows them time to found and care for the family. Divi said with a twinkle in his eyes that India is still male dominated, (Frankly I think that he enjoys the admiration of the women in his life!) but the scene is changing slowly. Both Budhi and Divi told us personal stories of how their marriages were arranged. We all agreed that a solid foundation, a

---

2.   Libby, the librarian

common value system and education base is more important for a marriage than the so-called initial infatuation that many inexperienced young folks call love.

12. Oktober

From the coolest…early in the morning…

Mystery of the Garland…Libbi…At Budhi's…Indian meal…4 times a day…Sari, Western, North Indian…

The **mystery** of the garland is solved. People buy it for their altar at home to worship Ganesha, the elephant god of good luck, or other deities. So, I was a walking altar the other night, and the guys found that extremely funny. Since I am informed, now, I took the garland off around the ashtray, built an "altar" with family photos I had brought along, and hung the garland around it.

Libbi (the librarian) let me work on his computer when the students came in, so I am all caught up on my Indian report, but only half way through on my computerized Greece report. Libbi is also a journalist. He can't write directly into the computer either. "Creative thoughts flow out of my pen", he said. They admire my stamina, here. When I work, I work. It's that inner driving force. As I said earlier, it's not always good. You need to take care of yourself in between. I am looking forward to when it becomes a little cooler. Yesterday Hemant said: "It is pleasantly cool, today, Mam", when he picked me up from the Ayurvedic clinic. "For YOU!" I said. It was maybe 2 ^{0}C cooler, and he wore a long-sleeve cotton sweater. I couldn't believe it. I call him "my adopted Indian son".

Last night, we were invited to **Budhi's** house for dinner. He and Hemant picked us up in the white Government SUV. He lives in a modern apartment house with his wife and two daughters. Indian wives don't sit down with their guests for dinner; they eat afterwards after the guests are fed. It was a **fantastic meal** with two kinds of freshly prepared bread: Spinach burri, which is deep-fried and chapatti, which is a puffed up flat bread, Indian spinach fixed with cubes of fresh homemade cheese, curried cauliflower, rice pilaf, mixed vegetable, lentil soup, joghurt with little crunchy balls, salad which is a raw vegetable plate, and a fruit salad for dessert. Not to forget the appetizers we had with our Indian light beer, which is very refreshing in that heat.

The **hospitality** and friendship is incredible: "Please come over for lunch, anytime, my place is your place." His wife cooks four times a day, every time fresh. Both daughters spoke English very well. The youngest is in 11th grade in Junior College (=10th-12th), and she is a certified Indian dancer. She showed me pictures of her dance exam. The older daughter is a computer programmer in

Bombay. She came home around 10 p.m. Every day, she spends four hours on the bus. The whole family is highly educated. Budhi also has a son who works at CSU with my friend from Argentina. He was introduced to me on New Years, but since I didn't know Budhi, yet, I didn't make the connection.

Budhi told us a story over dinner, which is significant in any kind of **translation**: He owes it all to his Grandma. She took him to school when he was very young, and gave his birth date in Hindi to the teacher. S/he did not know about the Hindi calendar (New Year starts now), and s/he put down Budhi's birthday in February instead of August. The school officials also made him older, since he probably looked pretty wise for his age. "Good thing", I said, "Now you can retire earlier."

From my observation he works twelve hours a day from 8 to eight. He walks in the morning, does meditation, takes homeopathies, helps his wife and is very fond of his daughters. No wonder the oldest doesn't want to go to America (yet). It is (too) cozy around Daddy! Not to mention the incredible work the mother puts in every day. She knows about Ayurvedic medicine and can prepare it herself. She misses her hometown in North India very much. She wore a golden-yellow sari, Budhi was dressed in Western attire, and the daughters wore the traditional North Indian outfit with loose cotton pants and a loose-fitting cotton dress over it. They want to go shopping with me, since I expressed the wish of wanting to wear the Northern outfit here. The US micro fiber is not suited for this climate. It's best when you wear all cotton, which absorbs and breathes.

Around 1 p.m.

Medicated oil...Fakir table...Synchronized massage...The dripping thing...Medicated hair wash...Cool doshas...

I just got home from my Ayurvedic treatment. My husband is fixing lunch for me, since I look pretty beat up. The treatment is very intense. Every day, they cook up special **medicated oil** for me, another herbal tincture for the head dripping bowl, and a bucket full of other herbal water to wash my head after the treatment. For one and a half hours you lay on a **"Fakir" table**, which is traditionally made of mahogany, a tropical hardwood. This one is from duroplast, but nonetheless just as hard.

First, the two women who have a four-year-college degree rub the medicated oil into you for fifty minutes. They do this in a **synchronized massage**, leaving no part of your body out, except the tanga area. They work like machines in broad circular strokes, changing direction after forty strokes, and then integrating the massaged part with the whole body. It is pretty painful at times; depending on how many emotions you have packed into your muscles over time. You'd think your whole body came out bruised, afterwards, but actually the skin looks pretty lustrous after the massage. Dieter and Hemant say I smell like an herb shop.

After the massage they treat the head with a **medicated liquid, dripping** it on your forehead while the bowl above your head is moving, and the liquid runs down on a cord. This gets you pretty fast into an alpha brain wave state where you can rest, dream or make psychic contact with people at the other end of the world. My aching back wakes me up from time to time. I shift my weight and do some stomach exercises; then I can hold out for another 15 minutes. The only things I can't endure are the strokes on my feet. I start to giggle, since it tickles, and soon we are all laughing together.

After the head dripping treatment I slide down the Fakir table like an oil sardine, and take a shower and a **medicated hair wash** in the bathroom. After dressing you sit down for a while to drink a glass of pink purified water. After the first treatment, yesterday, they had **cooled** down my **doshas** so much that I longed for a hot shower, before going to dinner at Budhi's house. In cooling down the doshas they could stop the pelvic inflammation. I saw the results within a few hours in spite of my four-hour computer marathon. This whole procedure is called Panchakarma, and I have to read more about it.

Missing laundry…Shared clothing…Tropical hygiene…

I'll tell you the story of the **missing clothing.** Practical and non suspicious as I am, I put the dirty laundry in a plastic bag and hung it outside on the doorknob. While leaving my key at the receptionist I told the house manager that there was laundry hanging outside the door for the laundry boy to pick up. After that I left for town.

Two days later I inquired how long the laundry normally takes, and they said it alternates days, but they didn't know anything about the laundry bag. Two more days went by. I had already said Goodbye to my laundry internally: 'Well", I thought, "Let them have the clothing. They wouldn't steal it, if they wouldn't have a need for something." When our favorite house manager came back he had already heard about the missing bag, and had me write down the items: One pair of black DCNY socks, my beloved army shirt from my boys, one white bras, one black cotton-silk man's shirt, one night gown.

A few hours later, when I came up from the computer lab my laundry bag was sitting on the couch. Our favorite house manager had conducted a very effective investigation in which the boys contradicted each other. They had already **shared** the clothing among themselves, and my husband said jokingly: "I wonder who opted for your oversized T-shirt (nightgown)." It was even too big on me, but perfect for this climate.

Tropical hygiene

Mohammed knew exactly what he was prescribing in the Koran for his brethren: The cleaning with pure water after every visit to the toilet, if small or big, is of utmost importance here. Things that work in the US don't work here at all. Baby wipes create a stink when confronted with tropical heat, and panty liners can lead to a yeast infection, because they don't allow enough circulation. There are many religions living peacefully side-by-side in India: Hinduism, Buddhism, Roman Catholic, Sikh, and Islam. Tolerance is a very important principle in India.

Father of Indian Democracy...Pollution...Celebration...Robbed...School Director...

Tonight, we visited a Buddha temple by the seaside in Bombay where the **Father of Indian Democracy,** Dr. Br. Ambedkar was cremated. He died in 1956, and was said to be close in spirit to Buddha. When we entered the temple barefoot there was a ten-day training camp for Buddhist monks in session. I asked if the color of their sari had a meaning. It was orange-red. "Sacrifice", they said. "Sacrificing earthly life in order to lead a spiritual life?" I asked back. "Yes", they said with a Buddhist smile on their faces.

We took a walk by the seaside. I was glad it was dark, so I wasn't able to discriminate the tons of garbage, which was swimming on the shore creating this offensive smell. I prayed to Allah, Buddha, Jesus Christ, Mother Mary, Mother Teresa, and all the enlightened entities, which had walked this earth to lead mankind to a major clean up, so that paradise could return on earth once more. If you imagined the **pollution** away, it was like any other beach in the world: Children playing in the sand, families sitting and eating popcorn, vendors selling their snacks in little booths, teenagers making out, young lads playing soccer.

After our beach walk we had a light Indian dinner in the restaurant "Celebrations". A nine-day celebration is starting today. Bombay and BARC look like Denver on Christmas. We'll be watching the Indian dancers tomorrow night.

Budhi said I **robbed** him of the pleasure of paying for dinner, tonight. I folded my hands in prayer when we departed for the night and asked his forgiveness. He never stopped smiling, so I hope it wasn't that serious of a cultural trespass.

For Monday afternoon, the science advisor to the Prime Minister who is also a scientist at BARC has arranged for me to meet the **school director** who was an Indian ambassador in Austria in former times. I'll suppose he'll speak perfect German.

Sunday, 13. Oktober

From the coolest…Hard to keep my cool…

Lose a son…Serene place…Pollution…"Noesthetics"…The Beauty in everything…Solution?…

I am not going anywhere, today. I have no desire at all, but to stay in the cool, comfortable cocoon of our apartment. I wasn't ready to talk about this, last night, but after discussing it with an Indian businessman at the treatment center, this morning, I am ready to digest my stark impressions of last night. He said: "I have a brother in the US. I had a chance to go to Canada, too, but I made the decision to stay home. I will send my son to the US. I know I will lose a son, but I want him to escape this desolate situation. There is a highly educated force here, but no opportunities."

Now I know why Budhi hardly ever goes to Bombay. He is longing to retire in **a serene place** in the mountains with clear streams and lakes, with fresh air to breathe. (Does that sound like Colorado or what?) When we drove into Bombay, last night, his daughter got headaches from all that **pollution**. Traffic was heavy on the major road, because it was Saturday night and the beginning of the nine-day celebration of "Dussehra". People "camped" out everywhere, especially on bridges. I guess it is a little cooler there. Women were cooking dinner over little open fires. Apartment complexes are fenced off along the road, keeping poverty out and confined to the sidewalks of the main road. Downtown Bombay is loaded with modern shops, but there is **no esthetic** landscape around it. You are constantly confronted with stark contrasts.

"There is beauty in everything", goes a Buddhist saying. It is hard to train your eyes while your stomach is revolting. "What is the solution?" I asked the businessman who worked for a French oil company. "Getting the masses off the street. Organizing health care and education for them, and stopping the overproduction." Just when it was getting really interesting, he was called in by the therapist. I hope I can continue this conversation next Sunday, when he comes for his weekly treatment.

14. Oktober

From the coolest…

Durga Puja…The Goddess…Festive atmosphere…Sauna… Traditional Indian dances…Soul of a people…

Last night, we had dinner at Budhi's, and afterwards we went with another family from the institute to see the **Durga Puja** festivals in New Bombay (N) and then in Old Bombay (S). It is a nine-day festival in honor of the **Goddess Durga,** her two sons and two daughters. One son is Ganesha, the elephant god for good luck. Durga defeated the evil guy and that's when the new world started.

We were nine people in the spacious SUV with two broad backseats. Lively conversations were going on and lots of laughter. The teenage daughters of both families were friends in school. At each place we visited, there was a fountain and an altar built up to honor Durga. People stood in line to approach the altar and share some sweets. At the last place, they motioned us in front and placed a round cookie in our hands, which looked like marzipan. We had Budhi share it with the rest of the party, since we are only allowed to eat cooked foods from controlled establishments.

There was a **festive atmosphere,** lots of booths with different foods and handicrafts. People were dancing with two colorful sticks in their hands. I liked the last place in Old Bombay best. It had a serene atmosphere, and it was already a little cooler, when we arrived there. Can you imagine being in a sauna for three and a half hours? Pearls of sweat were running down my back and my legs. The good thing was that I didn't have to use a public toilet. In the last place, in Old Bombay (S), we watched the **traditional Indian dances** as well as modern dances and music. I have heard soft and hard rock in four countries now. Each country has its specific traditional undertone. It would be an interesting musical experiment picking one popular song around the world and having it performed by different nationalities. Through music one can feel the **soul of a people.**

In the evening

School director/Ambassador...Staff developer...26 languages...Hindi...Mam...Uniforms...Discipline...Copyb ooks...Concentration...Family value system...Progress... Many cultures...

This afternoon at 3 p.m., I had a meeting with the local **school director.** No, he did not speak perfect German, since he was ambassador in Austria for only two and a half years. You can't learn a language in 2 1/2 years. To speak it at a sophisticated level you need 10 to 14 years of training. We communicated in Standard English. He and his assistant, a teacher trainer, were easy to understand. When Budhi and I arrived, he was on the phone with his feet up on the desk, and he didn't even notice us at first. "Relaxed guy!" I thought. He gestured that we should make ourselves comfortable at the conference table. After he ended his telephone call he came over, greeted us, and ordered some tea. Just when he switched on the air conditioner (just for me!) a huge butterfly (Pfauenauge in Ger.), symbol of transformation, lifted off into the warm air. Then he called his assistant in. From what I understood she was a **staff developer**, teacher trainer etc., a well traveled, beautiful woman in her 40s. He was in his 60s, I estimate, with white curly hair, light skin and fairly European looking. He appeared to be a little tired in the afternoon and so was I from my Ayurvedic treatments in the morning, but we picked up in temperament in the course of the conversation. He talked about the difficulties they are experiencing in the Indian system (It all sounded familiar to me!), and asked me a lot of questions about the German and the American system.

The DAE (Department of Atomic Energy)[3] operates 35 schools for 30.000 kids around the country. The rest are government operated and private schools. In DAE schools they teach the children in English and Hindi as a foreign language. For most kids both languages are "foreign". There are **26 languages** spoken in India, but **Hindi** is the common language of the country and English of the educated middle class. About one quarter (250 million!!!) belongs to the middle class.

After an introductory conversation with the Ambassador, the teacher trainer took me over to 1.grade. On our way I noticed the clean, esthetic environment. No trash was lying around anywhere. They were especially proud of the **school**

---

3.   DAE is devoted to **peaceful use of Atomic Energy!!!**

garden, a nature-learning path for the children who also take care of it them-selves with the help of gardeners. In 1.grade I was greeted with "Good afternoon, **Mam!**" The principal and assistant principal had also joined us for the classroom visit. The classroom teacher offered us chairs in front, but I had already headed for those cute little benches I sat on in first grade. So we all ended up sitting in benches. Budhi looked pretty wise sitting in a school bench. And he was paying attention, too, when I looked back and so were the children. I did not detect one ADD kid in that hot classroom with about thirty kids in neat **uniforms.** They were taking a test about conjunctions and prepositions within sentence contexts. The kids wrote in neat little booklets (copybooks), like I right now, with clear standard printed handwriting. It was a clean, orderly, **disciplined,** but very friendly environment conducive to learning.

For any kind of arranged school visits insiders know that you get to see the "chocolate side" of the institution, as the Germans say, but the school director confirmed later that there are practically **no discipline problems,** since the chil-dren are imbedded in a strong **family value system.**

After the 1.grade visit we went over to the 3.grade class. Again, perfect man-ners and a high level of **concentration!** The boys looked so handsome with their shirts and ties that I as a teacher would have to consciously concentrate on the girls in order not to give preferential treatment. It is a researched fact that boys receive more attention in school.

I bet the teacher chose the story "Der Rattenfaenger von Hameln", "The Rat hunter of Hamlin" on purpose, since she knew I was a German teacher. The kids responded well to her reading, questioning and clarifying words for them. I regis-tered a **good progress** from level one to three. The children spoke clear Standard English. Just when I was thinking "This little boy in the first row (sitting periph-eral) really needs a turn now, the highly aware and sensitive headmaster gave him green light to express his thoughts. He was speech impaired, but his English was clear and his thoughts profound.

After the 3.grade visit we went to the principal's office where they served water and lemonade. The teacher trainer had attended school in Maryland from 5th to 10th grade, and her father had taken her to **many countries and cultures.** The principal had also been on an exchange to the US in 1998. She remembered cooperative learning groups and a less structured and less disciplined environ-ment in contrast to the Indian system.

Last, we went over to the school director again and talked some more about teachers' salaries, status in society and the role of the teacher in the classroom. First, I want to finish my observations, ask more questions, and then I will write some more about BARC schools. On Thursday, I will go back to watch secondary schools.

15. Oktober

From the coolest…

Durga Puja…Boss of 30 000 DAE students…Ambassador…

Tonight was the closing ceremony of **Durga Puja** at the square in the colony at BARC. It feels like New Year in Germany or 4th of July in America, or the 14th of July in Paris. The fireworks are still rumbling on, celebrating the new beginning. The bad guy has been burnt tonight. His insides exploded with lots of fireworks going off in his belly. The burning puppet is a symbol for getting rid of the evil in this world. In the schools they celebrated Durga as the Goddess of learning. People brought little gifts to the temple, today. All day you could hear Indian drums and chants.

Indians love celebrations. The school director, who is actually **the boss of the 30 000 DAE students around the country**, as I learned tonight, said that when he was a boy they had around 70 something holidays[4], but they cut it down now. The parliament recently passed a mandatory school law, but they are not sure how to enforce it, if it should be the parents' responsibility or the state's.

Now I understand why the science advisor to the Prime Minister arranged that meeting with the "Ambassador" for me. It is my feeling that he found it very refreshing that I treated him as a human being and not as a "swamikunanda-mangolinibanasabu". When I 'contradicted' him I saw that twinkle in his eyes. "Scientists, doctors and high administrators are regarded important in this country. Teachers are not considered very important", he said. "But they are", I replied, "They change lives forever!"

He also interfered when Budhi wanted to give a long introduction about my husband's work: "We are not here, today to talk about science, but education." I have the feeling that he is a strong supporter of women and that his assistant could very well be his successor, the Director of some 30 000 DAE students around the country.

---

4.   Including weekends

17. Oktober

From the coolest...

Secondary school...English medium school...ESL...Radio production...Comparing Indian, German, American school system...Boston schools...The Nightingale and the Frog...Focus: Learning...

Today was my second observation day in **Secondary school.** (8-10th) Hemant picked me up at 10 a.m., and drove me over to Central Administration to meet the "Ambassador". I'll call him the Ambassador for Education from now on. I read his introduction to an English edition for level I, Primary English instruction, which he and his staff developer had designed together, and I noticed that our teaching philosophies matched, for example, that kids (pupils) <u>need</u> to be corrected, so that they become aware of their mistakes and can fix them, next time. He clearly analyzed the state of English in this country: English is the language of commerce, politics and opportunities, and the <u>only</u> language, which binds all Indians together; however it is not the mother tongue.

All BARC schools are **English Medium schools**; that means all the subject areas are taught in English. For that one needs teachers who are firm in their subject area as well as excellent speakers and teachers of Standard English. These teachers are hard to find if you consider that the training of a Foreign-language teacher takes up to fourteen years, from the time they start to learn the language. Tonight, his assistant (and staff developer) is going on a business trip to recruit teachers. The three of us chatted over tea. I asked the ambassador if he would be interested in a direct exchange with our superintendent, and he stated that he wants to travel India. I think he has been around the world a lot, and wants to retire in peace. But the teacher trainer expressed that she wants to stay in contact through e-mail and exchange ideas of how to teach English as a second language (**ESL**) more effectively.

After the morning tea break with the Ambassador, a driver from Central Administration drove us, the beautiful lady in the sari and me, over to the secondary school to meet the principal. His English was hard for me to understand yet my Indian colleague had no problems understanding him. After a brief introduction, Sari and I visited two 10th grade classes.

The first class was performing a **radio production,** which they had worked on for ten days. Every pupil had a role in that production: some longer, some shorter, some simpler, and some more complex according to his/her abilities. They interviewed two "teachers" in their role-play and you could hear and feel how much they value the teaching profession. Some students sat in "overcrowded" benches, yet there was no shuffling and pushing, or fighting for territory. After their play the teacher asked me to talk to the class. I gave a quick introduction, and encouraged them to ask questions. They hung on my lips with every word and asked intelligent questions about the comparisons between **Indian, German and American system**. They were especially interested in testing, and if the American portrayals on TV (**Boston schools**) were true.

The teacher and all the students spoke clear Standard English. It was the same in the second classroom where they dealt with the fable "The Nightingale and The Frog" written in verses. It is fun teaching in a class like this where you have this amount of attention and willingness to learn and absorb at all times. Sure, they are noisy during passing times (the teacher passes), but once the teacher enters the classroom it is "Good morning, teacher!" and the **focus is on learning**. These are not only the 7000 kids of scientists, but also of middle level employees and service personnel. And you could not tell one from the other, since they all wear their school uniforms.

The **uniting factor is learning** here, not socializing and fashion shows. The principal said that there are no discipline problems. They love and respect their teachers, and sure enough two students ran into my husband and me, tonight at the market place. They greeted me with a big smile, and we chatted for a while. Wouldn't YOU love to teach in such a place? On Monday, I will go back to observe Junior College (11th-12th). The Ambassador, Sari and I are already looking forward to our Monday morning teatime.

From the coolest...

Mushroom cut...Buying power...Master cutter...YOUR heart...Surgeon hands...Live heart-surgery...Mammal arteries...Trauma...Ceremony...

On Friday, I dared to go to the hairdresser, called beauty salon, here. When I made the appointment I asked Hemant to come with me so that I could show his haircut and explain how it transferred to me. It's a **mushroom-style** haircut with short neck hair and long deck hair. The "Chef" was a master cutter, very light to the touch, and the short neck hair feels good in this heat. Best of all, it cost me $ 2 = 100 rupees. Reflecting on **buying power**: A BARC teacher's salary is 10 000 rupees ~ $ 200. An Indian teacher spends 1% of his/her salary on a haircut. How much does an American teacher spend? Let's see: Average net salary ~ $ 2000, average haircut ~ $ 20, also 1% of the salary, although mine costs between $ 27 and $ 38, depending where I go to.

The **Master cutter** switched over from Indian to American music while I was there and had tea served for me, although Indian music is totally agreeable with me. He wore Nike jeans (didn't know that they made jeans now) and Western boots. He had been in the US and his saloon was modern and clean. It had been recommended to me by the Ayurvedic clinic. The Master cutter wasn't much of a talker, so I kept quiet and observed his skillful hands, which moved like a symphony through my hair.

Last night (Saturday), we attended a talk in the air-conditioned lecture hall of the guesthouse: "**YOU and Your Heart**", presented by two famous heart surgeons from Bombay and their assistants. When we arrived at the lecture hall after a shopping outing to Bombay with our host family, it was already ¾ full. We took seats further in the back, but were motioned to the front seats when the guests arrived half an hour later. Although I wore white dress shorts and felt a little underdressed being exposed to the shrill lights of the press, I was glad to get a close view of Dr. Goyal and his staff: One meter ninety tall with **surgeon hands** and fine intellectual features he was the most impressive figure of the whole group. He radiated wisdom and calmness. His delicate humor during the talk pointed at our human weaknesses in regard to diet, exercise and anti-stress-life style, which prevent heart attacks.

His assistants gave short slide-show presentations about nutrition and lifestyle, but any BARC 10th grader could have done a better job. Then his colleague, the other fine surgeon with a real long Indian name gave a scientific power point presentation, which he had prepared for a medical congress, and not tailored, to this audience. Towards the end the slides were repetitive, and the talk dragged out too long, so, many of the scientists sneaked out the lecture hall. HIS English was the best, and you could see that he had experience in the international scene. His short clips from **live heart surgeries** were very drastic and educational. He specializes in open—heart surgery with the heart beating while he replaces the damaged arteries with the **mammal arteries.** Both men and women carry a right and a left one. The mammal arteries are able to expand (nursing mothers) and carry a lot of blood through the pump.

His objective as a surgeon is discovering how to achieve long-lasting repairs (15-20 years) in a damaged heart. As the heart beats the mammal arteries expand. He said that this method causes the least **trauma,** although the picture show was pretty traumatic to me. I do not want that done to my heart if I can help it! Compared to the West there are more **ceremonial aspects** that go on in India before and during the lecture, which gives it a very festive atmosphere and special frame.

October 21

From the coolest place in the apartment…

Junior College…50 students…Note taking skills…Attention span…Teenagers…Montezuma's revenge…Good Bye Dinner at Grand Central…Crazy Monday mornings…

Today was my last observation day in school, because we will travel the day after tomorrow to Gujarat, Mangalore, Bangalore and some spiritual place up in the mountains, some five hours away from the city, to Mt. Abu. The morning tea with the Ambassador fell through, since he had a visitor, so Sari and I went directly over to the **Junior College** in a government vehicle to meet the vice principal. He spoke very good English, but Sari kept on "translating" or clarifying what the two of them had been talking about, which was very funny, as if they had spoken in Hindi. Sari and he had many common topics to talk about: Colleagues, their kids, Sari possibly coming back to the Junior College after her special assignment, etc.

At 10:50 a.m., Sari dropped me off at an 11th grade English class while she went to a book exhibition. There were **50 students** in the classroom with fans running and sounds bouncing off the walls. The English teacher, a younger guy around 35, with jeans and a dress shirt, taught **note—taking skills** in a voluminous voice. His lesson was skillfully crafted. He summarized frequently in chorus fashion and prompted his students to write down the <u>important</u> notes. He kept the attention of the kids for 40 minutes with his vivid body language, clear English and catchy anecdotes. Indian kids have a long **attention span,** so lecturing, note taking and summarizing suits them well. Sari said they had tried cooperative learning groups for a while, but moving the heavy furniture and the noise level in the 50–60 student classrooms was bothersome, so they abandoned it again.

These 11th graders definitely reminded me of American **teenagers,** but more like US 9th graders in their behavior. 11th graders in America are already settled after their stormy years in 9th and 10th grade. It was so hot in the classroom that the teacher's shirt was totally perspired. I am always hot, too when I teach. In retrospective, there was no sweaty smell in the classroom, in spite of that crowd, probably because of the mostly vegetarian diet and the good tropical hygiene.

I did not observe a second class, since I was overheated. In the morning, **Montezuma's revenge** had caught up with me and I was debating if I should go to school at all. On our way out, Sari and I had a look at the book exhibition, which frequently takes place to encourage students to read outside of class.

Back at Central Administration, we met up with the Ambassador again. He asked me about my impressions, and said that there was a problem with the date of our **Goodbye dinner** at Grand Central, since it was his friend's birthday on the 13th. His friend **is** the science advisor to the Prime minister. I said: "Don't break good traditions, we'll find a common date to meet again." He excused himself with a smile, since he had been requested at another meeting ten minutes ago. (Crazy Monday mornings!)

I am glad I got these observations in at the right time, because after we return from our travels the students here have a ten-day break, and we'll return two weeks earlier to my husband's hometown, since mother-in-law needs to go to the hospital. We will take care of his father (Alzheimer's) for two weeks before moving on to Italy and Spain.

October 22

Since the English teacher requested a written statement about my observations yesterday, I said I would give him a printout of my last chapter. Generally, I do not use real names in my literary travel report. Naturally, my computer draft would go to my proofreader in Chicago ☺ first, an American <u>native speaker</u>, before being released, but I will make an exception in this case.

GOING ON TRAVEL

24. Oktober

From Sardar Patel University in the State of Gujarat...

Flight cancelled...Rerouted...Contribution to science...Gujarat...NO escort...

I am writing from our Indian host professor's office at the physics department of the Sardar Patel University. My husband has to give a talk in about one hour. "We need to make some money," he says.

Yesterday, we wanted to fly out of Bombay National Airport with Indian Airlines around 5 p.m., but the flight was **cancelled**, just like that. "But my husband has to give a talk at 11 a.m., tomorrow." I pleaded with the head-cheese in his heavily guarded office. If you think the American security procedures are strict, wait till you come to Bombay. "I will reroute you on Jet Airlines", he said graciously. What you have a right to demand in the West will not work here, only patience, diplomacy and a smile. And since I have more of it, my husband sends me off to the frontlines. "Thank you, officer", I said "You are making a great **contribution to science** getting my husband to Gujarat on time!" So, one and a half hours later, we took off. The flight was short (ca. 45 min.) and pleasant; they even served a vegetarian sandwich and a dessert.

Our Indian host professor picked us up in a white University limousine with a driver, and greeted us with two beautiful flower bouquets. From Vadodara airport we drove about one hour to Vallabh Vidyanagar in the state of **Gujarat.** The environment here is much more harmonious, spacious and esthetic than in Bombay. "Any climate in India is better than the one in Bombay," said Libbi yesterday. True! It is less humid here, the air quality is better and it cools off at night, slightly...

After freshening up in the guesthouse we met up with a group of Indian Profs, including the chairman, in a vegetarian restaurant. The dinner was excellent, but my sleep was not, since my husband is a restless soul when he comes to a new environment. Now, I shall go downtown to explore the 55 000 inhabitant town.

They wanted to give me an **escort**, but it is safe to walk, so I refused. I miss going out by myself, exploring, discovering and taking a risk; a small calculated one…

25. Oktober

While walking on a dirt road among holy cows and school children coming back
from school:

Walk the soil of a people barefoot
And your heart will stay connected forever!

Original MOM

In front of the air conditioner dressed up in a salva…

Salva…Presents…In love…House tour…

I am waiting to be picked up for the official function, a general assembly, with the vice chancellor = (president) of the university, all dressed up in a salva. I got this salva last night as a present from our host professor's daughter, where we were invited for dinner. A **salva** is a Northern Indian outfit with light, lose-fitting cotton pants, a tailed long dress with high slits and a stole (shawl) around your neck sailing in the wind.

I have to watch what I say, because whenever you admire something you get it as a **present**. I said: "I would have worn my yellow golden salva tonight, but there was no chance to get back to the guesthouse to change after our evening excursion." Immediately, the daughter grabbed a shopping bag out of the cupboard with two salvas. "Try these!" she said. They had so much fun dressing me up Indian style that I gracefully accepted the present.

Before, I had worn a white outfit with pants and a lose fitting linen shirt which matched exactly to our host professor's evening outfit and his little grandson's, too. So the three of us posed for pictures. The baby boy was a cuddly, vivid little three-year old with velvet skin, thick black hair in his cute little white outfit. The white Grandma fell **in love** with him. The daughter of the house was his mother, who had cooked the marvelous dinner, together with the prof's wife. His son and his granddaughter also lived in the 2000 sq.-feet house. Brother and sister were totally devoted to nourishing the guests. They were quite a team! We had waited up for Budhi to arrive from Bombay. He had a worse trip than us having been detoured to another city before flying into Vadodara.

Since we had lots of time before Budhi's arrival, our Indian host professor gave us a **tour** of his **house**. You always leave your shoes at the door and enter the house barefoot. The stone floors keep your feet cool and the street dust out. The kitchen looks a lot more functional than in the US and Germany. Everything is very well organized, and you can grab the utensils faster. Indian women cook a lot from scratch, so a kitchen workshop is just what they need. There was a bathroom with a floor toilet, one with a Turkish toilet with a self-cleaning system, and a separate shower. On the first floor of the house there was a fully equipped, stored away classroom, because the prof had taught science and math to school children in former times.

What is different from Western living, are the built-in stone shelves in the walls. When I admired the bedspreads with Indian prints in the son's bedroom, they presented us with two sets over dinner for our bedrooms at home. They are locally produced with great Indian ornaments. I especially like the elephants.

27. Oktober

From Ahmedabat Airport, capital of Gujarat, back to BARC Trombay...

Our host professor from Gujarat just dropped us off at the airport of the capital: Ahmedabat. He and his faculty provided us with many memorable experiences during our five-day stay: A visit to the local temple, to the monument hall of the founder of the university, Sardar Patel[5], an official assembly with the vice chancellor (=president), a visit to the house of another Indian Son, a fourteen-hour trip back and forth to Mt. Abu, visiting four spiritual centers with an overnight stay at a friend's house.

When you have to digest so many impressions in the course of five days and do not have enough time to write—tomorrow we'll leave again for Mangalore—you have to condense it down to the essentials and the personal encounters, which left footprints in my heart.

You wouldn't believe whom we just met: Just when I was writing the word **heart**, the famous heart surgeon from Bombay, Dr. Goyal, who definitely left a footprint in my heart, walked down the isle in the boarding room and greeted us. He gave another talk here, he said, and we've visited Mt. Abu, we said. It was a brief and happy exchange. An airport feels quite homey when you run into a familiar soul.

---

5.   He was the Prime Minister with the iron fist, uniting this country which was composed of many kingdoms

28. Oktober

At Bombay National Airport flying out to Mangalore...

Indian sons...Rick...

Mangalore is the Garden city of India. I am curious. Continuing the 'familiar soul' topic from last night, many **Indian sons** were drawn to the white Indian Grandma with her silver hair and her salva. Actually, you feel like a teenager again when you get so much attention from males of all ages. When I sat in the back of the SUV (we rotated around with 6 people and luggage in the car) other jeeps were chasing us and honking their horns, only to get a good glimpse of the white queen in the back. Their contact felt quite flirtatious, but it could have just been Indian happiness. Then again, only the guys behaved like this; the girls were waving and smiling. Half a school class (boys, of course) on their way to school posed with me for a picture. I am quite intrigued by their smiles. There is definitely a mutual affinity.

I adopted a second Indian son, a 28-year old computer programmer and head technician of the Physics department. I will call him **Rick** here. When I encountered him first in the white limousine I thought: "He is not a service driver; he is his own boss", judging by his sovereign body language and fine demeanor. And sure enough it was so: He owned his own air—conditioned luxury car and made it a point giving service to the department. "Actually, all you do for others, you do in reality for yourself. It makes me happy to be of service." He said. So he was our companion for three days at Sardar Patel University, driving us places for lunch, for sightseeing, and a visit to his house.

Boarding time-!

29. Oktober

From the guesthouse at Mangalore University...

Health hazard...Education minister...A frog and a cricket...Lord Krishna temple...Elephant blessings...

In Germany and the US, it would be called a **health hazard to** reside in this building. It is full of moldy spots on the walls and ceilings. Not in our room, though, which is laid out like an octagon. Since the climate is so humid, close by the sea, and because of the month-long monsoon rains, it is hard to keep up the buildings properly. But where there are scientists there should be a way: How about inventing mold-resistant building materials? (If they don't exist, yet.)

The **education minister** is coming next week. What's good enough for him is good enough for me, right? But if they want to attract international guests, they must offer international standards, at least a three star! Last night, when I wanted to take a shower, a **frog** hopped over my feet. I caught him with a plastic bag, and we released him outside. Just when I wanted to turn on the shower a huge green **cricket** hopped onto the faucet. Again, we released her outside. Jungle is all around us, a beautiful green luscious jungle. As long as I don't have to handle poisonous snakes in my room, I can manage. Actually, it looks pretty romantic with that mosquito net draped around my bed. It must have been a gorgeous house when it was new. The architectural layout is pretty interesting, mostly octagonal.

The lecturer[6] of the department took us to a very famous Hindu temple, last night, 60 km away from here in Udupi, named **Lord Krishna temple**. Our host professor didn't have time, because he is leaving in a few days to the US for a two-month stay. This morning, he will pick us up for breakfast at his house. In the Krishna temple, a guide who spoke Indian English, showed us around. I didn't understand everything, but most of it. He showed us the various deities in the shrines, decorated with diamonds, the huge kitchen, the lecture hall, and the milk dairy. They cook some 6000 meals for the poor every day with firewood, which is stacked neatly in the yard. The temple lives from donations all around the world. I determined that my donation would go to primary education. You even received a computerized printout for your taxes. In front of the temple I was

---

6.   English system: reader=assistant professor, lecturer=associate professor, then full professor

blessed by an **elephant**, which put his trunk on my head to thank me for the coin for his master. It is quite an experience when you can touch these mighty noble creatures, which forget neither a good nor a bad deed.

Noon

Confined to the premises...Writing from my bed...

Hermit...Indian guys...Indian bathroom...Nutritional meals...Ceremony...

The breakfast at the professor's house, this morning was lovely, although I could only eat small bites. Actually, the problems had started after a non-vegetarian breakfast on the plane. I think I could not tolerate the sausage link; however, it is hard to track down. So now, I have to stay close to a toilet, and I don't feel like eating at all, today. Since I am not dead, yet, I can write. But this time, it is more serious than last time, because I feel that my small intestines are involved, too, my head and muscles are aching, and I am freezing. It's good that I can be a total **hermit** by nature, so I actually enjoy the downtime. Originally, I would have observed a primary school in the neighborhood and visited the computer lab to check my email and work on my computerized script.

The prof's son picked us up for breakfast in his own car. He had come home from Bangalore where he studies computer science, in order to see his parents before they went to America. Educated **Indian guys** have great manners: 'Mam' and holding the car door, serving attentively over breakfast, carrying your backpack, and all with a ground shaking smile!

Immediately after breakfast, I had to go to the bathroom. **Indian bathrooms** have no toilet paper. The cleaning takes place with water, soap and hands. A bucket with a little plastic can is standing near the toilet. I am getting better now at that, taking my stole off and securing the long dress of the salva. It's a matter of practice. Indians wash their hands a lot. Right by the dining table was a sink for washing hands before and after breakfast, since the food is mostly eaten with hands. For us they always put a fork or a spoon, but sometimes I join in scooping up my food with the chapatti bread. Indian housewives take great pride in preparing **highly nutritional meals** for their families.

After breakfast the professor's wife performed a **ceremony** with me. (In case anybody hasn't noticed, yet, I am special...banter!) She put a red dot on my forehead on the third eye from plant powder, handed me an apple and a plate with Ganesha, the elephant god and folded her hands for Namaste: I greet the god head in you. Very moved I did the same, thanked her for the presents and the delicious breakfast. Then the prof's son drove me back to the guesthouse where I enjoy catching up with my literary travel report.

A little later

Indian sons...Family bonding...Harmony...Spiritual focus...Guru...My native son...feet kissed...

I just threw up and actually I feel better, now, at least in my small intestines. I suspect motion sickness is also involved, since the diesel motor had a rhythm between constantly accelerating and slowing down, yesterday. It was the motor itself, not the driver with the gas pedal. My husband and a group of scientists are having lunch right now in the dining room of the guesthouse. I won't touch anything, besides bottled water, black tea and some coke till my body gives me the green light in form of an actual feeling of hunger.

I wish to come back to my Mt. Abu experience: The night before we left for Mt. Abu, we were invited to my second **Indian son's** house in an upper class neighborhood. I enjoyed swinging on the porch. His lovely wife, his three-month old son, and his parents live together in a spacious modern town house. Being a computer guy he had all the modern gadgets, of course.

Family bonding is very important in India. The son leaves it up to his mother to pick the right wife, since they all must live in **harmony** after the wedding. But Rick found his wife himself. Marriage is based on common values and family backgrounds. Actually not a bad concept, if you consider that the failure rate is very low. There is a strong support system for every family member. His wife can finish her Ph.D. in electronics while Grandma and Grandpa take care of the baby. In return, Rick will care for his parents till they die. It's his duty, he says.

Rick feeds his son biological cow milk, besides Bianca breastfeeding him twice a day. When I held the tall, muscular little guy in my arms, I felt all the love and care he had been born into. His parents have a strong **spiritual focus,** and know that the ultimate love from the Source Light is always available when you keep the connection through prayer, meditation, and service: In what church, in which temple, through which specific practices, it all doesn't matter. "We don't need another **GURU!**" I sang subconsciously one night under the shower. (Beatle song!)

Rick took me on a tour of the ground level of his house. "These are things tourists never get to see. It's an honor showing you around, since you have a genuine interest in learning about other cultures." "I feel honored being in the sanctuary of your home having things explained to me by a native son." (I am not sure now whether I said **MY native son**!) Rick and Bianca gave me a rice-light string for Diwali; the festival of lights, and later Rick presented me with a little bottle of jasmine oil, which gave me comfort in many situations, later.

When we departed for the night in front of our guesthouse we almost banged heads. Since he bent down to the ground, I thought something had fallen down. My Indian son had actually **kissed my feet.** I could watch the ceremony with my husband once more, how gracefully he honored his "elders".—Indian sons and the white teacher from America-!!! I shall take a nap now for a speedy recovery.

To Mt. Abu...

Baked...Now I believe...BARC Gamma Ray Observatory... House warming ceremony...Swastika...Hindu temple on Mt. Abu...

Our host professor, his wife, his graduate student (who attended to our every need in the guesthouse), the driver and us, took off at 4 a.m. in a spacious Toyota SUV. However, with the luggage on the foldout seats, three had to sit on the backbench and one in the luggage compartment. So we rotated around, cooling off in front of the air conditioner in the front seat. In spite of the air conditioner it got awfully hot, especially when you were **baked** in between two people.

The 350 km-drive took seven hours, since you have to slow down in between driving 90—100 km, because of pot holes, speed bumps, bridges, little villages, cows, camels, dogs, pigs, children, Ottos, motorcycles etc. There is a story going around in India: Before the Russian President Putin came to India, he didn't believe in God. When he saw all the members participating in this insane traffic, he said: "**Now I believe** in God! There must be one All Mighty directing all this chaos."

The purpose of our visit was seeing the **BARC gamma ray observatory** and four spiritual centers on Mt. Abu. When we arrived at the very top it was pleasantly cool and breezy. However, we were in the wrong place, because we were at the infrared observatory with an air force base right beside it. So we drove ten minutes down the mountain where we found the BARC gamma ray observatory with the huge parabolic mirror. We arrived just in time for the official function, the blessing of the newly built staff apartment house. We were fully included in the rituals: First, you had to take off your shoes, (how much Dieter loves that!) then you got a red dot on your forehead as a blessing, and then they wrapped a friendship bracelet around our wrists. My husband had to pick up a coconut and smash it at the entrance of the house over a **swastika**, a sign for good luck.

Signs are signs. They are neither good nor bad. It depends how a people interprets and uses it. For the Hopi Indians the swastika simply represents the four directions. For the Germans it is loaded with bad history of which they don't want to be reminded. After the entry ceremonies, a professor from BARC gave a talk, congratulated the architect and showed us around. The major building material is stone, to keep the apartments cool: concrete, granite and marble. It is more functional than in the West, but it depends on the owner to make it a home.

After the **house warming ceremony** the Prof and students wheeled out the gamma ray observatory for us. The research is on gamma rays in the universe, detecting pulsars. They feed all the data into computers, which are also connected to BARC in Trombay. (Our place!) The gamma ray observatory was constructed and built from scratch. Once a year, they have to take it apart for polishing and to replace the broken parts of mirror in the huge parabolic dish. Avant-garde research is being done on finer and finer substances now, until we finally find the ultimate cosmic ray, you'll see. (Totally unscientific, futuristic, intuitive opinion of the author!)

After lunch and a brief check-in at a friend's house where our host professor had arranged quarters for the night, we went to a breathtaking **Hindu temple** dating back to 1486. It took only 18 years to build—European churches are built over centuries—carving out every column with filigran religious ornamenting. Everything was made of marble in that temple, which reminded me of the one in the university town in Gujarat, but that was entirely made of stucco.

30. Oktober

From my bed...Feeling more stable...

Food poisoning...Indian doctor...Two PhDs...Coconut... Land of contradictions...Tolerance and patience...Mt. Abu, paradise on earth...

I love these early morning hours when the jungle awakes. This is the only time when you can open the windows to let the cool fresh air in. Later it gets too hot. Last night on the way to the good-bye dinner, our host professor took me to his family physician, a relative of his. The doctor motioned us in immediately. I felt sorry for the folks waiting, but they seemed all right with it. The state of my health was more serious than I thought: **Food poisoning** (non-vegetarian airplane meal!) and a 100 Fahrenheit fever, which is 101.8 for me, because I'm normally at 96.8 0 F. The doctor, a very warm and friendly man around 45, put me on white, fresh linen, and listened closely to my pulses and to my stomach with his stethoscope. This praxis reminded me of my childhood, when medicine was still centered on human touch instead of machines. He gave me a shot and explained, to my "men" how to take the medication (remember it is a social affair!), while I was having another attack in the bathroom. The physician refused to be paid, so we will think of something from Germany or the US for his praxis. He accompanied us to the car and waved Good Bye.

During the treatment the whole party of ten in two cars waited patiently. Their humor and laughter distracted me from my internal turmoil during the half-hour drive. At a gourmet restaurant we met up with five more people from the institute to celebrate two **PhDs** and our Good Bye. The meal looked fantastic: Fish, prawns, and interesting vegetarian Indian dishes. For me, they poured fresh coconut juice directly from the coconut. That's all I could have. Did you know that coconut juice is so pure and sterile that it can be injected directly into the veins? I enjoyed watching the party dine but had no desire to do so. After the shot my stomach stabilized and my fever diminished, so that I even enjoyed participating in the conversation. Humor is another common denominator around the world. They have plenty of it.

The car we drove in was a TATA, an Indian built car. It is very well built and gets 6 l/100km = 45mpg. The driver was a fellow professor with a smooth driving style on the bumpy roads, sent by an angel just for my sore intestines and me. He said: "India is a **land full of contradictions**. You have high tech and no tech, side by side. This is the only country in the world, where you can observe people living in the first century up to the 21st Century." I have a lot of hope for India, because it is a very spiritual country with a lot of **tolerance**. People have plenty of **patience** here. Otherwise living would be impossible in these overcrowded cities.

Back to Mt. Abu...PARADISE ON EARTH

Besides the temple, we visited three spiritual centers for World Peace. These were **paradises** within themselves. They produce their own solar energy with a very sophisticated system, built by a German and Swiss brother. Everything was built out of white marble, and the visitors or students from all over the world all wore white outfits. In these centers, they study **metaphysics**, probing the deeper questions in life. It is very clean and esthetic. Gardens and meditation places are everywhere. In the kitchen they cook up to 35.000 meals per day and the whole operation runs smoothly. There are many volunteers helping out from all around the world. If you don't meditate and follow the program, you can't cook, because the food takes on the vibrations of the cooks. I can confirm that from my own experience, because when our cooks didn't cooperate in harmony, last school year, I got stomach problems. (But then again, the experiment is not reproducible, and my stomach is not Thy stomach...) These spiritual centers up in the mountains are very serene and a good example how we can establish **paradise on earth** step by step.

30. Oktober, same day

From my bed in the guest house in Bangalore, the Silicon Valley of India…

International standards…Silicon Valley…

After a one-hour drive to Mangalore airport, and a one-hour flight to Bangalore and a half-hour ride, I am now in the guesthouse of the TATA Science Institute in Bangalore. This facility agrees with **international standards**. I survived the trip without having to run to the bathroom. I have only had water and black tea, so far and a little bite from the roll in the airplane. I decided to stay here, while my husband gives a talk, because I still feel a bit shaky.

I had a one-hour nap, black tea with lemon, and I am feeling back to normal. Bangalore is the **Silicon Valley** of India. I saw very few shacks on the way from the airport to the guesthouse. The climate is pleasant, around 25 Celsius, and I actually slept with two covers. The body has to adapt to the colder climate. It's winter here. I neither need the air conditioning nor the ceiling fan to stay cool. The windows are open, and I hear the jungle sounds. When you arrive at a place they (the boys or employees) take care of you immediately, until you've settled in. They brought tea, hot water, four bottles of mineral water, and two bitter lemons. I guess my Geezer is hot now, so I can take a warm shower and wash my hair. Hopefully tonight, I will be ready for an outing, again!

Shopping outing...Lower class people...Saree...Going nuts...Coconuts...Vegetarian...

Tonight, we went on a two-hour **shopping outing** with the driver from the TATA institute; Tata, an industrial magnate, was the founder of this place. The driver had clear instructions of where to go, and that he should stay with us every step of the way. But he wanted to drive us to a fancy shopping center. After half-an-hour drive we got impatient and said: "We should have been there 20 minutes ago!" Maybe I confused him with my directions: "Somewhat between the institute and the airport." But I don't think so, because later, at the shopping market, he said: "Only **lower-class people** shop here." Well, that was just fine with me, because I found a beautiful saree for 10 bucks at this "lower-class" place. The driver **drove** my husband **nuts**, because he disappeared in between, and Dieter doesn't like crowds in the first place. When I motioned the driver into the shops, there was no escape. You have to give them clear instructions (commands), and we are not good at that, but I just imitated the masters out of necessity. We wanted to find a silk shirt for my professor, but Dieter thought $ 20 was too much for local conditions, so he passed buying one. Men and shopping!!!

On the way back we bought two **coconuts** for my evening meal. I added a little rice, yoghurt, and some red-beet-carrot vegetable. A professor from Madras, who was having dinner with us in the guesthouse, explained the spicy dish, which I skipped: Unripe bananas cooked as a vegetable. It was delicious, said my husband. There are numerous ways of **vegetarian** cooking. When I am back home, I will become very creative in this. The doctor said: "Always order vegetarian, because you are on the safe side with it in this tropical climate." In spite of the carefully composed meal, I had to run after dinner. My warrior is sound asleep. Traveling and giving talks are wearing him out. It's not my bedtime, yet, and it is too noisy in the hallways.

31. Oktober

From the rose garden of the guest house...

Beauty...Song of gratitude...

I just walked my husband over to the Physics department. I know that when he discussed physics last night on the way back with our host, he didn't pay attention to the way. It's such a beautiful campus, embedded in its natural environment. This city, which has all the money, but beauty doesn't come from money alone: It comes from deep down in the soul of the tenants to <u>make</u> a place beautiful. BARC needs to do a better job in this. I heard it's beautiful behind the hills, in the secured area, but the town itself has areas devoid of all beauty.

Song of Gratitude

My soul sings a song of gratitude
With beauty, harmony and nature
All around me.
I shall devote my life
to creating Paradise on earth
in thoughts, speech and deeds.
I shall walk this earth
With an open heart and open eyes
To see beyond the Sir-face
Into the face of God.

potawi

31. Oktober

From Mangalore Airport flying home to BARC Trombay...

E.T. home...Nehru Science and Research Center... Arranged marriages...Guests and Gods...Education budget...Deputy Secretary...Silk shirts...Next time...

When I write BARC on my cabin luggage, they check me through faster, I learned. We just want to go "**home**" and sleep, now. My tummy is still rumbling, but I didn't have to run, today. I could fully participate in the program.

Today, I saw another science and research facility where art and nature were incorporated in the design. The equipment was state of the art and comparable with the Max-Planck-Institutes in Germany, or NREL, NIST or Los Alamos National Lab in the US. It was the **Nehru Science and Research Center**. We met an old, actually young acquaintance there from the 1996 Gordon conference in New Hampshire. He was one of the best soccer players of the Gordon team and he stormed Mt.Cardigan with us back then. He beat us, of course, being a younger professor in his forties, now.

While my husband discussed with another scientist, I clarified some cultural uncertainties with the young professor: "How do you feel about **arranged marriages**?" I asked him. "It's shifting more and more towards an agreement on all parts. In former times, it only worked, because the women suppressed their individuality. There is still a strong family bond, but it can't be forced or ordered."

"When you are a guest in a place which is incompatible with your health and you want to move into a hotel, is that an offense to the host?" "They will be very unhappy, because **guests** are treated as **Gods** in India and attended to personally."

"How much percent of the gross national income goes into science and research, **education**, and military defense?" "0.5% goes into science and research, less than half of that into education, and an unpublished high percentage into military defense." "I hope we reach that state as a human family soon where we can pump all that defense money into education and research."

After touring the Nehru Institute the young professor took us to lunch in an exclusive restaurant on the 13th floor, overlooking all of Bangalore. I couldn't eat much, but I enjoyed the view. The seven-million people Silicon Valley looked like a modern city, wide spread with some high rising buildings.

After lunch we went to the State Capitol, an outstanding architectural structure in Parsee style, where we had a meeting with the **deputy secretary** of treasury who had issued us a personal invitation at Mt. Abu, where he had taken a one-week class in metaphysics. He gave us a tour through the upper levels, and had the state minister's conference room unlocked for us. I recognized pictures of Gandhi, Nehru, Indira Gandhi, and the current Prime Minister Vajpayee, who by the way visited BARC, this morning. This deputy secretary was also a good friend of our host professor in Mangalore as we heard today. It's really a small world!

On the way to the airport, we finally found the **silk shirts** for my prof for $12 a piece. The university driver stopped at his "cousin's" place (Thought I wouldn't notice?), but that worked out fine, after all. I am glad we have experienced hosts everywhere, who give us a deeper insight into the culture of the country. We have visited four states, now: Radjastan, Gujarat, Karnataka, and Maharashtra. We had invitations to the south tip of India, to the beautiful state of Kerala, and to Delhi, but that will have to wait for next time, since we both want to finish our work, before we attend to the parents.

Midnight

Home, finally home! As I said earlier: When you come back to a place two or three times, it already feels like home, at least like a home base. I took a shower and I am sitting here with the cool air conditioner running behind me (27 ^{0}C), and a castor oil pack on my belly to remove those toxins faster. Babarao, the senior driver picked us up from the airport. It sure feels good to see an old, reliable friend at night.

From the coolest...Only fans running, now

Diwali...Sweets...Mothers and sons...Close nit...Corruption...People are the same...

Today, Indians celebrate the most important holiday of the year: **Diwali**, the festival of lights. It looks like Christmas, everywhere, but at the same time we have New Years. Since dawn, last night, fireworks have been blasting into the air, all through the night into the morning hours. (This will go on for several days!!!) Animals are howling. They are suffering a lot and some go deaf. Our cat always hides inside on 4th of July and on New Years. I bought my Indian son a present for Diwali: A hip Indian CD and a light string with ten programs.

Last night, when he drove us home from a dinner at another prof's house, he stopped on the way to buy us some **sweets** for Diwali. That was very sweet of him! "It is a pleasure working for you", he said to us. "It is a pleasure driving with you, son!" I replied. I couldn't refrain from teasing him: "Sir, it's pleasantly cool tonight." And we all had a good laugh. My husband said he has never heard Hemant talk like a waterfall, and he speaks really good English, too. "**Mothers and sons**, that's the secret!" I said.

Last night, we got another glimpse of the **close-knit** Indian family structure. Since the prof's wife is an <u>only</u> daughter it is her duty (and pleasure) to care for her parents. So they all live together with their two daughters in a four-story house. The grandparents are around eighty years old and fully participate in daily chores. Grandma and the prof's wife cooked a delicious dinner. I ate very little, but with great appetite. The main job of the daughters is to study hard. The prof had spent some time in the US, and six years in Finland where the family visited for vacations. The prof's wife is a chemistry teacher in higher education, and a highly spiritually aware person.

Many of the problems in India are deriving from **corruption** in the government, they said. The caste system is still in place after half a century of democracy. We witnessed one case of corruption with our own eyes coming back from Mt. Abu. The police had built a traffic barrier and the officer wanted to collect bribe money, but you should have seen our host professor telling him off. When you pay bribe money, they don't search the car for alcohol, which you are not supposed to take into Gujarat. The officer didn't even dare to search our SUV after the prof's thunderstorm. Besides, we didn't have any!

It seems we are lacking good leadership all around the world. **People are the same** all around the blue planet: They want to live in peace, economic well being, in a clean environment, and they want the best for their kids in the future. If we all want the same in principle, the wall of corruption, economic injustice, and pollution should crumble down like the Berlin wall in 1989. Sometimes I think: Which is worse: The pollution in Bombay or the pollution on the Internet? I think the physical pollution is the visible pollution of the mental and emotional pollution around the world. Each and every one of us is responsible for clean thoughts and a clean environment. The main responsibility is on the so-called developed countries not to deplete the resources any further, waste energy carelessly, and dump their waste in "third"-world countries.

We all need to get involved in a major clean up in thoughts, speech and deeds. Then we can celebrate Diwali around the world: "The Festival of Lights", "**The Festival of an Enlightened Mankind!**"

Student activities

1. Describe the most important holiday in India. Compare it with local holidays.

2. Describe a close-knit Indian family structure. Describe the family structure in your culture.

3. Why does Hemant talk like a waterfall?

4. Have you encountered corruption in YOUR culture?

5. What do people yearn for around the world?

6. What do YOU think, which kind of pollution is worse?

7. Could Diwali become an International holiday?

7. November

Body language in different cultures…

Head shaking…Turkish NO…Traffic rules…Brilliant job…Tolerant coexistence…

Body language is very different in each culture and hard to interpret, sometimes. At the beginning, the **head shaking** in India threw me off as a NO or MAYBE, while in reality it is a confirmation, a YES. You have to have a very loose neck to do this motion. It is not a rotation as in the Western NO. It is a movement from one shoulder to the other with the head swinging loosely on the vertebrae.

In the **Turkish** culture a strict **NO** is done with raising the eyebrows. "Which part of NO don't they understand?" we thought when street vendors were still running after us, until we learned the eye movements from Shirkan. Since we are not used to that, it looked very funny when we expressed the NO with the eyebrows. But if you want to survive in another culture, you have to learn these things fast.

Nonverbal language, common conventions, and registration of will power take place in **traffic** all the time. In Germany and America traffic rules are fairly reliable, and everybody more or less follows the rules. In Greece and India they drive much more flexible and care less about the rules. If they drove in India like in Germany they would have severe traffic jams all the time. Considering the very different traffic members in India: 4 wheelers, 3 wheelers, 2 wheelers, cows, dogs, pigs, camels, oxen carts, sleeping people, street vendors, beggars etc., they do a brilliant job in taking care of each other.

On the phone you become the most aware of how much is conveyed through body language (60%), because you are deprived of it. Reading people and thought projection are big parts of communication. The guy in the other car knows exactly when Hemant has decided to cross the intersection. They use their audio signals all the time, because it is safer when you are warned by a horn. They also have excellent peripheral vision here, seeing out of the corner of their eyes. Simply taking care of each other and a **tolerant co-existence** is the secret to the relative peaceful Indian traffic (without road rage) in overcrowded cities.

Student activities

1. What is the meaning of "headshaking" in India?

2. Demonstrate a Turkish NO!

3. Discuss silent (unwritten) traffic rules (conventions) in your group. Record!

4. A huge part of communication is based on.........Give me examples when and how you communicate non-verbally.

5. What is the secret to the relatively peaceful Indian traffic?

8. November

The Present of Friendship

No strings are attached
To the present of friendship
Not wrapped in a box, or in paper;
Open to share the heart with a friend.
No monetary value involved:
It is priceless!
Trust can't be bought
And caring and love:
These gifts are eternal
They come from the source.

A present can be stored away.
Friendship is a living entity.
It must be nourished like a garden,
Cared for by the gardeners,
Watered and tilted with
Caring and truth.

Who else is to tell you the truth,
if not a dear friend, to spur on your growth?
It must be fertilized with love,
For love is the heart of source light.
Without love humans can't grow.
Without care they shrivel.
Without truth the ego grows,
But not the heart.
The heart of a friendship is:
Truth, caring and love!

Potawi

Student activities

1. What is the most important aspect/component in a friendship for YOU?

2. Write a friendship poem and share it with somebody!

10. November

From the coolest…

Last days…Homeopathy…Health care…Oath of Hippocrates…Patient oriented…Cricket Club…Synopsis…Writing authentically from…SHE…Contradictions…Who are we to judge…

These **last days** in India are racing by like Greyhounds on a race—track. This was the fastest weekend ever. Since my husband had a lot of vegetative heart problems, they (Budhi and his team) brought us to a famous **homeopath** on BARC. The medicine to lower his blood pressure worked almost immediately without side effects. Again, the doctor did a pulse diagnosis. He gave my husband medicine for a whole year to reprogram his body. He also convinced me that another DNC would be superfluous, if I'd apply the medicine for half a year. He is an M.D. with a specialization in homeopathy, and has given many international lectures and received many awards. Germany is also avant-garde in homeopathy[7], where the original herbal medicine is thinned to the 11th part, stimulating the body's self-healing capacities, oscillating between the physical and the ethereal body.

If you have a life-threatening condition, Western hospitals and surgery are life saving, but long-term stress related conditions could be healed best by herbal Ayurvedic or homeopathic medicine with fewer side effects and for one 100th of the regular cost. And the billion—dollar pharmaceutical industry is surely not interested in that.

Health care should not swallow more than 1 % of our monthly income, because the body is capable of staying 99% healthy, given a healthy life style, diet and exercise is observed. All the doctors I have encountered in India held up the oath of Hippocrates ethically: The patient always comes first and the money last! They are skilled in pulse diagnosis, tongue diagnosis, inquiring and listening to the patient; everything our olden-day family doctor did in the 50s, when medicine was still **patient-oriented** and not machine, lab and money centered.

Saturday night, we were invited by the Science Advisor of the Prime Minister to the Cricket Club, a prestigious establishment in South Bombay. Cricket is

---

7.   The Father of Homeopathy is Dr. Samuel Hahnemann!

related to baseball. The British left it behind and the Indians love it. It took us one and a half hours to crawl across town in that heavy traffic, and 45 minutes back, later at night. Wizard (as my husband calls him) was a wonderful host, and his wife across the table was my only female counterpart. It's a male-dominated society, as Divi said earlier. He and Budhi were invited, too. Many dignified high jet society members were dining in the club. You were not allowed to take photos in there, only outside. The dinner was excellent and the conversation stimulating. I can see why Wizard is filling that position fully and sovereignly: He is a funny, very accessible man. He has synoptic capabilities of seeing the bigger picture, and pulling specialists together to create the whole artwork from puzzle parts.

He stressed a very important insight for me, which I mentioned earlier in my literary travel report: Subjective experiences in another culture don't ever reflect an objective, or whole picture of the country. So, I warn my readers again: **My** specific experiences in a specific culture at a specific time do not reflect the whole truth; it is my perspective, my truth of how I experience the people and the country through the lenses of my culturally preconditioned glasses. However, me **writing authentically from my heart**, takes you with me on a journey where I can offer one perspective of my truth to you, and take you on an adventure through my inner landscapes (see title!) of being shocked, shaped and enlightened by different cultural experiences.

"India is surely a **SHE!**" I said one night in a trance state, traveling home in the rocking car. She is full of contradictions: Rich and poor, high tech and no tech, finest and lowest, culturally refined and close to the dirt, beauty and garbage, luxury cars and oxen carts, villas and huts, high education and no education, atomic energy and simple wood fires, cell phones and old fashioned telephones, sophisticated machines and manual laborers, kings and beggars…Her majesty is the full expression of our earthly, dualistic experience, where everything exists in contrast.

If we measure a life experience by the unit of happiness and contentment, then many of these simple Indian people, who live a basic life, would fall into this category. And **who are we to judge** if a life is rich or poor? India, her Majesty, has left tiger prints in my heart, and I am barely beginning to comprehend the richness and diversity of this country.

12. November

From the coolest...Early morning hours...

TATA Institute...NO Secrecy...Thinking outside the box...Cobra King...Down Town Bombay...Scientists...

This is our third to last day in India. Yesterday, we drove all across Bombay, over two hours from BARC to the South visiting the TATA Institute. Riding across town is a major stress on our health in this pollution and heat. I have no desire to ride for more than half an hour in the car, anymore. The TATA Institute, right by the seaside with beautiful gardens around it, was also founded by Homi Bhabha and sponsored by the industrial magnate Tata. This setting is another example how art, nature and beauty are combined with science. In the spirit of Bhabha there shall be **NO secrecy** in science. Everything should be accessible and shared among scientists around the world. I photographed his creed, right beside his picture, and I wonder if certain institutes are still operating under his will.

I stayed for my husband's talk in the small lecture hall, which was cooled down like an icebox; the same waste of energy as in the US! He sure can capture an audience with his wit, well-prepared transparencies, audience-involved style, temperamental, voluminous voice, comparisons of the international scene, good advice for young scientists, his straight-forwardness, and modesty and honesty about problems arising in research. **Thinking outside the box**, being creative and cooperating with neighboring sciences like biology and chemistry were some of his recurring themes. He does not get to read my raw script, so he has no idea about this paragraph, yet! Not for a long while, at least!

After the lecture **Cobra King**[8], with whom I talked a lot over lunch, also about Indian music, brought me a CD where he explained the music and instruments, written out on an accompanying letter. I wished we could go to a live-concert with him, but time is almost up. Talking about synchronicity: The evening before we left Greece, I had watched a two-hour special about Indian music on National Geographic. Indian music is much more polyphonic than European classical music, because they have quarter—tones.

We left the TATA Institute in the late afternoon, and Budhi took us sightseeing in **downtown Bombay**: To the Tajh Mahal, right by the seaside, and the Gate of India, a monument of George V and Queen Mary (1911). This was a rel-

---

8.   English version of his Indian nam

atively clean area of Bombay with no offensive smell from the seaside although lots of trash was swimming on the water. Later we took a walk through the Hanging Gardens, a beautiful recreational area in midst of government housing. The Science advisor (Wizard) lives near by. Crawling though the heavy rush hour, we arrived home just in time for dinner. Over lunch in the TATA Institute I said I would devote one-whole chapter to writing about scientists as I experience them:

Scientists...

have minds, which want to explore and find out about the elementary nature of things, material things. They are **truth-seekers** in our three-dimensional world. Their playground is the laboratory=lab. When they show and explain their **playground** to each other, it gives them a tremendous amount of joy.

Sometimes, they are very **cooperative** in sharing ideas and equipment, and other times they are very **competitive**, shortly before a publication. It is very important to note who has done what for the first time, because s/he who succeeds first, is the grandfather of all...such and such, and quoted over and over again in literature. Besides really **good papers**, which document thorough research, there are a lot of **junk papers** out there. (Did you know that around 50 % of published papers are never read?) This happens when they jump on the bandwagon of a hip topic and publish too fast. Sometimes, they even need to renounce their findings if the experiment is not reproducible.

But in general, they are truth finding, honest people, who do careful measurements and theories, which can be reproduced and examined by fellow scientists. It also can happen that a scientist is ridiculed by other scientists, if he has found something unusual, which they have no explanation for. And when this scientist later substantiates his/her findings, then the mocking scientists sort of need to repent. It also can occur that somebody claims authorship or patent first, while in reality another scientist's paper has been delayed through **politics**. Then they fight it out in the science court in Geneva.

They have their **own language** and get very irritated when another non-exact science uses the same expression, but with a different connotation. Many scientists are **divas** and not the easiest characters to live with. I come around. I talk to other women. Many scientists love **music** and **art**, **cooking** and **history**, and have a wide range of topics to talk about. **Who says** women talk more? I don't think so! Just watch a political show on TV and measure the talking time of women versus men.

Many scientists are very **spiritual** people, but they will hardly ever leave the three-dimensional playground in the presence of other scientists. But since I get to talk to many of them around the world individually, after a long day in the lab, I know about their deeper yearnings.

There are very few **women in science** and they need to work double as hard as men to get there. I have talked to them! My science VIP is a "feminist" you could say. He works often and very well with women, especially women who contradict him, strong women; that's why I am married to him! (Banter!) "We'll not get away easily!" was my husband's comment yesterday after my announcement that I would devote a whole chapter to scientists.

Student activities

1. How is the pollution in your area and what do people do to keep it to a minimum, or to improve their air quality?

2. Does the TATA institute remind you of other places near your hometown or in the author's book?

3. What is Homi Bhabha's creed? Do you think that that is a good policy?

4. Discuss the waste of energy in YOUR house/neighborhood.

5. Which three things are important for innovative research?

6. What does the author mean by synchronicity?

7. Research which role George V and Queen May (1911) played in Indian history. (If that should be your chosen research project…)

8. How long does it take you to get from one end to the town to the other? How is traffic? How could it be improved?

14. November

From the coolest...Last morning...

Last talk...Privileged Island...Good-bye dinner at Grand Central...Birds of Passage...The Ambassador...Heart connections...

Fresh air is streaming through the open windows. I only have the fan running so that I can listen once more to the jungle waking up. My warrior is sound asleep, now, after all his talks are over. Yesterday, he gave his last one in the small lecture hall behind the hills. They gave me a special permit, too, yesterday to get a glimpse into the secret area. After a 20-minute security procedure I put on my badge with the photo ID, and was taken to my husband's office.

Thirty minutes later he gave his **last talk** in India, a moving farewell. After he folded his hands for Namasté it was quiet like in church. Wizard had come back from Delhi, Divi attended, as well as many friends who had taken care of us during our six-week stay, some other brilliant scientists from the field, and of course Budhi, the organizer and host.

Over lunch Divi showed me the area from the roof of the banquet dining hall: Two reactors, an extra huge water tank to cool the reactors down—just in case—the AD building, and the research tracts. All the buildings were imbedded in sculptured gardens in a huge area right by the sea, a **privileged island** of civilization. Only the heavy security wouldn't be in the spirit of Homi Bhabha (+ 1969), but times have changed.

Last night, we invited about twelve guests to the Grand Central for our **Good-bye dinner**. I was extremely delighted to see the Ambassador again, who had taken some time in between an all-day principle meeting and a formal dinner with his princes at night, to come with his wife for a drink to say Goodbye. The day before, he had sent his signed book **"Birds of Passage"**, a hilarious novel with insightful, sharp observations, mocking Indian bureaucracy. Wizard described it as "Indians laughing at themselves". My husband and I take turns reading it while bursting out in uncontrollable laughter at times. Women do not get away easily in his first novel, so he is planning on writing a second one depicting strong women with equal rights and standing. It's such a privilege knowing **the ambassador of education** and the author of "Birds of Passage". While reading the novel, I get an insight into his sensitivity, creativity, humor, wit, and value system etc. Although it is fiction, the author will always shine through his opus.

Divi, to my right at the dinner table, kept me entertained with his historical and hysterical tales about India. He is a walking history book and knows at least six languages. He owes it all to the Classical British education, he said. History comes alive for me in his sparkling eyes, at night. I was also glad to see his wife, who had taken a retreat from society because of her brother's death. She is busy packing for Delhi, because Divi retires from BARC in six days to join Wizard's team. Divi's wife presented me with a very stylish leather purse.

While driving home in Divi's car so that there would be more room for the people in Budhi's SUV, I already missed my "Little Brother". So I called him from the guesthouse and thanked him for organizing this last day so delightfully. People make your stay memorable, not buildings or monuments. It is through people who **connect with my heart** that I learn most about other cultures. Good Bye, India, Your Majesty! I am a Bird of Passage taking the love of the people with me in my heart.

Student activities

1. Tell me about an incident where you got a glance into a secret area.

2. Does the secret BARC facility remind you of other facilities in YOUR area or in the author's book?

3. What is Homi Bhabha's opinion on secrecy in science and who is HE? Use your computer or library for extensive research, if you choose him for your research project.

4. What information have you collected about the Ambassador in your "persona gram"?

5. Discuss the author's statement "Although it is fiction, the author will always shine through his opus" in a small group. Write out your findings and give examples in literature or current readings.

6. How do YOU learn most about other cultures?

End of part three: India

PART IV
Alzheimer's, Italy

From my bed…Early morning hours…

Father house…Multicultural education…

The Indian rhythm is still in my system, so I wake up very early. We are now in Germany, Flörsheim, 20 km away from Frankfurt airport in my husband's **father house**, (Vaterhaus in German), not mother house, so let's call it parents' house in the 21.Century. The central heating is on; the outside temperature is about 5 Celsius, and I am sitting in my bed on top of a sagging mattress with a fluffy down cover. On Monday we'll buy new orthopedic mattresses for our aching backs.

During my early morning meditation I got the inspiration that I should use my travel report for something educational. The script with the short chapters could be utilized for **multicultural education** if the author added student activity tasks at the end of each chapter. So, I will practice that now in a few chapters where I left enough space at the end, and I'll tell you later if I find it to be beneficial or not.

Yes, it works fine and the pedagogue in me has so much fun with this! I can visualize teaching a lively, very effective multicultural course with my literary travel script. Let's do it! Just do it™_!!! (I can't find that Nike check mark anywhere)

Student activities:

1. What do the expressions father house/motherhouse tell you about a culture?

2. Make a weather chart! Climate in November in India versus Germany.

3. What was the author's inspiration?

4. How does the author achieve the didactical aspect of her travel script? Look up words first and then answer!

5. What does the author mean by "Just do it!"
    What was the author's original motivation for this literary travel report?

When did she add another aspect and why?
Go back to the India report and check out more student activities!

18. November

Early morning hours...

Alzheimer's...Refuse any outside help...What to do?...

Alzheimer's is a creeping disease. It never will get better, it will only get worse. It has been going downhill with my father-in-law over the last six weeks: He doesn't bathe anymore, doesn't shave, soils his bed slightly, and has some coordination problems while feeding himself. He watches less TV, sleeps till noon and dozes off many times during the second half of the day. I hear him get up less during the night, which is beneficial, because he'll drink less wine, this way. One liter has been his night "ratio" since the illness started; he never was an alcoholic, before.

Alzheimer's is a tricky disease. Step by step certain parts of the brain are rendered immobile through plaque deposits around it. Since Mother has been the only caretaker—she **refuses all outside help** or presence of another person in the house—we wanted to send her to "Kur" (medicated spa) for recuperation, but the most she agreed to, was getting rest in the hospital for two weeks. She is getting weaker, now, has no appetite, except when we are around.

What to do? We both have about six to eight years until retirement. Starting twice in two cultures puts you behind and the service years don't amount to a reasonable salary unless you put in 20 years, at least. What are the options? There are Polish caretakers who would live in the house, but the parents don't want this. We had to rehire the cleaning lady for her once-a-week assignment, because Oma (my mother-in-law, actually: Oma= Granny) wanted her services only every fortnight, and that's not enough to keep the house in order.

Meals on Wheels don't suit them either. Another option is eating hospital meals in a nice cafeteria setting only 100 meters away from here, but Opa (my father-in-law, actually Opa=Grandpa) doesn't shave and Oma is ashamed to go there with a "gorilla". You can't do anything against their will either, nor do we want to force or talk them into anything. Unless they are in a stage of surrender and express what they need, one cannot help, except during summer, spring and Xmas break, and during emergencies.

19. November

From my down bed...on an orthopedic mattress...

Outer environment...Inner landscapes...

I am a lousy traveler during transitional times. Why? For many reasons: I am not in charge of my **outer environment**. One can't restructure somebody else's home to make the energy flow according to Feng Shui.[1] I live partly out of my suitcase and have to adjust to different foods again. My intestines are revolting. It is pitch dark at 5 p.m. in Germany in the winter, and the month of November was always difficult for me with its damp, overcast weather leading to depression for many people. There is too much negative energy in this house coming from the pain of three generations. My house in Colorado gives me the energetic framework to support my happiness and my longing for esthetics. I would not leave my home for a whole year again, except in a small motor home, furbished to my needs to explore America. But now that I am writing it in retrospect, there is also that adventurous driving force in me, so I am not sure about the "never".

However, I am in charge of my inner environment, responsible for my **inner landscapes**. I should be nicer to my hubby, but I am crabby at times. A huge part of my satisfaction comes from work, from an energetic work out of solid achievements and satisfactory accomplishments. I can't work on my computerized script, right now, but tomorrow, I will take over the household, and we'll take care of Opa while Oma is being checked over in the hospital and is getting some rest.

---

1.   The art of placing objects for the maximum flow of energy

20. November

From the kitchen table...

Broken record...Clean per definition...The sandwich generation...No artificial life support...

It goes **every five minutes**:
"Where is Mother?" Me: "In the hospital."
"In which hospital?">In Rüsselsheim.
"Why? What is she doing there?">She is being checked over and treated. She is getting weaker. She is exhausted.
"I must go there to visit her.">Yes, we'll do that, the day after tomorrow.
"How do I get there?"> We'll drive you in the car.
Tears, crying, a one-minute break, and then it starts again. It's like a little boy who has lost his mother. I was mainly cleaning, today, besides answering back patiently: Changing all the beds, theirs and ours, running two washing machines and two dryers; vacuuming dust balls in the bedroom from who knows how many months? The cleaning lady hasn't gotten to it, since Opa is always sleeping around 10 a.m. We'll have the bedroom cleaned thoroughly, next week, as long as Oma is out of the house. (A good opportunity!) They think it's **clean**, but it's not. We cleaned out the whole fridge and found moldy stuff in there. I also cleaned the drawer with silverware and washed everything out. Theoretically, they would need Assisted Living, but they say they can manage fine. I would like to maintain my independence as long as possible, too. The standard of cleanliness is defined differently by everybody. Even different nations have different **standards of cleanliness**. People usually don't die from dirt, but many die from the sterility of homes and hospitals and careless treatment.

The **Sandwich Generation**: Sandwiched between job and family responsibilities and caring for the elderly and all that being over 10.000 miles away. There is no planning out of anything, because they don't have a plan. All the decisions will be reactive. They used to live in this house for generations. Since the 1500s they live in this village, now town of ca 25.000 inhabitants. This was the first time that the "young" generation went overseas. Nowadays—parents need a plan: They need to plan out their (g)olden days as long as their minds function solidly. I don't want unnecessary life support, ever! No artificial breathing and feeding tubes! Why is a cowboy giving his companion horse a bullet to end his suffering?

Why do we bring our pet to the vet to put it to sleep when it has no quality life anymore? Why don't humans have more say over their own lives? From a spiritual standpoint I know that every soul needs to mature to a certain degree, and maybe those last years of seemingly senseless suffering are necessary to achieve just that.

From the kitchen table...

Tricked...Marriage per definition...

I exchanged the old wax-kitchen-table-cloth, which had holes from cigarette burns for a new seasonal Advents cloth with golden stars, white candles and fur branches; an esthetic backdrop for my diary. He misses her badly, breaks out in tears when he hears her voice. Opa is happy and funny at times when he forgets about Oma being in the hospital. We drove him to the barber, today, for a hair wash, cut and shave while we went grocery shopping.

So far, he has been pretty cooperative, has tried to help out, at least symbolically. Last night, he walked down the stairs twice (good exercise!) to ask us where Oma was. Dieter got out of bed again to sit in the upstairs living room till Opa fell asleep. Fortunately, he slept through the whole night, because he thought Oma was sleeping right beside him. I plugged in a nightlight by his bed, and in the half dark he thought the double folded bed was Oma. Tonight, I will put a big teddy bear on the cushion. Hopefully, we all can sleep through the night again! He doesn't complete his crossword puzzles anymore, but he is still doing one of his favorite leisure activities. He used to crack every puzzle.

Oma has just been in the hospital for one day, and she already wants to come home again. Go figure, old people: At home they behave like a dog and a cat, and when they are apart they cry for each other. Another definition of marriage?

22. November

From my favorite window seat in the downstairs kitchen...

Dictatorial...Stuff...Saturation...Maturation...

Opa wandered around half of the night upstairs. He did not come downstairs to wake us up, but I listened into the sounds many times, and nothing sounded unusual. He has kept his bed clean so far; knock on wood! He is looking forward to seeing Oma this afternoon in the hospital. So he has an incentive for shaving. Oma sounds very impatient on the phone, almost **dictatorial**, since they have not progressed with further examinations over the weekend.

The house is so overloaded with material things that in every cupboard I open, **stuff** is stuffed to the max and frequently falls on my head like from a deranged airplane compartment.

Germany is in an economic freeze, they say on the news, because the growth rate is only 0.something percent. Maybe people have reached a state of **saturation**. Maybe we need to get to a stage of **maturation** and grow in a different direction, not materially, but spiritually. I have enough stuff, too, at home, more than enough stuff. Who says an economy has to grow, and what is that growth worth when our salaries don't grow at an equal rate? How about maintaining a reasonable living standard, and putting our energy into educating and caring for the children instead of working for more material goods, and getting sick in a competitive, stressful work environment? Half of all Americans suffer from sleep disorders. I am sleepy, now; woke up at 4 a.m. hearing Opa rumble. I'll take a nap after lunch while Dieter takes over babysitting Opa.

22. November, same day evening

From the corner bench…upstairs…

The game of codependency…Challenge to death…Back-up plan, a MUST!…

Kitchen benches are typical for German furniture. They are very cozy, especially in winter times, when the whole family chats around the kitchen table. Yes, we've been at the hospital visiting Oma. They greeted each other as if they had been apart for half a year. A moving sight indeed, if you don't know the background. They have played the **game of codependency** for over 60 years, now.

Now that Opa is totally dependent on Oma, she doesn't like the game anymore, but they still know how to push each other's buttons, because a half a century old practice doesn't die. Opa doesn't play those games with us, because we don't fall for his manipulations. He can maintain intelligent conversations in the moment (well, it depends on the time of the day), but two minutes later he does not recall any content. Yet it is important to challenge his memory and to train his muscles with little chores. With us around he is more alert and self-reliable.

If he were <u>my</u> husband I would **challenge him to death** while at the same time give him all the necessary support, but close relatives wear out since they are emotionally involved. Family members are the worst caretakers of Alzheimer's patient, they say in the medical profession. I wonder how Nancy is managing with Ronald Reagan. Though chore! The social worker made it very clear to Opa and Oma that there must be **a back-up plan**; that they must apply for Pflegestufe 1 (health care step 1), so that mobile services will come to their home when needed. We'll see to it that it's done, even if Oma says otherwise.

23. November

From the upstairs-kitchen table with the Xmas cloth...

Blasting...BMW...Island of retreat...Complex linguistic transaction...Afraid of the dark...

The TV is **blasting** in the living room around the corner. Opa is hard of hearing. Since his retirement around 60, he refused to wear a hearing aid. Oma's voice is hoarse on some days. He telephoned Oma five times, but has no recollection of this: "Why doesn't she call? Are 20 cents already too much?" (These were the prices in 1950!) The phone in the hospital by her bed is card operated: € 1, 30 rent per day, and € 1, 30 long distance calls, although the town of Rüsselsheim is just across the river Main.

Friends took me to the Northwest shopping center for a few hours in a **BMW sports car**. Racing on the Autobahn is fun, but the suspension is too hard in a sports car for my back. The NW shopping center in Frankfurt is huge, with many specialty shops, covered with mighty glass vaults, very stylish, very clean, and very esthetic. I was looking for a portable CD player to listen to all my CDs I had bought or gotten from friends in different cultures. But I didn't buy one, yet. I want to look around some more. I don't want to spend more than € 50. I have a fancy CD player at home. All I need is an **island of retreat**: My music with headphones on my ears. What I actually bought was a new watch for Opa, since he constantly looked at his wrist in the hospital and his old one is kaputt (defect). It belongs to his complete dress-up when he goes out, and somehow he misses it.

Thank God that I date back 35 years in his memory, so I am stored in his upstairs computer. Our daughters-in-law and his great-grandchildren are non-existent in his brain. Everything that has happened in the last decade is not stored in his memory. But he is still receptive to humor, which is a pretty **complex linguistic transaction**, because you need to compare and contrast the superficial meaning with some underlying meaning. Sometimes, I would like to look into his brain with a computer encephalogram to see what exactly is going on and which areas are blocked. It is 8 p.m. He went to bed now but it will take him two hours till he settles in. Every 20 minutes he'll go to the bathroom and glance into the living room like a kid procrastinating his bed time or being afraid of the dark. With many Alzheimer's patients day and night are reversed.

24. November

From the upstairs kitchen table…

Misses her…His dose…Hizzifits…Free will?…Oh, what a night…

He misses everything about her: Her voice, her presence, her breathing, her scolding, and her cooking. Yesterday, I fixed cauliflower with spaghetti Bolognese. Of course, the cauliflower tasted and looked differently than Oma's. It was fixed with egg yolk and Boursin, while my husband wanted his Indian style with curry and hot spices. So Opa said: "Oh, that potato salad looks good." "That's cauliflower, Opa!" Then he starts eating: "Why is that potato salad warm?" "…because cauliflower is supposed to be eaten warm." It's pretty funny if it weren't sad at the same time.

Oma gets bored in the hospital. So far, they haven't found anything alarming, but the check-over will continue on Monday. Tonight, Opa came into the TV room and said: "Hey, can you tell me…I am married, right? Then where is my wife?" I cooked him lots of green tea with lemon, tonight, so he wasn't "thirsting" for wine and stayed pretty alert. He'll probably have his **dose** later, at midnight. I can't take it away, because Oma won't follow through. If it were my husband, there wouldn't be a drop of alcohol in the house under these circumstances. Every time Opa consumes alcohol, I can clearly see a stronger disorientation and weaker coordination. But it's that old power game: Oma can't take his bottle away, because the kid (Opa) will react with a hizzifit.

My daughter-in-law, who is concerned about her own mother also, although for different reasons, raised a good question, tonight: How far can we go along with respecting the old folks' free will, and when is it time to simply step in? Well, we already stepped in two years ago, when my husband smashed all the cognac bottles in the sink. Somehow that must have stuck in Opa's mind, because from that time on, he was content with wine, "only".

11:30 p.m.

Oh, what a night! He has come downstairs already three times asking, "Where is mother?" Dieter went upstairs to plug in his nightlight and to tuck him in. I went upstairs just now to see if he would take a Baldrian (Valerian) pill. "No, it's alright", he said, "You must go to bed now, it's late, the wine will calm me down." I am afraid my green tea had just the opposite effect. Trial and error!

25. November

From the upstairs kitchen bench with the nice Advents cloth...

Accidents...A chore...CD...Slick and sly...

Oh, what a night! The result of the green tea with lemon was: A restless Grandpa, three downstairs walks on his part, three upstairs walks on our part, soiled underpants, a smeared flannel sheet, and an interesting, artistically looking bathroom floor.

In spite of all these **accidents** due to my missionary efforts, Opa was so considerate as to wash out his underpants by himself. Maybe he will get more and more restless as the days progress without Oma, and it had nothing to do with the green tea. In any case, I will keep everything normal, tonight, and if it gets any worse, we'll consult our house doctor for a light sedative around suppertime. He is cute in his own ways, but it is a **chore**, I tell you! When we arrived in Flörsheim he slept half of the day. Now he is out and about all day. Fortunately, he doesn't run away, yet as other Alzheimer's patients frequently do. We keep everything open during the daytime, so that he doesn't feel restricted. He frequently walks around in the yard "tanking fresh air" he says. During the day he has clear moments, but at night his memory deteriorates completely and the same part of the CD (**C**omprehensive **D**ementia=my invention!) runs over and over again. At the same time he is also slick and sly. Dieter had to put Oma's phone number away, because he was constantly trying to call. It was rather amusing how he tried to talk me into giving him the phone number. He even appeared with a big pad and asked me to dictate it. "Tomorrow!" I said; then he finally gave up.

26. November

From the upstairs corner bench...

Aggression...A lover?...Sedative...Psycho terror...

As the time progresses a good portion of **aggressiveness** comes in. This morning, after one-liter of wine at night, Opa threw a hizzifit about Oma not calling him from the hospital. Then he directed all the aggression towards his son (Dieter) "This bone (Knochen) has put the telephone number away." We had to, last night after he bothered Oma seven times on the phone. This morning, he was trembling with fury, but since we were not impressed—I was concerned though about his breathing—he calmed down after half an hour. Their house doctor stopped by later upon our request to prescribe some sedative drops (Atosil), and to talk with us about supportive solutions for Oma.

Tonight, he got furious with his wife, since Oma told him off on the phone. "Where does she work? In Rüsselsheim?"> No, she's in the hospital. "Why does she have a room there? There is something wrong! She has **a guy in her room**." "Opa", I said, "You have been married to her for over 60 years, and I have known her for 35 years. This is ridiculous!"

Now I will take the phone # away. He has called her four times within one hour and 15 minutes. He has scouted for the phone number, but he didn't dare pressure us, since we had a visitor. We applied 25 drops at 7: 30 p.m. as the doctor had prescribed. He dozed off twice at the kitchen table, and finally went to bed at 9:30 p.m. Now it is ten to ten, and I hear him rumbling again. My husband is sound asleep. He is exhausted. The doctor said we should not wean him off the bottle, since he could run amok. We'll see if the **sedative** has any effect tonight. He is a restless soul. He needs some sleep and we, too.

With Oma they haven't found anything concrete, yet. Tomorrow, she'll have a colonoscopy. The doctors think it is mainly the "Vegetative Nerve system" (psychosomatic), because of exhaustion. She is more receptive to finding solutions, now, like applying for Pflegestufe and assigning herself and her son as a legal guardian for Opa. But she'll leave the steps of action to my husband "to save face" as the doctor disguised it in words. It is just too much for her. Opa is executing **psycho terror** over her, and she is not able to distance herself emotionally. As I said earlier: Close relatives are the worst caretakers of Alzheimer's, because of the emotional involvement.

27. November

From the corner bench…

Lost functions…What a surprise…How do men get away?…Life supporting decisions…Broken record…

Opa was shaving just now, but then, all of a sudden, he didn't know how to unplug the sink. That's Alzheimer's, alright! Certain **functions** get **lost,** just like that, and it may vary from day to day. The night was fairly quiet, because of the drops, but **what a surprise** in the morning! I ate a solid breakfast first, before I started cleaning up the mess. Subconsciously, the little boy who cries for his mother all the time, had soiled his bed badly, and he was all in tears about it. He used to be a very handsome looking man—he still is when he is shaven and dressed up—who always kept himself very clean. So first I equipped myself with rubber gloves and Sakrotan (The German Lysol) and a bucket to wash the bathroom floor and clean the toilet. Then I started one load of laundry, set on 95°, boiling hot, with pre-wash and Sil (bleach). Opa did not protest, this time, when I put him in an herbal bath. He managed by himself, mainly. I just put out fresh laundry for him and put fresh linens on his bed.

How do men always get away with avoiding the messy stuff? Of course, they have more important things to do, like work and deciding the big politics of the day. Mine is excused, today, but only for today! He has to regulate all the legal matters in Hochheim, and I take off in the afternoon for Kaffeeklatsch[2] with the Colorado Club[3], only the women of course; the men have to work and make the **life supporting decisions** of the day.

Now everything is clean and in order, again: The laundry is flying in the wind and sunshine (wow, it really does shine today!); Opa is sitting in his armchair, shaven, bathed and freshly dressed, watching TV; lunch is ready to be served. The lady of the house took a shower, too. What a delight one can get from cleanliness and order! Thank God I have my writing, reading, and music. A Woman needs to stay content to mend the broken CD patiently (remember: **C**omprehensive **D**ementia)!

---

2.   Exchanging the latest news over coffee break. Klatschen: Talking behind one's back
3.   Group of 10 couples for whom we plan the USA trips every 3 years or so.

At night

From my fluffy down bed…

Learning process…This bone…Can't reason…Flipped out…Police search…In the center of the storm…Robbers…Locked in for 24 hours…Steeling money and food…Dementia>distance…

I never knew that there would be so much to report about his intermediate phase, but it's really an interesting **learning process**. First of all, I can understand Oma much better now, and secondly I have learned how to deal with an Alzheimer's patient, not effectively, yet, but I am learning.

When I came back from the Kaffeeklatsch, we changed shifts. My husband was being picked up by a friend to workout in a nearby health club, so there was no time for a briefing. When I came upstairs, I found Opa very aggravated. "**This bone** (Knochen), locks me in (everything was open!), and hides the phone number. It's worse than in the military!" He kept on rumbling and rumbling. You **can't reason** with Alzheimer's, this I learned today. You need calm stereotypical short answers. He said he wanted to say Good night to Mother (You recognize the relationship of a husband to his wife already by the address!), so I dialed for him. When he aggravated Oma, I **flipped out**. "If you don't calm down, I'll call the doctor." I shouted. "Then I'll go to a hotel." he screamed back. "OK", I forced myself into a calm voice. "Here are your shoes. I'll have the **police search** for you if you get lost, because I am not running after you!" Then I went about my household chores like preparing supper and ironing.

I never knew that ironing was such a great activity to calm down, to stay focused in the **center of a storm** and to meditate. When he went to the bathroom, I put 25 Atosil drops into his beer, but unfortunately Oma called again to tell him off, so the aggravation started anew. But this time I let the storm pass by and stayed centered, ironing the load from this morning. The drops take two hours to grip. One has passed and he is fairly reasonable, but has asked again to call. "It's too late now." I said, continuing to write in my 'book' as he calls it.

You wouldn't believe what tricks the German bureaucracy would play with old people, if they didn't have somebody to stand up for them: Today my husband went to Amtsgericht (Court of law) Hochheim to apply for legal guardianship of his father, with Oma and him in charge of decisions. "She is too old", they said, "And you are in America, so we need an official Vormund." What that means is that the state takes over and gets access to the bank accounts and estates **instead of old people being protected from robbers**. It happened to our friends in Boulder who have a mother in Frankfurt. So my husband threatened to go to the judge right away if the officer didn't comply with his orders. Then she caved in.

At the Kaffeeklatsch a friend said, the Sozialstation would also apply tricks of allowing the least amount of money per diem for the lowest step of Pflegestufe (home healthcare). In the presence of other people Opa will never show his true face. This team of examiners should be **locked in** with him **for 24 hours**; then they would get the picture. This morning, I found the telephone register in the fridge on top of the cold cut. All these slips could be dealt with easily, even the mess, if he were manageable and agreeable. The running-away part has yet to come, and being accused of **stealing money and food** from them. These are the usual topics you hear from dementia and Alzheimer's patients.

During my engagement time when I was a young woman, I helped Oma, over the weekend, clean up the mess in HIS (Opa's) mother's room. I see the same behavior, manipulation, and bully patterns. Not with ME! But I still get involved emotionally, while I should distance myself. The same sounds can be found in *dementia* as in *distance*, only in a different order. In order to deal effectively with *dementia* one needs to *distance* oneself emotionally!

From my favorite window seat in the downstairs kitchen…

Oh what a night!…Favorite appetizer…Pall Mall without filters…Structures…

Oh, what a night! I slept between 12 and 3:30 a.m. The rest was garbage: Opa came up twice to the TV room to ask where Oma was and five times downstairs. You think you hear a ghost roam through the house, stepping with heavy boots down the stairs. Then he calls for "Gabi" who is his daughter. She used to live downstairs, but is now living in Texas with her family. "I can't believe she's in the hospital. There is something wrong!" "Opa, try to get some sleep. Oma is coming home tomorrow." Tap, tap, tap upstairs, then tap, tap, tap downstairs and the broken record runs again. And in the morning your **favorite appetizer** is being served before breakfast: A soiled sheet, a smeared nightgown, a painted toilet, and a bathroom floor with tracks.

Oh Lordi, Lordi, Lordi, I hope he calms down now that Oma is home. And what did she search for right away: Her **Pall Mall without filters!** Dieter had thrown one packet away, and she knew exactly where it was stored. "He must buy a new one. No, I am not giving up smoking!" Some people can't be helped. They must live out their own program. She doesn't even have stained lungs. There is nothing wrong with her organically. It's all psychosomatic! We offered to take her to America whenever she needs to recover, three weeks to three months, while Opa will be in short term care, but there is no rational response. "Oh, I am going to die anyway. Don't go through all that trouble. Don't even cry at my funeral! I am not hungry. I am not going to eat that stuff!" (I had baked Leberkäs, potatoes and Kohlrabi-carrot veggie) "It's OK, Oma; then you'll be extra hungry for supper."

The truth is: Old people can't live our life-style and we can't live theirs. We can only set up the **structures**, so that help is available when they need it.

1. Dezember

From a Gasthof (B&B) in Brannenburg by Innsbruck...

Advent...B&B

It is the **first Advent**, today. Germans count down the four Sundays before Christmas by lightening the respective candles on an Advents wreath. (1, 2, 3, 4) After the fourth candle has lit the way for the Christ child (Christkind), he arrives on Christmas Eve, on the 24th, which is the major celebration day at night. Children open their presents and families have a traditional light supper, because the next day, on the 25th, there is a big meal, usually goose with all the trimmings. On the second day, the 26th, families traditionally visit relatives. Germans celebrate Xmas for three days.

I am in the Alps now, close to Innsbruck. My mother used to ski around here when she was working in the hospital. The German **B&Bs**[4] are fairly inexpensive (€ 60), compared to the American B&Bs, which are fancier. It is very clean and cozy here, with a modern bathroom, but no TV and phone, which I don't miss. After breakfast we'll take a hike with my husband's "Old Math Prof" and his wife, who live in Munich (München), and own two vacation apartments near our B&B.

---

4.   Bed and Breakfast

From the fluffy down bed at friends at Ulm...

Stud...2. Spring...Mud pie...Cycle of Alzheimer's...Cost of care...Spirit goes where?...

It was time to get away from the old folks to live our own lives again. Wow, Opa is quite a **stud!** I envied my husband, who was sound asleep the day Oma came home, because he didn't even hear the rumbling that was going on upstairs. I listened to my Indian CD with great joy, following Kobra King's descriptions, after I had formed my own opinion about the piece. Once in a while I took out my earphones to listen if Oma needed help upstairs. The idea of a **second spring** never crossed my mind, until Oma made a remark over breakfast the next morning.

During our strenuous hike with the math Prof and his wife I slipped on a muddy path making a **mud pie** on the right side of my body. I would have needed hiking boots for this, but I had only my Keds with me. I let the mud dry on my butt while focusing on the rather relevant topic of Alzheimer's. The Prof's wife had gone through the whole cycle of Alzheimer's with her mother:

"Losing muscle control and soiling the bed belongs to the profile of this illness. Alzheimer's patients are gripped by an elementary fear of losing control, losing a familiar person, or environment. In many patients there is a stage of endlessly moving around, an enormous force for motion. After that comes a stage of settling in, surrender and calmness, at a point when they lose total sense of reality. Even in a nursing home Alzheimer's patients experience the precious life of sharing joy, sadness, simple tasks, company and routine. The nurses there don't wonder about anything. They are endlessly patient. Close relatives are not suited for this in the long run, because nobody can give 24-hour care with interrupted sleep and emotional involvement." My friend suffered from sleep disorders for one year after her mother was admitted to a nursing home where she seemingly enjoyed living in for another five years.

The **cost of full-time** care is 3.000 € at that time in Germany, which amounts to 210.000 € over five years. The average Rente or Pension (Social security or pension) is around 1.500 €. Part of the health care cost is covered by health care step 3 (Pflegestufe 3) which leaves the patient and her/his guardian with 500 € times 60 months = 30. 000 €. Most middle class people have considerable savings and estates, so the financial aspect wouldn't be the issue, unless one prefers money to having a life. Not all of us are Mother Teresa, and at times I have seen warehousing of elders and inadequate care at home instead of professional care and lovingly letting go at a time when it would cause the least amount of pain for the patient.

I think I would rather die from a heart attack at an earlier age, because if we age to a hundred years old, we'd all get eventually Alzheimer's. Alzheimer's means a total surrender of one's personality and spirit. Energy doesn't get lost; it always transforms into something else. So **where did his spirit go**? Into his soul account, the combined accumulations of all his earthly lives and experiences? We'll all find out some day, sooner or later!

3. Dezember

From the fluffy down bed in Ulm…Early morning…

Happy Birthday, Max!…Donkey hill…Attitude problem…Ulmer Xmas market…Glow wine…German Adventskaffee…Catastrophes everywhere…US Island…Language joke…

I am writing from a cozy attic apartment in a spacious light/flooded house of friends in Ulm/Ost, Thalfingen, who have been spoiling us for two days with delicious breakfasts, dinners and Swabian wine.

It is my middle son's birthday, today, the one who studies medicine in Bethesda, Maryland, and raises a family of three (15, 3, ½) together with his wife, Laurie, who finished her degree through distance learning, while nursing babies and keeping his back free. **Happy Birthday, Max**! (Nick-name) Max wrote the second best medical entrance exam in the whole US. So the Air force released him so he could participate in a full-time medical study in one of the finest hospitals in the US, where all the royalty and presidents are treated. After his MD degree he has to devote another four years to the air force, where he had been a business manager and then a PA[5], practicing the medical profession, already.

Yesterday, we visited the University of Ulm, where my husband had substituted for the chair during the three summers of 92, 93, and 95. The Uni is located at the Eselsberg (**donkey hill!!!**) in a beautiful campus setting, overlooking Ulm. While driving on the Autobahn and speeding up to 180 km legally, as my husband was dozing off, I frequently confirmed to myself: Germany is really a beautiful country. The communities, towns and cities are embedded snuggly into the generously wide-open landscape and surroundings. Everything is very clean and the Autobahnraststätten (gas stations and restaurants directly by the Autobahn) deliver superb service.

"Germans are whiners", a friend said recently, "It's such a rich nation, yet they complain all the time about the recession." I agree: in contrast to Americans, Germans always see the glass half empty instead of half full. They have an **attitude problem**! I am totally amused when I see structures imported from America, and

---

5.   PA=Physician assistant

then they wonder why it doesn't work as well over here. It's very simple: Germans have their own characteristic way of working and reforming, and a more critical outlook on life. One cannot simply take the structures from another culture and expect the same results.

Yesterday afternoon we strolled over the **Xmas market** around the Ulmer Münster (Cathedral). The smell of roasted almonds, Bratwurst, **Glühwein (glow wine)** and the festively decorated booths of handcrafted items put the visitors in the mood for Xmas. We all had a glass of Glühwein[6]. My husband claimed that most of the alcohol had evaporated, but our driver was careful in pouring half of it out. I was glowing alright after that glass of Glühwein. It was pretty cold, yesterday, so the hot wine warmed us up.

After our Xmas market stroll we all went over to another professor's house—an old friend of ours, who always organizes our summer bike rides—for a typical **German Adventskaffee**. His wife had baked plum cake, a delicatessen in the middle of the winter, and Stollen, the traditional German Xmas bread. The first candle of the Advents wreath was lit of course, and nice festive classical music was playing in the background. Since we had missed the bike trip, this year, working in Dresden, the Prof showed us the photo album of their Elbe trip from last year.

"Everywhere we go there are **catastrophes**", my husband said. "In Dresden there was the flooding; In India the Pakistan conflict and NO monsoon in some areas; In Catania the Etna is spewing on Sicily; Near Santander (300 km away), there is this horrific oil spill." Our Ulmer host professor said: "I couldn't roam around for a whole year like you guys. Half a year at CSU[7] was just enough for me!" These old geezers smooth the way for the young cocks in getting international experience in science and research. But the fact is that Americans are far too homebound, and Germans are more enthusiastic about going overseas. I am coming back to my old sermon: The reason is the **US Island-attitude** in regard to learning foreign languages. They think English and maybe a little Spanish, that is sufficient. But if you want to experience the world, you must make an effort in learning other languages and cultures, even if your host country speaks English. A few words and sentences open whole doors into the hearts of "foreign" people.

There is a joke going around the world about America's attitude in regard to learning foreign languages:

---

6. Hot red wine with rum, sugar and spices
7. Colorado State University

What do you call a person who speaks three languages?   **Trilingual!**
What do you call a person who speaks two languages?   **Bilingual!**
What do you call a person who speaks one language?   **American!**

4. Dezember

From Villa del Bosco[8] in Catania...

Sucking energy...Spewing Etna...Black ashes...Light earthquake...Jugendstil...

When we arrived last night in Flörsheim to repack for Catania, Opa and Oma were **sucking** the life and **energy** out of each other. Within four days Opa looked totally run down, again. I was sitting quietly at the kitchen table, watching their psychodrama. They are both involved: Oma can't distance herself emotionally, and look at the whole situation as an illness. Opa makes impossible accusations, and she is responding to it as if he were in charge of his faculties. Nobody can imagine the drain unless they have actually lived with an Alzheimer patient. I didn't...before I had the opportunity.

Opa came downstairs at 4:30 a.m., again, to ask us where Oma was while she was sitting all along in the upstairs bathroom. We were up anyhow, so it didn't matter. I did not get any sleep last night, because obviously I can't distance myself very well, either. This can't go on for much longer. He is in that restless motion stage. The doctor has prescribed another sedative, since the Atosil had only worked for one night.

We left for Catania at 7 a.m. from the Frankfurt airport to Rome. The flight was pleasant with Alitalia. The Roma airport is generously designed with many modern shops. I considered buying a spiral notebook, since I had forgotten my pad in the pocket of my suitcase, but I dropped it like a hot potato when I saw the price: € 17.50. From Rome to Catania they put us in business class where you felt like a human being and not like a sardine. Fortunately, we could fly into Catania at around 11 a.m., since it wasn't raining ashes from the **spewing Etna**, but one could see the dark cloud coming out of the volcano's crater. Everything is dusted with black ashes and people either stay inside or run around in umbrellas when the residue falls down. They also had a **light earthquake**, last night, but the people here are not concerned.

When we went out for lunch in a near-by bakery (panificio) to eat a slice of pizza, I felt hard particles on my tongue from the ashes. The hotel is very pleasant. It must cost the university a fortune, judging from the prices of the hotel

---

8.   Bosco=wood, versus Don Giovanni Bosco, a Saint, known as Don Bosco.

menu. Our large room is furnished in Jugendstil=style[9] with TV, telephone and a luxury bathroom. With a two-and—a—half hour nap I caught up on my sleepless night, and don't feel so groggy anymore. At 7:30 p.m., our Italian host professor, whom I will call Verdi from now on, will pick us up for a visit to an authentic Italian restaurant. It is 6 p.m., and I shall splash around in that fine bathroom.

---

9.   Style around the turn of the century: playful, curved, and elegant…

5. Dezember

From Villa del Bosco…

St. Nikolaus…Theme pizza…Corso Italia…International breakfast…

Tonight, in Germany, it is **St. Nikolaus**. He was a bishop in Smyrna around 400 A.D. who looked after neglected kids. So tonight, children put out their boots and stockings, and expect them to be filled with sweets and little presents. Bad kids get a spanking from Knecht Ruprecht, Santa's helper. Well, that used to be in the olden days! When my boys were little, I used to run out the veranda door, around the house to the front door, made a hell of a noise, ringing the bell and knocking on the door. Then I ran back into the house through the veranda door, while they were standing in awe before their filled boots and trying to find Santa. I was standing right behind them admiring the gifts from "Santa". Now you know the secret, guys!!! Do you still believe in Santa? I DO, in the spirit of Santa, that's why I'm a teacher!

The Italian dinner, last night was excellent and the wine superb. After an anti pasta appetizer I ordered a **theme pizza**. The character was out of the novel 'I Viceré', by Giovanni Verga, a local author, and the restaurant was named 'I Viceré'. It tasted pretty close to my home baked pizza with hearty dough and fresh ingredients. The red wine had 14% alcohol, and was glowing in the glass like a ruby. A tourist would have never found that restaurant in a side street. Only Italians dined there. In Catania very few people speak English. After dinner we took a stroll down to **Corso Italia**, a major shopping street with all the high cost designer shops. In spite of my long nap I was tired again around 11:30 p.m., and had a deep night's sleep on the firm mattress in this cozy Jugendstil room.

The breakfast hall was cold, this morning, but gorgeous and light flooded, overlooking Catania far out to the sea. You find an **international breakfast** buffet in almost every good hotel, nowadays. So everybody can find something to his or her likings. I observed, however, that Italian men go for the sweet stuff in the morning, which dominated the Italian buffet, while I prefer something hearty, first. Now, we'll explore Catania by bus and on foot.

5. Dezember

From a little Cappuccino place by Villa del Bosco...

Poor US teacher...Hidden aspects...Six languages...Annoying cell phones...

I just purchased a local Italian spiral notebook for € 2.50. He wanted to sell me a € 10 spiral notebook, but I said: "I am a **poor US teacher!**" Then this good-looking Sicilian businessman said in half Italian, half English that US teachers are not <u>that</u> poor. He also wanted to know, how I could afford living in that expensive hotel over there. "The university pays for it", I said, "My husband is a scientist. He is giving a talk at the university. That's why we can afford to stay there."

I could learn Italian easily if I stayed here for a whole year. I figure out most of the written language from Latin and French, which I had in High school (German Gymnasium: 5th-13th) for six and three years respectively, and the latter for two semesters at CSU.

I stayed downtown for the whole day, while my husband had to ride back on bus 429 to Villa del Bosco to change into his suit for his talk at 3 p.m. Piazza Duomo (Dom=cathedral) was fenced off for reconstruction, so I strolled over to the market place with its delicious and sensual displays of fruit, veggies and fresh fish. I often wander the little side streets with their irregular cobblestones to discover the unusual **hidden aspects** of a city. Climbing up some back stairs, I landed in the judicial part of the university. Nearby was a speedy Internet café from where I sent some emails home. Right by the Internet café was a native Italian ristorante; by native I mean non-touristy! It was a family-run business, and the father spoke six languages. Well, I didn't check on which levels...There, I had Prosciutto with Ananas, light vino rosso and fresh bread for € 7.50. After my late lunch, around 3 p.m., I took a stroll down to the seaside. Catania is as hilly as San Francisco. The railroad station and the commercial harbor were right by the seaside. Since there was no sea promenade in this stretch I tried to return to Piazza Bellini. I got a little confused, since bus 429 was leaving at the Bellini statue, but there was another historical Piazza Bellini nearby where people had sent me. Next time, I will follow the city map on my own, because people would have sent me in the wrong direction twice, if my fair sense of direction had given in.

"Buonasera!" I just replied loudly to another customer entering the café with a sonorous voice. Don't you love those guys who dominate the whole café on their

cell phones? Very irritated I started a battle of voices the other day in an Ulmer restaurant, conducting my conversation with our friends in the same decibel as the phone guy. Finally he noticed and toned down. I better go take a shower now, since we might be invited, tonight. Buonasera! Good night!

Student activities:

1. Compare the headlines of part 1 and 2 with the headlines of part 3 and 4 in regard to the narrative. What has changed and why?
    Think of various newspapers!

2. Which language could you learn easily and why?

3. Tell me the Italian words for: Cathedral, wine, restaurant, red, good evening, pineapple, bakery, court, Italian ham, wood. Look up please and thank you!

4. Compare the prices of spiral notebooks in different countries.

5. Why can the author afford an expensive hotel?

6. Research the volcanic activities of Mt. Etna in the library or on the Internet. Make a diagram on a transparency and give your talk by heart.

7. How do YOU use your cell phone in a café or restaurant? Or other public places?

8. Research the entities Don Giovanni Bosco and Vincenzo Bellini.

9. Describe a typical Italian meal: Appetizer, soup, salad, main course, and dessert.

10. What are the benefits of Internet cafes? Where are they located in your area?

6. Dezember

From my bed in Villa del Bosco...

Expensive sleep...Parking chaos...Confession...Seismograph...Hard like a brick...Illness...Wellness...Elephant poem...

Wow, it is € 150 a night in this luxurious Villa. No, I wouldn't dream of **sleeping somewhere for € 150 per night**, but I do like luxury and style, even better when I can create it for one tenth of the cost. The busses drive round tours here, in one direction, not in both. So it takes me 45 minutes to get into town and 15 minutes back, given there is no car parked in a no-stop zone where the bus needs to turn. Today, I waited eight minutes on the bus for the driver to show up to move his car. It's like in Greece: Cars are **parked everywhere**, but Italians are more attentive and generous towards pedestrians.

I should have become a pastor. People frequently tell me their life stories and I hear their **confessions** at bus stations, subways, museums, wherever. Yes, I am on alert, at first, until I feel it is genuine. Maybe I look "available", because I have time. The math professor's wife thinks I am endlessly patient, emanating calmness and serenity. My outer disposition does not match my inner landscape. Internally I react like a seismograph in expectation of an upcoming earthquake. In India my heart was fine. In Germany it started to act up, again. I need to stay away from stressful situations, but then life is no challenge. I'll just ignore the pain and enjoy life to its fullest. Maybe there's one last test I shall take: a special blood test, which they developed three months ago. It shows the enzymes that are in the blood in case of a hidden attack. My back is a lot better after the work with the Greek physio. I have been living without massages for quite a while. It is all tension and stress, which make the muscles hard like a brick and press on the spine. My uterus lining needs to be checked over in Spain. But I'll stick to the homeopathic drops from India, unless there is something unusual. I <u>must</u> be getting older. I am talking about illnesses. I always thought I was invincible, health wise, when I was younger. Let's talk about wellness:

I am a well of joy and creativity.
Nothing can shake me off my elephant
'Cause I stand on four solid columns.
With the trunk of my nose
I can smell camels and donkeys[10]
From far away.
I don't step into shit easily.
I am a peaceful vegetarian (almost)
With a memory of an elephant
But only the relevant memories
Are glued to my brain
Burnt in my soul.
I guess me and the elephant
Are verwandt![11]

THE ELEPHANT POEM
BY potawi

---

10. Animals are attributed with certain human qualities, but they are a bit different in each culture. So pick what you choose…
11. Ger., related

7. Dezember

From my bed in Villa del Bosco...

Art attack...Trattoria...Antipasti...Light-weight Verdi and his aching Fiat...Lava flood in 1693...Modern preservation of history...Fainted...Image versus substance...

My Prof has decorated the two Delft[12]-ceramic-candle stands with two Mandarinen[13], crowned with stems and green leaves. One mandarine is reflected back to me in the crystal mirror in a golden frame. "What an **art attack!**" I said. That's quite an improvement from hanging washcloth through our Indian quarters, I thought. After I protested enough he took it off.

I am slowly warming up after a long hot shower. The fabulous Italian **Trattoria** (it. Taverna) where we had lunch with Verdi was nippy. They don't heat much over here. In the Trattoria the waiters put about ten different **antipasti** on the table, among those a basket with five different salamis and 5 kinds of meats. I always thought antipasta meant everything <u>but</u> pasta, but actually it means: before the meal (anti=before, pasta=meal). Since we have been invited by Professor Renato tonight (No, that wouldn't be ME!) for a major pesce dinner, I only had a lentil soup after our antipasti buffet; Verdi had pasta, Basta! And Dieter had nothing, since he had ploughed himself through 20 antipasti items.

Before the meal, Verdi had chauffeured us with his cute little Fiat towards Old Town. This poor little Auto was making aching noises when I boarded the car. I guess it's mainly used to **light weight Verdi**. (Don't you love those Germanic alliterations?) Finding a parking space close to the old Benedictine cloister was a task. A foreigner would never know that you need a special parking card where you rub off the date and time. The University of Catania has purchased that Benedictine estate which was flooded by lava in 1693, as was the whole town. The rebuilding of the second largest city of Sicily, now with over half a million inhabitants, began around 1700. Therefore all the older buildings are uniformly built in Baroque style. When I entered the inside yard, it felt very strange hearing Rockmusik coming out of the window of this Ba-Rock building (German: Barock, Engl. Baroque), which is now used by the students of the university.

---

12.   Famous Dutch porcelain
13.   Nectarines, clementines, around Xmas time in Germany

Over 100.000 students study in Catania. Another famous university town is Palermo.

It was a bit difficult to find the entrance to the catacombs, the well-preserved original structure of the Benedictine cloister with an underground Cistern, kitchen, laboratory and seismograph. The original structures are imbedded in modern architecture, heated and moisturized to preserve history. More and more historical findings are preserved this way nowadays. The Anne Frank house comes to my mind in Amsterdam, which was totally embedded in modern architecture when I visited a few years ago, also in Greece; the tomb of Phillip II was surrounded by protective underground structures. When we were in the first underground level, somebody fainted below us. After the one-hour guided tour I probably didn't look so good either, because Verdi offered me his arm to hold on to. Actually I did feel oxygen deprived. Verdi is a young Italian professor with a high level of sensitivity. On one hand I enjoyed his attention; on the other hand I didn't want to admit to any deficiencies. My youthful image is fainting away. After all "image" is not "substance"! Ripe grapes have substance before they shrivel and frost to provide the Winzer[14] (wine grower) with the best material for Eiswein, a very expensive dessert wine.

---

14.   Christ is often referred to as the Winzer in the Bible.

8. Dezember

From my bed in Villa del Bosco…early morning…

Renato…Nero d'Avola…Tomato meditation…Raining ashes…Big mistake…Antipasta/Pasta/Antepasta…Prickly pears…US Air force base…Tipsy Verdi…Mrs. Etna…

I have been awake since 4:30 a.m., while my husband has been sawing down trees in his sleep. So I stayed quiet and meditated. Professor Renato, the department chair, had ordered a superb Sicilian wine, last night in that exclusive little fish ristorante. It comes from the little sea town of Avola, and its name is **Nero d'Avola**, because of its almost black color. Renato said that the grapes take on that special taste of the sandy soil there. This was one of my topics of my meditation, this morning: Living organisms taking on the flavor of the local soil. In India the **tomatoes** tasted differently: They had less acidity, less liquid, were more meaty and redder. The same holds true for human beings taking on the flavor, energy, and vibrations of the local soil, water and sky. We are born into special grids to support our internal mission. I definitely feel more energy in some places and less energy in other places. Anyhow, back to the opulent dinner from last night:

When Verdi was picking us up, he brought us a box of sweets. That was very sweet of him. Stepping out of the Villa, I already felt hard particles on my nose and cheeks. "Oh, oh, it's **raining ashes**." When Verdi engaged the windshield wipers you could see a handful of black sand gliding down the glass. The Etna "sand" is very edgy under the microscope, said Verdi, while sea sand is well rounded by the erosion. Since we arrived at the ristorante in a side street off Corso Italia ten minutes early, we decided to take a stroll around the corner. Verdi offered his arm and a safe place under his huge umbrella. Going around the corner, I looked up to read the street sign. That was a **mistake**. One of these edgy, black particles flew into my eye and was grinding uncomfortably. So we went straight back into the restaurant. I went to the bathroom, and eventually it was flooded out by tears.

Meanwhile Renato had arrived, and was choosing the fresh fish to be prepared for our evening meal. I greeted him with a red eye and a sniffing nose. During the **antipasti** courses of frutti di mare and various fried fish dishes I forgot all about Etna's curse. The wine had high-alcohol content, but tasted light, fruity and earthy. After the antipasti courses they served seafood pasta with ricci[15] di mare and swordfish sauce. The seafood in pasta is finely grinded and almost invisible; so don't expect big chunks of fish on your plate. It is mainly to bathe the spaghetti in these various flavors. There is also black spaghetti, dyed in octopus juice. Following the pasta **course,** wonderful fresh fish, sautéed in seawater, tiny flavorful tomatoes, herbs and other spices was served separately. Fresh, crunchy bread was always available from the breadbasket. Breaking his own rules, Verdi was having a few sips of Nero d'Avola for "prosting" (saying cheers) to the host.

After the main course, I tried **prickly pears**, fruit from the cacti, while Renato was having a smooth cognac, and to my husband he recommended local lemon-herb liquor. The prickly pears tasted delicious, but I wouldn't recommend them to people with third teeth, because they have a lot of kernels. After my light dessert I had a smooth Italian espresso. The meal was well rounded, light and delicious. The dinner was leisurely, but the departure was hectic. For some reason, Renato who lived just around the corner, needed to head home fast. So there was barely time to thank him for the delightful invitation. Maybe he expected a call from his girlfriend, or he had digestion problems, or he doesn't like Good byes in general.

Over dinner I learned that there is a US Air force base of utmost strategic importance, here in Catania. Heading home in the little Fiat, we had a few good laughs about the evening. Since Verdi was tipsy[16]from the few drops of red wine, he couldn't stop laughing while I was squeezing myself backwards out of the Fiat. The vehicle squeaked a sigh of relief, when I de-boarded.

It's a beautiful morning. The sun is up, and we hope to be able to fly out of Catania at 4:30 p.m. But one never knows if Etna will agree. If he doesn't—or is it a SHE, spewing fire—they would bus us to Palermo, and from there aviate us to Roma. In any case, we plan to be "home" in Flörsheim around 10 p.m.

---

15. Black stingy urchin, looks like a black ball with spikes
16. Not really: He is a cool and careful driver!

Same day 5:30 p.m.

From Palermo airport...

In the center of the storm…What a mess at Palermo airport! Catania airport was closed, so they (Alitalia) bussed us to Palermo. The bus toilet was conveniently closed, again. Somebody should sue for physical and emotional torture. I am referring back to my poem on p. 31 *Travel as long*…part 2…*Travel as long as your bladder can hold three liters*…

9. Dezember

From Mythos Hotel in Milano…early morning…

Etna Odyssey: Catania…Bus to Palermo…Plane to Milano…NO plane to Frankfurt…Stuck…

From **Palermo** they (AirOne=Alitalia&Lufthansa) put us on a plane to Milano, and from there we were supposed to fly to Frankfurt at 8:15 p.m. The plane took off from Palermo with one-hour delay after waiting for a group of American kids. (Yeah, yeah, they are afraid of the American suing business!) Alitalia was incredibly helpful in assigning a personal airport attendant to us who raced us and another *lawyer* lady (here you have the *real* reason!) through security-check, and through endless hallways of the **Milano** airport to the gate to Frankfurt. When we arrived there with our tongues hanging out, eight minutes <u>before</u> departure, they told us that the airplane had **just left**. So we had a short night sleep after a late Pizza dinner. AirOne is paying for this ****hotel and the mess-up. They will pick us up from the hotel at 6:15 a.m. in order to catch the flight **to Frankfurt** at 7:45 a.m.

In the air

Flying with Alitalia from Milano (Mailand) to Frankfurt...

Dolomiti...Hannibal...Holding over Frankfurt...Geography from an eagle perspective...

It's a gorgeous sight: Underneath is a sea of fluffy clouds, but the rugged tips of the **Dolomiti**, where our counselor hiked, this summer, rise and shine in the morning sunlight. The Alps are a young mountain fold from the Tertiary, ca 5 million years old. They are not rounded, yet, like the Rockies, which have been shaped by ice, wind and weather over a long period of time. It's hard to imagine that **Hannibal** crossed the Alps with elephants around 120 B.C. There are not many convenient pass ways. The airplane took off from Milano with a fifty-minute delay[17], because of alleged difficulties at Frankfurt airport. So the whole odyssey from Catania to Flörsheim will take us 24 hours by the time we arrive "home". Under regular circumstances it should be a four-hour trip.

Italy has become quite expensive. It used to be a favorite vacation spot of the Germans in the 70s. Last night in the Pizzeria, I paid € 35 for a small pizza, herb pasta, a large beer, salad, a shrimp cocktail, and one dessert to share. The breakfast on Alitalia was ice-cold everything, except the coffee. Fortunately, we already had an early morning café in the four-star hotel with crunchy warm croissants, chocolate and apricot, and a strong milk coffee, because the airline crew was already out and about. The captain just announced that there is another 15 minute holding over at the **Frankfurt airport**, which is the busiest in Europe. Every two minutes planes fly over my parent-in-laws' house. They don't register it anymore, but when we arrive early in the morning from America and want to get some sleep, it is bothersome.

Circling over Frankfurt, I get to see the middle mountain area "Taunus" from an **eagle's perspective**. I can identify the river Main, which flows into the Rhein by Mainz. Now, we are flying over the "Spessart", another middle mountain region. Wow, the high rising bank buildings and TV towers of Frankfurt come into the picture of the airplane's bull eye. The runways of Frankfurt airport look like an artistic geometric design. The forests appear partly green and partly brown

---

17. When you don't need a delay, you always get it!

gray, damaged from acid rains and pollution. Now, we are exactly at Mainz where the river Main flows into the Rhein, the second longest river streaming into the North Sea and originating in Switzerland. I never knew a holding could be that entertaining. One can only identify geography from the air, if one has paid attention in class. We are getting ready for landing. I heard the landing gear roll out.

From the upstairs corner bench...

Nervous breakdown...End of the ropes...Plot...Torture...

In the center of the storm I stand to hold onto my inner compass.

The health evaluation service has left. Mother had a nervous breakdown and is resting now, that is, if Opa lets her. Every ten minutes he says: "What did I do to you, tell me!" "Can't you tell me what I did to you?" "Why can't you tell me what I did to you?" The doctor has seen the truth: A woman at the **end of her ropes** and a constantly, nagging, helpless, dependent, aggressive Alzheimer's patient.

During the evaluation process he was full of mistrust that a Grüne Minna (restraining car) would come to pick him up. My husband was gripping his heart three times while being accused by his father of being an accomplice in this plot against him. My Prof is also too involved emotionally in the whole situation. Opa just shouted, "Elli!" while she was sleeping right behind his armchair on the couch. Can you imagine that **torture** for 24 hours? She can't even go to the bathroom for two minutes, and he is right behind her.

The middle-aged, very compassionate woman doctor has arranged for immediate services. A nurse from the Sozialstation will come every morning to administer medicine, bathe Opa when necessary, and most of all to support Oma psychically. The house doctor has issued a transfer to a hospital in Kittrich for Opa to wean him off the bottle and to find the correct dose of medicine for his state of mind. It cannot be done, right now against his will, because Oma needs legal guardianship first, and secondly, she does not want to send him away, yet.

11. Dezember

From my fluffy downbed…

Network of services…Step 2…Extortion…Your choice…Tender darling moments…Emotional channels…In his own ways…Traditional roles…

The structures are set up for Opa and Oma to live independently, but with a **network of services**: The cleaning lady will sweep and shine once a week for two hours; The nurse from the Sozialstation will home visit every day and on call to survey the intake of medicine, and to report to us about the "state of union". A visiting service from the hospital will support Oma in establishing rapport with someone who has gone through the cycle of Alzheimer's. A "Civi" (Civil Service) helper will assist Opa with bathing and shaving once a week and help Oma with shopping. Opa was put on **health care step 2**; that means Oma will get € 1000 for additional health care services at home[18]. She'll also get legal guardianship for Opa to conduct official business.

We delayed our departure for Spain for two days to be present for the medical and legal evaluation, and to drive Opa to Wiesbaden to a Neurological MD to get that new medication prescribed (Resprisal). I hope they will develop a certain routine for the next half-year, and acknowledge that they need help now.

While Oma's nervous breakdown was a serious cry for help, the house doctor made it clear to my husband that it was also extortion, subconsciously, to make her son come home. She does use other tactics of extortion, too, like: "I am not hungry. I will not eat" "OK, Oma then you'll be extra hungry for the next meal." I never made a fuss with my kids either. The meal was being served. They could either eat or leave it. No extras for anybody, and no in-betweens! We never had fussy eaters, only healthy boys with a healthy appetite. So Oma starts eating eventually, if nobody pays attention.

Tonight—the last night here for us—she said: "My cigarettes and a bottle of schnapps will see me through." "That's **YOUR choice**, Oma!" I said. "Just think it through for a moment: You'll fall down the stairs. They'll get you to a hospital, find alcohol in your blood, and revoke legal guardianship, then what?" After that she was all quiet and switched to another topic.

---

18.   Home health care is less than one third of nursing home care.

Besides being a nerve saw (Nervensäge), Opa has **darling tender moments**. When Oma rested on the couch, he played her favorite Xmas song on a Spieluhr (Jewel box). At the kitchen table he frequently takes her hand. "That's his way of thanking you for holding on." I said to Oma. Of course, she wants to shake it off, but I am trying to interpret *his* side from what I see and feel. Since he can't reason, anymore, everything comes through his **emotional channels**. His emotional receptors are very acute. He sees right through people and their intentions. Feeling, sensing, and touching are his strong channels, now, to convey messages, since the logical brain is giving up more and more functions. He wants to hug her frequently, while she often freezes. He loves her very much **in his own ways**, which seems totally ego-centered to her. They live out the traditional roles of marriages, sealed during WWII: He is the breadwinner and she is the housewife. She spoiled him in every way, so he was never used to caring for himself. And after retirement, it was too late to change the roles. So they live out the roles on the stage of life, which they have set in motion sixty some years ago. We can support, but we cannot live out their lives. Tomorrow, we'll leave for Spain.

END OF PART 4

PART V
Spain

From a hotel room behind Lyon…

Stuffed Corsa…Counting beds…Prices going overboard…€ 8.50 chicken leg…Professional evaluation service…Good old house doctor…

We managed to complete half of the trip today and leave half for tomorrow. (Or so we thought-!) After packing for four hours, we left around noon in our blue Opel **Corsa, stuffed** with our belongings for half a year in Santander, Spain. We looked like two students on the move from one dorm to the next. I have **counted the beds** I have slept in for the last half year: At least fifteen. It was smooth driving on the German and French Autobahn, today. While German Autobahns are free, we have already paid € 25 on the French Auto route.[1] Each country finances their streets differently. Eventually, the European Union should find a common modus vivendi.

It was freezing cold in Frankfurt, this morning (-8ºC), but rather mild in the Rhone plane (+8ºC). We drove on Autobahn Karlsruhe-Basel, crossed over at Mühlheim (Mulhouse) direction Marseille, and are now 60 km behind Lyon. I had the most expensive cafeteria meal ever for € 15. French **prices are overboard**: A small plate of salad for € 3.50, one herbed chicken leg and two legumes: haricots verts (green beans) and carrots, and a flan. I should have stayed with the veggies. That was the **most expensive chicken leg** I have ever had (for € 8.50). Next time, I will check the prices before I order. At least I got some fun out of ordering in French.

Good-Byes are always emotional for Oma, but when we called them around 5 p.m., Opa seemed happy that he had Oma all for himself now, and Oma sounded fine, too. Looking back on the **legal and medical evaluation process**, I must say that the doctors were very professional, compassionate and precise in their findings; which means: Dr. Renate fully agrees with the diagnosis. Our house doctor stopped by Oma's house, before we left. He was on the run, too,

---

1. It amounted to over € 75, altogether. The stretch through the Pyrenees not included.

leaving for a medical congress. We exchanged phone numbers and emails. This **good old house doctor** sees right through the curtains of this house. His analysis is precise. The man is compassionate, but not involved emotionally. He tells it as it is, and some people don't like that in Flörsheim. I am getting tired now, and we want to aim at an early start for the last 700 km, altogether 1500 km, or so we thought. Bonne nuit! Good night!

13. Dezember

FROM A HOTEL IN ZARAUTZ BEHIND THE FRENCH BORDER ON SPANISH SOIL...

2000 km...Pyrénées...Wild driving...Seven Dwarf Motel...Travel lightly...Angel rider...Stung by...Sleep disorders...

The trip is longer than we thought: Nearly **2000 km**. We could have gotten an Internet printout, but with all the last minute arrangements for the parents, we only took a quick glance at the map. Since it would have been too late for our host professor and nerves were running thin, we decided to make a second overnight stop in Zerautz. It is somewhat cheaper on the Spanish side, but still quite expensive. Warm winds are blowing inland from the seaside, and it is still 12.5 Celsius at midnight.

In order to save some toll fees on the French Auto route and to see some of the landscape, we drove right through the **Pyrénées** with their thousands of vineyards via Montpellier, Perpignon, St. Gouden, and St. Sebastian. We wanted to dine French style in a little village, but it was already after 2 p.m.[2] So we had baguette jambon (ham), baguette saucisson (sausage), un vin rouge de pays (French red country wine), un cappuccino, et une espresso, all for € 12. The baguette was crunchy and fresh, the butter delicious, right from the local cows.

The Pyrénées reminded me a lot of the Rockies, an older formation. The detour through the countryside took about four hours. On the autoroute we would have saved two. A car needs to fit like a bicycle, and this one is definitely too small for my husband. He frequently gets cramps in his legs, but when I take over, he gets "cramps" in his heart from my **"wild" driving**. I call it flexible and sporty. While we housed in the "**Seven Dwarf Motel**" last night, as my husband called it, this room tonight is very spacious. It is just big enough for Dieter's oversea suitcase, while my small leather backpack fit into the "Seven Dwarf Motel" all right. What in the world does <u>one</u> need for <u>one</u> night?

Before I die I shall get rid of all my earthly belongings, of all that extra baggage, which is totally worthless for the last journey. Maybe I'll keep a piece of art, some music and a book, probably my fluffy down-bed; that's it! Talking about

---

2.   French lunchtime is from noon to 2 p.m.

angels: They are surely helpful for your last journey, but they also appear in earthly situations. Just when my husband wanted to turn back to the autobahn, feeling lost in a commercial area in Zerautz trying to find a suitable hotel, a **bike rider** appeared, escorted us to this wonderful ***hotel, and disappeared so fast that we couldn't even thank him. I better get some sleep now, since my restless sleeper costs me two hours of sleep every night. This morning at 4:15 a.m., he jumped out of bed like he was **stung by** a tarantula. "Is it time, yet?" and fell right back to sleep while I was awake for nearly two hours. I really need my very own room back. I am starting to get **sleep disorders**.

15. Dezember

From the pink couch overlooking Santander...

Panorama view...Picture book landscape...Philipp II...Armada...Terrible oil spill...Colorado sun...Marriage survival training...Lysol freak...Spanish class...More employable...

We settled into our spacious, beautiful apartment in Santander. For those of you, who have ancient old standing credit: The bank of Santander was one of the first banks to give out that tempting plastic. From this pink, sagging couch I have a **panoramic view** from old town, to the sea and to the snow covered peaks of the Cantabria Mountains. Santander has a gorgeous city landscape with very steep hills. Fortunately, it never falls below zero. All the cars would slide into the Atlantic. It is indeed as blue, turquoise, green and white here as **pictured in the book** our Spanish host professor gave us last summer at the NATO Conference in Pingree Park. I'll call him **Prince Philipp II**, and his wife **Armada**. They took us out for a Spanish Sunday lunch at an excellent fish restaurant around 3 p.m. Every thing is very late in Spain: Dinner is around 9 or 10, even later in the summer. People go to bed past midnight. University starts between 9 and 9:30. Lunch is approximately at 2 p.m. on weekdays.

After lunch, Philipp the Second and his wife Armada gave us a tour of Santander, down the hill along the seaside with its beautiful beaches and turquoise water. Parts of the **terrible oil spill** from the Province of Galicia, about 200 miles around the corner of the West of Santander, have also reached the city's beautiful white sand beaches. They already did a thorough cleanup. I do have my Colorado sun back. I really missed that brightness for the last half year. I also have my private room back and my very own bathroom, which contribute a lot to maintaining the fire in my **marriag**e. But the fact that we can **survive** in dwarf motels, facilities with one bathroom, in a shoe box (car), in busses with locked toilets, on cotton-cloud and brick-mattresses, in sauna and north pole-weather conditions shows that we are still fit for traveling as a couple, although it is more tedious than in our younger years. One wants more comfort now, space, privacy and solitude.

Last night, we unpacked and set up the apartment 'till 2 a.m. I can live in my own "dirt", but not in other people's dirt. So I cleaned everything out, before I stored it away. Dieter helps a lot with this. Virgos are **Lysol freaks**. I sure appreciate his love for ovens. It looks like new now. When we leave in half a year, the apartment will be even cleaner than after we "messed" it up. No, no, no, it was not messy or dirty, just unused for a while. As I said, it's a beautiful apartment.

On the late-afternoon-lunch walk along the sea promenade I talked with Armada about taking a **Spanish class**. The semester had already started in October. We'll see what the Language department has to offer. She is taking an English class at a state institution, but it's hard to get in, because a lot of jobless people are taking foreign language classes to make themselves **more employable**. (CHECK THIS, American kids!!!) On Monday, Philipp II will run all the bureaucratic errands with us. I am looking forward to a working routine again.

16. Dezember

From my favorite window seat overlooking Santander...

Countdown 8...Lost without...Survival strategies...Feel at home...Commotion lately...Toning down...Garbage collection...

Wow, only **eight workdays** till Christmas! Kids get their presents on the sixth of January, here, the day the Holy Three Kings presented their presents to Baby Jesus. Christmas is a family celebration for two days just like in America, but there is that extra day on January 6th. I had to get away from that sagging couch and straighten my back, sitting on two chairs, legs up, right by the window in 1. Floor, loge seat, like in a theater, overlooking the bay.

We ran all the errands, today, with Philipp II. **Without** a Spanish native we would be **lost** dealing with the health insurance and rental agencies. The university is just ten minutes from here when I run down the steep hill and up maybe 15 or 20 minutes. My husband has a nice office, and Philipp II will help me in the language department, tomorrow and arrange for a computer space.

We did some more shopping, today with the car, after we had received the garage door opener from the house manager. Shopping takes a long time in the beginning, because you have to figure out all the labels and locations. In our home culture we do so many things automatically and half consciously, but in a foreign culture it takes that constant awareness operating with **survival strategies,** rudimentary words and phrases, combining all the knowledge intelligently that one has accumulated in 50 some years.

I **feel** very **at home** in Spain. Actually, my artist rhythm is the same: I start working at around 9 a.m. in my workshop in Colorado when I happen to be home for summer break. I labor until 2 p.m. Then I have a late lunch and a siesta, because there is absolutely no creativity flowing out of my system between 2 and 5 p.m. From 5 p.m. on, I can work creatively up to midnight, if nobody disturbs me, and family duties don't call.

Coming from the university, I took a nap today, too. My heart is not strong, lately. Traveling for two and a half days in the car seems to be much more stressful than flying. There has been a lot of **commotio**n, lately. I think a daily routine will help in establishing a more serene disposure. What did the Barock (Baroque) people say during the 17th century: "The only steady thing in life is CHANGE!" I used to be very athletic, but now when I don't rest enough, my muscles and bones start aching, even the soles of my feet. The need for **toning down** is hard to accept.

I just heard the **garbage collection**. It comes here after 10 p.m. Isn't that a clever idea? I bet the job can be done in half time when most of the cars are off the streets for Spanish dinnertime. Buena noches! Good night!

17. Dezember

From a cute Italian restaurant downtown...

Little brother...Used laptops...Azúcar...Old wreck... Shopping malls abroad...

It is my brother's birthday, today. He is three and a half years younger than I. **My little brother** is a Kriminalkommissar (detective) for the Frankfurt police. With his soft, cunning, intelligent, inquisitive style, sooner or later hard criminals always confess to HIM. He is a very successful investigator. Actually, he is my little half brother. We came from the same mother and grew up together in Frankfurt. I have two more half brothers from the same father, but he never cared to show up. Happy birthday, Lothar! Feliz Cumple años!

After working for two hours in an Internet café catching up on business, I ironically landed in an <u>Italian</u> pizzeria for my lunch. The Internet guy gave me an address for a second hand computer shop by City hall. I have to find that place after lunch. I want to check out **used laptops** (should have asked my "rich" district for one at the beginning of the trip), because I could utilize a lot more "odd" working hours when I am in the mood. It really is fun working when you don't <u>have</u> to.

I could live here forever if I spoke Spanish fluently, except I do miss my family and friends of course, and beautiful Colorado! The wo/man on the street usually doesn't speak English. I have to learn Spanish fast. The Pizza was superb, and now I am enjoying a smooth espresso with a little **azúcar**. This word is a perfect synthesis linguistically between German and English: (azúcar: Zucker + sugar). I also need to buy a Spanish espresso machine for the stove, since I ruined that **old wreck** completely. Wanting to repair the handle with a Phillips the brittle screw broke off. Well, it was worth a try. I use things till they fall apart[3] and I love to repair stuff. Now I will scout Ol'Town.

---

3.   Like my husband. Oh, oh, now I am in deep trouble!

7 p.m. at night

If you think Wal-Mart is huge or Sam's, try Carrefour in Santander, Centro Commercial. I bet my husband got carried away shopping while I am already waiting (writing!) at the coffee place. I found my little espresso machine for € 7.50. It makes six espressos, equals three cafés leche. I fill it up with hot milk in the morning. That's the Spanish way! We had a little trouble figuring out the bus system, because some busses take round trips and others go straight. We did not dare to take the car, yet, because you go through endless round-abouts (how Americans love those!), organized along the bay. Finally my shopper showed up with two bags of groceries and a large trashcan. When I saw it on the way to the espresso machines, I knew exactly that he would buy it, because it was on sale for € 6. Carrefour is not cheap at all. You've got to experience the **shopping malls** of other cultures. In my section there is a Mc Donald's and a Häagen Dazs. People enjoy sitting down here and talking. In our neighborhood, on General-Davila Street there is a coffee place or Cafeteria every 50 or 100 meters, just like in Greece. People love company and take time for conversations.

18. Dezember

From my favorite window seat overlooking the Bahia...

Spanish rhythm...Siesta...Bureaucratic marathon...The "Spanish" way...International student...Full time occupation...Wrestling with keyboards...Brain-active people...Hard liquor...

Few have such a view! I feel privileged! "The **day** is clearly **cut in half** in the Spanish culture", said Philipp II today over lunch in a seaside Cafeteria with another spectacular view. The waves foamed over the white sand beach in the foreground, while huge fluffy white clouds were lingering in the foothills of the Cantabria Mountains as a dramatic backdrop.

The first half of the day starts around 9 a.m. at the University. At 11 a.m., Profs, students and support staff congregate for coffee break for about half an hour or longer. These informal talks are considered very important for social relations, out-of-department information, and getting to know "strange" people like us. At 2 p.m. it is lunchtime till about 4 p.m. Most people go home for lunch to meet up with their spouses and kids, or they go to a cafeteria. Many Spaniards take a **siesta**. (This is to demonstrate how sanely other cultures live!) After lunch break they pick up work again until 7:30 or 8 p.m. Most shops are open till 9 or 10 p.m.

We took Philipp II out for lunch today after another **bureaucratic marathon**. We barely made it to the police station to register before lunchtime. While my husband had no problems with his German passport, because Germany and Spain belong to the European Union, it turned out that I need a visa for staying longer than three months. I caught on to the officer's bubbling explanation in Spanish. Philipp II wasn't present, yet, to translate, because he was scouting for one of the scarce parking spaces. Later, he and the officer negotiated the "**Spanish way**", which means there is also a non-bureaucratic way to get things done. They have a good sense of humor here, and they know how to beat their own system. Legally we could procrastinate till the five months are over, but I bet my husband will do it the German way: Straightforward and efficiently. He already emailed the marriage license office in Frankfurt to get a copy of our marriage certificate. Once the Spaniards have a document showing that I am also German, the visa for me as an American is not important anymore.

After "anmelden" (registering, anunciar)—every American who has been in Germany knows that word—we raced to the International Student Office. The door was already locked for lunchtime, but Philipp II had announced his Majesty and Jesters, so they let us in. I am now an **officially registered international student**, hurray! My intensive language class will start mid February to mid March=60 hours, and a second course (if I want it) till May 8 for another 60 hours, that means 12 credits in three months, equals a **full time occupation** with lab studies, home studies and home work etc.

My morning was pretty productive, as they had set up a computer for me in the Physics/Geology computer lab. I started part 5, the literary travel report about Spain. (And right now, I am almost caught up!) I am still **wrestling with the Spanish keyboard,** finding specific signs and operations. All the computer commands are in Spanish, of course. This is now the fifth national keyboard I have had to figure out: Germany, Greece, Turkey, Italy and Spain. Hail to the British occupiers, because I had an English keyboard in India! I don't think I could have learned Hindi in six weeks. Everything takes time and a lot of concentration, but the Spanish work rhythm is very sane and humane.

Lunch was delicious in that seaside cafeteria. They have special plates for **brain-active people**, with high protein food and low carbs, which keep you active in the afternoon. We also stayed away from the almost mandatory red wine (vino tinto) and stuck to mineral water.

In the student Cafeteria, this morning over coffee break, I was <u>not</u> surprised to see cigarettes and alcohol, even hard liquor. It's a common sight in European countries, although I don't like it: the cigarette smoke, especially, is clearly constricting my heart. Every culture has plus and minus points and it all depends on your own value system whether it adds or subtracts to your personal happiness.

21. Diciembre, Sabádo

From my favorite "Bahia seat"...

Exploding population...Cruising seagulls...Flying laundry...Christmas party in the country side... Rambunctious chorus...Students celebrating Xmas...

The bay looks mellow, today: The Atlantic Ocean is gray blue and the mountains are a little hazy. On this side of the bay where we live, there are mostly high-rise buildings, 8-12 stories high, with the old low-rise houses imbedded in between. Santander has been **exploding** lately to 200.000 inhabitants. Since everybody wants to live in the city there is no space to grow except up into the sky. On the other side of the bay it looks like countryside with villages nestled into the foot-hills of the Cantabria Mountains. **Seagulls** are using the thermics all day, **cruising** elegantly in between the buildings and over the water. Maybe they are looking for "human" food. A city ordinance, issued recently, forbids that seagulls be fed any longer, because of the waste swimming in the ocean.

The sun is piercing through the clouds now. The balcony in front of the living room is facing south; that's where the spectacular view is, but even from the north balcony in front of the kitchen, I can see the ocean. So we are located on a land tongue. **Laundry is flying** everywhere on the balconies and in front of the windows on extendible clotheslines; even bed sheets are flying like flags in front of the buildings. Hardly anybody dries with dryers in Mediterranean countries. In Germany some people use dryers in the winter. Germans don't dry laundry in the dryer because of energy conservation, and in Southern European countries there is no need for dryers, because the laundry dries fast outside.

Yesterday, at the department's **Christmas party** out in the countryside, I learned more Spanish in three hours than during our first week here in Santander. In the morning I worked on the computer for three hours, and around 2 p.m. the whole department left for the Xmas party to a little village ca 30 km west from here. The tables in a rustic Mesón were festively decorated for our vivid party of ca 36 people. The massive building dated back at least 200 years and was built from natural stones and mighty wooden beams. A three-course Xmas lunch of excellent quality was served plus red wine, rosé, fresh bread, coffee and schnapps. First, you could choose between "sopa de pescado" (fish soup), and traditional bean soup. The main course was either Lubina (bass), hake, sirloin or lamb. For dessert they served tarta de orujo, (a typical Spanish tart with light cream and layers soaked in the traditional Orujo[4] liquor) or cheesecake or flan. By the Spanish expressions you can guess what I chose, because I couldn't store every expression in my head at the same time.

After the main course, the Ph.D. students and the younger Docs started to **shout rhythmically** in a chorus: "que hable directór!" trying to make the "shy" department chair give a speech, but he was still busy with his main course. When he was finished the Post docs and grad students started a second round: "que cante directór!" but the director did not sing. Putting more emphasis to their request they started to support the rhythm of the next round by banging the silverware against the glasses. "Que baile directór!" (Dance!) When that request went unheard, they shouted: "que fume director!" (Smoke!) Then they focused on another victim: "que hable subdirector!" (Who is our host professor, Philipp II) Then the chair rose and said in Spanish, which I caught on to: His assistant can't give a speech, because he forbids him to, which was a joke of course. Later when it quieted down, the chair rose at his own terms and said in Spanish: "I wish you a jolly party, a Merry Xmas and a Happy New Year!" **I** could have given that speech. Then the director moved to different sections of the table, talking to his rambunctious Docs first. He felt more comfortable that way than standing before the whole crowd.

After the postres (desserts), espresso or the Spanish cortado[5] was served. I skipped the schnapps, because I don't care for hard liquor, but Phillip II had the traditional Spanish orujo, which I had a taste of in my tart already. After la cuenta arrived, we all had to pay € 20 for our delicious Xmas lunch. Eating out is a major social event here with a lot of fun like in any culture.

Around 6 p.m., our sober, designated driver, Professor Dr. Hans Dieter, chauffeured us home. Philipp II had to finish some administrative business in the Uni while we were meandering our way up the hill to our apartment through endless crowds of happily delirious students, broken schnapps bottles, empty coke bottles, plastic bags, cigarette stomps and empty bags of chips. This kind of **student celebration** happens twice a year, before Xmas and before summer break. The whole point of it, said Philipp II, is getting drunk. The Saufgelage (Ger.: sauf=drinking heavily & gelage=lay around; Engl. rève?) is being watched over by the police, but not restricted or interfered with; therefore it is always peaceful. That's another way of having fun from the kids' point of view. I didn't

---

4.   Fermented with the skin of the grapes. Very fruity taste!
5.   =Cut in half: half espresso, half leche (milk)

experience any aggressiveness or rowdiness on the way up to our apartment, just kids being a little "out of space" and letting it all hang out, like one young man peeing into the bushes.

25. Diciembre
6 p.m.

From my bed overlooking the Bahia...

Howling winds...Gorgeous Xmas morning...Malena Peninsula...Sea ambiance...Tapas...Tapas finito... Schickeria...Working class people...White Cabbage Xmas...Que aproveche...Santander Xmas song...

I am starting my new <u>Italian</u> spiral although I am in Spain. The **wind** is **howling** around the apartment building and everything that is not bolted down is rattling, squeaking and trembling. I can feel the drafts from the rough sea winds through the windows. They don't build as solidly here as in Germany. The house quiets down past midnight. I can even hear the telephone ring upstairs and the lady of the apartment argue with Jesus. (Speak: Chesús) Poor Jesus! Whatever he did, he needs a break, especially on Christmas!

Christmas morning by the sea was **gorgeous**. Half of Santander was out and about, enjoying the sunshine and the foaming waves. Some "polar bears" were taking a dive in the ocean; joggers were running barefoot in the white sand; dogs were sniffing each other's behinds; children were playing ball; older folks were slurping along the sea promenade, and we were taking a hike out to **Malena Peninsula**. The sea branded against mighty rocks, which were layered into a parallel downhill fold. The hike meandered along the Atlantic Ocean, and from each angle the city looked ever more beautiful in the Xmas morning sunshine. Xmas by the **sea** has a different **ambianc**e than Xmas in the mountains; and Xmas in the desert is still a different treat. My son called from Maryland. They have snow, this year, and here we had 20-Celsius weather around noon.

After our three-hour hike we sat in a hotel café by the sea and had some **tapas**. When my Argentinean friend called from Ft. Collins, last night, she said that Dieter should take me out for some tapas. They are called Häppchen in Germany and garnished bites in the US. (Unless somebody has a better word!) Those little squares of white bread, garnished with cheese, anchovies, ham, caviar, hard-boiled eggs, cornichons, lox, ropes of mayonnaise etc. looked very appetizing, and they tasted all right, but I got an allergic reaction from the anchovies. (Probably!) For seven of those little squares we paid € 7.50. I can create a whole plato with much more interesting toppings at home. We'll just play "cervecería" at home one night with a plata of tapas and Spanish beer.

It was a task to get those tapas for my hungry husband. First, we waited for over half an hour for the only waiter of this covered outdoor café, and then he said that **tapas** were **finito**, but I didn't take his word for it. I went inside to another hectic guy behind the counter, pointed at my desired objects, accompanied by some fragmented Spanish phrases, and arrived back at our table with a plato of siete tapas and a delicious chocolate tart. What good was this CSU Spanish course anyhow, when a guy can't even get his tapas in Spain?! The ancient professor beat all the young chicks in class, but he never told them that he needed double the study time.

The waiter then brought the cappuccino and the café leche. The mineral water he forgot. Oh well, poor guy! Who wants to work on Christmas Day satisfying all these snobbish **schickeria** guests?! Well, them, not US of course, we work here! We belong to the **working class people**.

Yes, it was a lovely Xmas, very unusual, and now we are not even having turkey or goose; we are creating our own white Xmas: We just have plain, simple **white cabbage for Xmas**. It is the most delicious white cabbage I have ever cooked by accident, because it is fixed with very unusual ingredients: I used up the brick hard, rather expensive ham sausage which nobody could chew, and cut in my baked quince, which I couldn't finish yesterday. On top of it, the cabbage slightly burned on the bottom of the pot, because I am not used to gas. So it caramelized a little bit, and altogether all the creative mishaps contribute to the most delicious tasting cabbage I have ever tasted. And the irony is that my husband never wanted to shop for a white cabbage, but a Wirsing, another softer kind of repollo. Merry Xmas to me and all my friends out there around the globe! Guten Appetit! I am going to eat now! **Que aproveche!**

Around 11 p.m.

Santander Xmas Song (Sing!!!)

Oh, Holy Night
It storms, it roars, it thunders
Across the bay in Santander, Spain.

I wish you all
A very merry Xmas!
And for next year
Success and peace
And blessings!

Fall on your knees
And hear the ocean roaring
For Christ was born
To uplift this messy world
And you and me-e-e are free
to praise his (he-is) grace.

NOT an original MOM, borrowed from a church song.

From my favorite Bahia seat...

Home for Xmas...Examining Inner landscapes...Language barrier..."Shoulds"...Feel incompetent...Philipp II...European loopholes...United Germany...Mind-set changed...West messed up...

In-between the years..., in-between the old and the new...in-between work and slugging off: It is best to take off completely, for the sake of peace of mind. Period! People show up whenever at the institute during that transitional time to take care of the most urgent matters—and that's a matter of definition, of course—and we show up, too, since we have no desire to do any major traveling, right now. We just got here. Being **"home" for Xmas** and New Year is just fine with us.

Since my husband is still splashing around in the bathroom, I shall **examine my Inner Landscapes**: I've noticed recently that I keep on procrastinating with certain things because of the **language barrier**. I should make an appointment at the gyno; I should go to the post office to send a package; I should find out about massage therapy; I should go to the hairdresser. It all takes that extra effort and courage to make a fool out of yourself, to speak with your hands and feet, to just go out and do it—where is that little Nike check mark? I can't find it. Maybe I should do away with all the **"shoulds"** and let it all hang out. I just don't have the drive right now. You **feel so incompetent** without language skills. You always depend on other people's good will and helpfulness. And usually, the Spaniards are very sweet in helping out: Either, they rush by in a hurry like the New Yorkers, or they take their time in supporting your needs, like the guy at the foreign registration office. He established quite a rapport with my Level-one-Spanish-speaking husband. We literally went there four times with Philipp II.

—Oh, my God, the grandchildren are gone, and now she is arguing again with Jesus. Somebody slammed the door upstairs and I can hear steps coming down the staircase. He probably left to get away from his bitching wife. Why am I not on the women's side? That constant bitching gets on my nerves, especially as a spectator.—

Anyhow, poor **Philipp II** made the trip four times with us: The first time the office was closed. The second time they let us in five minutes before their lunch break. The third time they had moved to another location, and the fourth time, we finally got our official permit to stay legally in this country in expectation of my marriage license, which would arrive in three weeks. (As I told you: No procrastination possible with MY Prof…straight forward and efficient!!) The irony is that we never entered Spain, because there is no entry visa in our passports. We entered Spain within the European Union, so officially we are non-existent here.

Officials make fun of the **European loopholes**. Actually, we need all the loopholes or the lawyers wouldn't have any holes to leap through. Europe can't be created in one decade, of course, and it never will be a "United States of Europe", because of all the different cultures and languages. Originally, politicians had thought to create a **United Germany** in one decade, but now everybody understands that it will take two to three generations to get the whole **mind-set changed**. Dictatorial structures imply that "Father State" is in charge of the "infantile citizens". Democracy implies that the power lies with the people. The former Easterners need to go exactly through that process: They have awoken from infantilism, and are now in a stage of teenage protest, shifting the responsibilities back to the adults (West), while they want all the freedoms and amenities without the adult responsibilities of a democratic, mature behavior. Of course, that only applies to the masses, not to the intellectuals. The literary circles, for example, always had a critical "see-through" (Durchblick). And the **West messed** up quite a bit, too, in my opinion, integrating, swallowing up the East, annexing mindlessly in a hurry, instead of forming beneficial symbiosis between the systems. The East, for example, had a pretty good education system in place, and the West could have learned a lot by forming an EW school coalition.

31. Diciembre 2002

From the sagging pink couch...

Jesus gets a break...Spanish beds...Adult version...An apple instead...Hot Latin music...Ten grapes...

New Years is a family affair until midnight, I heard, and then the crowds move through the streets from party to party and bar to bar. We'll see what happens. It sounds like twenty feet are moving about in Jesus' apartment upstairs. They must have just sat down for dinner, because it is rather quiet now. **Jesus gets a break** at last!

Spanish beds are rather narrow. Have you ever slept on an eighty—centimeter bed? It seems that at least 20 cm are always missing to fold out my leg in a 90-degree angle in belly position and to fling my arm in the other direction. There is no rolling around or sleeping diagonal like in my American bed. Lovemaking is an art on those 90 cm beds in the Master's room. If you don't pay attention you fall through the cracks, because they move slowly apart. The sagging couch is too soft, the shoebox too small, the wooden floor too hard. One has to become inventive or eat an apple instead! For those of you barely over twenty, there was a time in our lives where none of the above problems posed any problem. There was room in der kleinsten Hütte. (In the smallest hut) But now one needs comfort, room and time. More time...

Depending on what I finally do with this script, there needs to be an **adult version** and a student version for educational purposes. But who says Spanish beds are not educational? Why not include sex education into multicultural education? Integrated, holistic teaching, connecting to all threads of life, will be more beneficial and motivating for a student than cutout artificial pies of knowledge. It was quite educational for me, also, to realize that 80something-year old people have sex, too. (See part IV!)

We had a nice New-Years Eve dinner with a variety of fresh fish: prawns, calamari, hake and some other muscular fish, along with salad, fresh bread and red wine. Now Dieter is sound asleep, but he will wake up before midnight—or I will move the beds apart—because the champagne is waiting in the fridge. If not he'll get **an apple instead**! I am listening to some hot Latin music on the TV and it is half an hour before midnight.

What do I wish for, next year? Number One is health: complete, restored health! Number two: Great satisfaction professionally, whatever I will do. Number three: Creativity and peace within. Number four: Family reunion. Number five: Deep-growing experiences for my soul. Number six: Working through obstacles with patience and grace.

Fin de año[6] 2002¡ Año nuevo: dos mil tres: 2003
Tiene un prospero año nuevo!!!

It is quite a spectacular view from up here: People light up their own private fireworks. I don't care about those loud ear-blasting bombs, but the colored star rain against the deep blue night sky is beautiful. On TV they did the countdown with 24 strikes of an old church tower clock, which reminded me of my Grandma's. Ten seconds before midnight you have to eat **ten grapes**[7] off a plate for prosperity and health. WE "klinged" (sonar) glasses with the exquisite champagne from Philipp II and Armada. Maybe we'll try the grapes next year, instead…or after…! Feliz dos mil tres ¡

---

6.   Never forget the enye: ñ or you are in big trouble!
7.   I wonder if they also raise the kundalini like the Indian Mangoes?

2. Enero 2003
Jueves (Th)

From my favorite Bahia seat...

Spanish toilets...Dear Madam...Stiff like a frozen towel...100% yourself...Cultural context...Verdi wait!...

One gets the oddest writing ideas sitting over breakfast, staring at the ocean. Today, I noticed for the first time that there is Ebb (tide) in the morning, because sandbanks are visible in the middle of the Bahia.

You want to know how the **Spanish toilets** are? (ASeos![8] or servicios) Very well, Sir/Madam, just like in the US, but with a bidet right in front or beside, just like in France. So, one needs to move his/her royalties over in the process. The Turkish toilets are still the best!

Before New Years, I received an email from an Indian friend, addressed with Dear Madam Misses Renate Hochheimer and signed with Yours Sincerely..., while I just wrote: Hi, so-and-so...his nickname and signing with: Love, renate. I am afraid I committed a serious faux pas, not knowing about the formalities (conventions) in Indian letter writing. His email letter was so perfect in style and form that you could print it out, fold it, place it in a wax-sealed envelope, and send it to His Royalty Juan Carlos or Prinz Philipp II. Then again, the content was so dear and appreciative that I think he didn't mind my informalities at all. (Or they just pardon those dumb foreigners gracefully, all the time) I think that's a typical American feature of mine being very informal.

I noticed that when we have German guests, or any other nationality, back home in Colorado, they can be very **stiff**, at first, **like a frozen towel,** hanging on a German clothesline in January. But in the process of communicating with my informal American entity, combined with my German directness (straight-for-wardness) and my Hessian[9] curiosity—a fatal combination!—they thaw up like the stiff towel by the fireplace, and become very flexible, soft, refreshing, open, entertaining and funny, like they finally found their long-lost child-like self. So, in being informal, open and a **100%** (well, 99%) **yourself**, you can open the

---

8.   Which would add another AS to the Ambassador's AS collection in his novel "Birds of Passage"

9.   Hessen: State of Germany with my hometown, city of Frankfurt

door for your fellow human beings to "afford" the same. I am writing, "afford", because it is a daring process. It takes courage.

But one still needs to know about the writing conventions in other countries, because <u>not</u> observing the conventions could also close the doors, like in a vitae, or a job application. So we always have to play within the **cultural context** in order to be successful in any given culture.

Now, I shall stroll down the hill to the university to update my Spanish literary travel report and to start part IV: Alzheimer's, Italy—not that Italy has anything to do with Alzheimer's-, because my Italian professor can't wait 'till it is ready. First, I considered extracting the Italian chapters, but then it doesn't evolve organically, and **Verdi** just has to **wai**t like anybody else. Imagine how long Sokrates had to wait for his travel report till it finally arrived for Xmas! Well, I couldn't foresee the erased-disc accident, but I could have taken precautions. Now, I have everything backed up 3 times, but I am still getting more comfort out of my old fashioned hand written script.

Sexto Enero 2003
Lunes[10]

From my favorite Bahia seat...

Introspection...Holidays and family...Swimming in an ocean of...Magdalena peninsula...Christopher Columbus...Victims of oil spill...Prenatal submarine...

No far sight, today! The Bay is mysteriously mantled in layers of thick gray clouds. The perfect day for **introspection**! Today is one of the highest holidays in Spain: Holy Three King Day, when the kids get their Xmas presents.

Holidays only make sense to me when you can gather **family and friends** around you. Yesterday, I was watching a young man bring his grandparents to the taxi stand in front of our apartment house. Suddenly a stream of tears was flooding down my face. Then I had to laugh about myself, because there is really nothing to cry about having the privilege of learning about other languages and cultures for one year. But the pain came back, and I allowed myself to **swim in an ocean of sadness** for a while.

Originally, we wanted to drive to a National Park, near by, but we'll save it for a sunny day. On New Years, we took a walk (rather a hike) on **Magdalena Peninsula** where they had built a summer residency in 1913 for the Spanish King Alfonso XIII and his wife. It is now a park and recreation area with a maritime zoo, a ship exhibition and beautiful, white sand beaches inside the bay. Around the peninsula, towards the open ocean, the sea brands vigorously against mighty rocks, leaving white foam on the shore, before being sucked back towards the horizon. The view is spectacular. There is no end in sight. You can just imagine yourself as a little nutshell, rocking on the ocean. **Christopher Columbus**' ship, which was exhibited as a reconstruction surely looked like a nutshell, compared to those mighty ocean liners, nowadays.

The maritime zoo was imbedded in the natural environment right by the sea. Sea lions, seals and penguins were the remnants of an originally bigger zoo. Judging by the deserted Tiergarten, they might have had polar bears in there. Two penguins looked yellow-brownish and gooey. They kept my gaze glued on them, 'till I figured out that they were victims of the **oil spill**. At least they had a clean

---

10.   You see why Mondays are a little deranged!

environment to recover in, but they looked like outcasts among all the elegant "pengs" in their clean white and black tuxedos. The sea lions were swimming with their bellies sunny side up and seemingly enjoying the warm sunrays on their layers of blubber.

Royalties know how and where to build their castles: Infinite ocean and horizon on one side, beautiful white sand beaches on the other, and towards the inland esthetic, green royal gardens. When it warms up, I will go there to write, sit on a bench by the rugged side with its steep rocks and wild branding, foaming ocean waves. This is the time in my life to fully absorb the sea into my soul with its vast graveyard stillness, its mild rocking, rolling waves, and its wild, violent, vigorous waves. The moody colors of the water range from brilliant turquoise, emerald green, royal blue, pitch dark blue to dreary gray. Many writers have finished their novels in solitude by the branding sea.[11] I think the rhythm, the sounds and the rocking have been branded into our memories in the nutshell of our **prenatal submarine**: our mother's womb. That's why the sea has such magnetism on many human souls.

---

11.   Like Thomas Mann and Ernest Hemingway

Noveno Enero, January 9

From El Corte Ingles...
Another Mall on the route to Bilbao...

Rebajas...WWII kids...Land of my Forefathers...Moody foods...Latinized...NO to US offer...Sugerentia...

Rebajas, Rebajas everywhere! It's that time of the year, right after Xmas, when smart shoppers buy their Xmas presents for next year. I don't need anything! I don't want anything! I have it all, except my family and friends and my health, and those are the most important, besides my number ONE inventory. My shopper is out there somewhere. He likes to shop with heart and soul. If he doesn't see a major mall, once a week, and a supermercado every other day, you'd really need to call the doctor, because he would be sick. We'll never run out of food. Should Santander be totally shut down, because of the announced snow in two days, who cares? You just go to the Doc's in-home grocery shop and you'll find it: All the commodities in storage.

Those are the **WWII kids.** They never want to run out of food, again, because they never knew where their next bottle came from: American powdered milk from the sky[12], or actual milk from the Alps or Holstein. These little hamsters have everything in storage as if the world would come down tomorrow. When I was born I did not feel the scarcity anymore. By that time, five years later, the American soldiers already distributed sweets and chewing gum to feisty little kids like me playing in the rubble. I had many American uncles and now, I am an American aunt myself. I always wanted to be an Indian when we played "Cowboys and Indian" in the rubble. Now, I've come home to the **land of my forefathers**.

My Prof just came back, happy like a kid on Xmas Eve. "Look, what I got for you!" "Oh, oh, I bought the same thing." I really needed that "flipper" to turn pancakes around. On the weekends, we have a good old American pancake breakfast. Well, I make the dough with harina integral, that's whole wheat, and so it's a bit germinized, i.e. Germanized, rather. **Food** carries potentially all the traditions, **moods** and tastes of the eater. He even found maple syrup in this Corte Ingles. Traditions and inner rhythms are deeply engrained. I still work

---

12.   From the US care packages at the end of WWII

right through the Spanish lunch break. For lunch I eat half a sandwich and I have a cortado (half and half), then I go back to work. However, our dinnertime has Latinized: It's getting later and later. But then I don't have to get up at 5 a.m. to start an American school day. The day starts here at 9 a.m.; that's when it gets barely light outside.

We have had a lot of rainy days, lately. Prof A., who sometimes joins us for coffee break, said that Santander has more rainy days than England. He has declined many **offers** to come **to the US**. "People form deeper relationships in Spain. I never have to worry about the health care system; it's government supported. We also have a saner life style here. Did you know that we have the highest life expectancy in Spain?" No, I didn't know that. It's even more surprising to me, since I see so many people smoking, especially women.

Today, in Corte Ingles, at the coffee place, I ordered "**sugerentia**", and the waiter looked at me like a question mark. Then I pointed at the black board by the entrance and said "special". Had I engaged my brain[13] I would have derived "sugerentia" from *suggest* or *suggestions.* So I ordered a bunch of *suggestions=sugerentia*, which were composed of: Little round potatoes in creamy garlic sauce, three slices of bread, and one glass of red wine. Pan and vino rojo I could read off the black board. The third *sugerentia* would be a surprise to me, I reckoned. I like surprises!

---

13.   My classes always chuckle, because I train them to look for cognates. "Where the heck do you see the similarities?" they ask in the beginning. After a while, they catch on.

Decimo Enero, January 10

From Suizo Cafe...

Coreo...Princess' Day...Centro de Estudios...Students' responsibility...What a concept...Milking the cows...Power to teach...Administrative Phalanx[14]...

It is Friday, late afternoon, end of the workweek, and every cafeteria in town is filling up rapidly, now. I am having my favorite coffee Vienna at Suizo Cafe directly by the bay. I just picked up a package from my Baby son in Colorado. At the coreo I instinctively went up to the right counter. "¡Paquete, por favor!" I handed her the slip; she handed me the packet; smooth transaction! The heart beating was all for nothing. Figuring it was my smooth, nonresistant **Princess Day** I followed with making an appointment at the hairdresser and massaje therapy, too. The trouble is that when I start speaking in Spanish—does it sound that real, already?—a flood of info in Spanish rolls over me. Struggling to drown in the waves of "Nix verstan" I finally admit with shrugging shoulders "No hablo español": Since it was an international beauty salon they graciously helped me out with English then, although I could have stumbled further along with: "Tiene usted una sita a la lunes en dis hora?" YOU figure out what I wanted to say, including the mistakes!

Everywhere I go in town I see these big signs on houses "**Centro de Estudios**". While walking up the hills—and there are many in Santander—to distract myself from my aching bones, I made up my theory about those Centros de Estudios: When so many kids and university students go there to keep up with their grades, teachers are there for teaching and holding up the standards. Then teachers are not responsible[15] for the students' progress, or for extra help and babysitting. It is the **students' responsibility** to learn, keep up their grades and meet the standards. "Is that so?" I asked Philipp II during coffee break in the presence of an American Physics professor from Washington who gave a colloquium that day. "Yes", he said, "We wouldn't have the time for this. We have a heavy teach-

---

14. Phalanx: Tight military defense line, shield by shield, first used by the Macedonian King Phillip II, father of Alexander the Great.
15. Like in government: Checks and balances, separation of competences!

ing load, up to 15 credits." In Spain it is the student's responsibility to learn and the teacher's responsibility to do good teaching. What a concept!

The "extra help" American students cry for is often disabling, because it supports procrastination, laziness of the mind, and shifting responsibility onto someone else. This "pampering" lowers the frustration level more and more until students have no tolerance for the slightest effort anymore. They want to be breastfed instead of **milking the cows** themselves, but that takes effort and initiative. We teachers must not deprive them of the pride of self-achievement after a period of struggle and self-discipline.

Imagine the track and field coach putting up 80 cm hurdles: He would teach the technique how to overcome those hurdles with speed, but he would not put little steppers in front of the hurdles and hold the sprinter's hand to "walk" over the hurdle. The runner would never gather the strength, follow his/her own pace, and learn how to deal effectively with thrown-over hurdles and falls. Why is everything so clear for our athletes in sports, and when they come to the classroom the same rules don't apply anymore. Intellectually they hang through like shriveled balloons after a nightlong party, while on the sports field their muscles are pumped with determination and drive for success.

We teachers must not take the blame any longer for lazy students or F's. We must not bow down to parents who try to interfere with the teaching process. In none of the countries I have been to, have I seen or heard about such kinds of interferences like back home. One would not tell a trained doctor how to operate on a patient. Teaching is a highly skillful art. Most parents would not survive for one hour in a High school classroom. American teachers need to take back their **power to teach**, and **administrators** need to stand strong like a **phalanx** to support that battle against mental laziness, shifting responsibilities, and blaming the teachers.

The American education system is especially vulnerable in this aspect, because of the power of small local school districts, where people in office are directly exposed to daily criticism and pressures, while in many European countries education is either centralized, like in France, or the authority lies with the states, like in Germany. Local administrators merely execute the policies, and local parents are not interfering with the teaching process, policies, or discipline rules.

14. Enero

SUNSET OVER THE BAHIA

A painter paints with colors.
A musician paints with notes.
A writer paints with words.
The colored symphony of
A Santander Sunset
Makes me speechless…

Potawi

15. Enero

From Cafeteria La Marina…

Spanish siesta…Water corpse…One Liter of Peña Castillo…Exotic taste…NO servants of time…Viva España…

I am still operating on a German/American schedule. At 4 p.m. I wanted to pick up a CD-radio player at Lidl's, a German chain, like Aldi's (see part I) with high quality items and low prices. But the **Spanish siesta** goes until 4:30 p.m. Since I haven't eaten anything yet, besides breakfast, I decided to have a late, late lunch at La Marina. It is worthwhile: Sitting upstairs behind a panoramic view window, I have a grand view over the harbor. Hundreds of seagulls are seemingly enjoying the warm afternoon sunshine after a weeklong cold spell (down to 3^0C), circling over the colorful sea ships.

I ordered plato del dia, which is easiest to order for a not-just-yet-Spanish speaker: You choose your first and second plato among four items. I pick those, which sound familiar or exotic, like sopa and dolce, today. If there are false cognates you might be out of luck, and get poison instead of a gift.[16] In any case, I trust that they feed me right. I am a recognized International student at Santander University of Cantabria. They cannot afford a **water corpse** (Wasserleiche) swimming back home to America, although geographically it would be possible. (See Christopher Columbus!)

My first course was **sopa** de pescado, served in a huge metal bowl, steaming hot. During all those chilly days I had dreamt (Brit!) of a hot soup. They trusted me with a whole bottle of vino tinto in front of me: **One liter Peña Castillo**. I wonder what would happen if I drank it all, besides me taking the bus to Bilbao in a delirium. I guess it is understood that you drink a reasonable amount of vino tinto or rosso with your lunch. I reckon that would be one to three glasses. Fresh baguette (pane)—my favorite is campesino—accompanies every meal.

My second course was thinly breaded beef in a wine sauce **dolce** with mashed potatoes. If it was tongue I don't want to know! It tasted delicious, and the sweet

---

16. Engl. *Poison*=Ger. *Gift (in French poisson means fish!!☺)*
     For your information: Where ever the smiley faces appear my editor in Chicago added an intelligent remark, or had an outburst of joy!

touch of the wine sauce was **exotic**. Now the friendly young waitress just served cafe leche and my choice of a postre, among four, which is a flat, fluffy, deliciously tasting almond cream square. All in all it will cost me € 7 plus 10% tip, an excellent value.

I will not be able to eat, tonight. The most I can do for my better half, thinner half, (—then it wouldn't be a half, would it?—) more intelligent, but not necessarily wiser half, is prepare the meal and dance for him to the music of my newly purchased CD-radio player, which I will buy now. Wake up, Spain, it is ten to five, and those schedule-driven Germans are coming!

In Spain **time serves** the people!
They are not the **servants of time**!

The sun is slowly setting over the Bahia. The snow-covered Cantabria Mountains are reflecting a tint of the vino tinto back to me. The Spanish Flamenco rhythm with the nut cracking sounds of castanets in this Marina establishment drifts me into another time and space. **Viva España!**

Jueves, 16. Enero
(Th) midnight

From the pink sagging couch...

Aseos...Inspiration...Gifts of each Nation...Fallen raindrop...Human Rainbow...Butterfly...

Aseos can be great places for unusual ideas. Artists are often inspired by nature's grandiosity and motivated by heart breaking calamities and pain. Homesickness is one of them. Women seem to suffer more from it than men, although there have been great male Minnesingers (minstrels) during the Middle Ages, and plenty of male writers during Romanticism.[17] Stricken with homesickness on the aseo, I got the **inspiration** that each country we travel through is giving me (has given me) **specific gifts**, and all the hosts and co-players reflect back to me certain teachings in the school of life.

Germany was about revisiting my childhood and youth, a worry-free time, and recovering from the stresses of Public school teaching. Our youthful German professor, Günther, in Dresden reflected back to me the time when we were raising small children, had boundless energy and optimism.

Greece gave me the gift of delving deeper into my soul through philosophical reflections with Sokrates and the Physio. Daily exposure to ancient **his**tory turned into **her**story in the classroom of life.

Turkey, the "Young Conqueror" charmed me with childhood fairy tales of 1001Nights, two Turkish Knights, and four nights and days of laughter, work, dance and memories.

India leaped me into my spirituality to see beyond the Sir-face into the face of God. A huge butterfly[18], symbol of transformation, lifted into the air, when the Ambassador switched on the AC for me. India, her Majesty, showed me the richness of life through powerful contrasts.

Italy taught me that man plans, but nature reigns. When Mrs. Etna spews one needs to stay under Verdi's umbrella, and <u>not</u> look up to the sky like in Greece. Playing Rock in a Ba-Rock[19] cloister is not an alien concept anymore.

---

17. Prototype: Werthers Leiden (sufferings) from Johann Wolfgang Goethe, although the "real" Romanticists like Eichendorff, Brentano, Fontane and others came later.

18. It was a Pfauenauge in Ger. (literal translation: peacock eye)

19. German: Barock, English: Baroque

Through **Alzheimer's** I learnt that parents need to draw up a living will and communicate with their children about old age and death. I saw a spirit fading away who once lived in that body, so it wasn't its home in the first place, only a hostel on the soul's journey. In the midst of the greatest shit, man is entitled to certain inalienable rights[20]: To be treated with dignity, compassion and patience. We are born into this world as helpless infants, and most of us regress into this stage of total surrender, before we are allowed to leave this planet again. The final stages of soul maturation are as important as the soul's first imprints.

Spain is teaching me the secrets of the sea: A tiny sand particle, being rounded and polished through daily grinding—A tiny water drop in the ancient sea pot of mankind: originating from the Source, swimming, paddling, rushing upstream, drowning occasionally, being swept under, meandering my way to the sea, evaporating into the sky to begin a new cycle someday as a **fallen raindrop.**

Hopefully, on its way Raindrop has stilled thirsty lips, watered dry fields, soothed crying eyes, smoothened aching hearts, cooled heated arguments, sprouted young seeds in the classroom, extinguished fires of hate and ignorance, and participated in the brilliant colors of the **human rainbow**. Then the journey was worthwhile: The journey of my sabbatical. The journey of my life as a little raindrop, which fell from the sky to travel through her Inner and Outer Land-scapes, to die, transform and fly up into the sky as a butterfly. Say HI when you see a peacock-eye-butterfly. It could be me…

The Ambassador emailed that my book should not stop with the last chapter. It seems that I have written my last chapter, tonight. I can always move it back…or invent a new closing chapter. (This is a beautiful section)☺

---

20. See American Constitution

17. Enero

From Rhim cafeteria at Magdalena Playa...

Next chapter...Purpose of a raindrop...Sand-walk...Gooey black spots...Windsurfing on the waves of life...Footprints...All Sickness is Homesickness...

If you wanted to close the chapter of your life you'd never know the content of the **next chapter**. It might be an extremely funny one, and I wouldn't want to miss a good laugh. Do we write our own life-scripts or are they written for us? What is the **purpose of a raindrop** in motion? Is it merely an endless cycle or are we getting somewhere? Light behaves both ways: corpuscular and wavelike. So I guess we are getting somewhere. Teilhard de Chardin's model is coming to my mind: Evolutionstheorie: Circular, spiraling upwards, ever expanding, never ending...I shall take a **walk barefoot** in the sand and cold water of the Atlantic along the playa till my feet get tired.

After coming home from my beach walk I washed my sandy feet in the bidet. Yes, they are useful for that, too! I had already wondered about my pitch-black socks and discovered two **gooey black spots** on either foot sole. I had to rub hard to get it off. In spite of being a Yogini, I can't get my feet up behind my ears[21], not even up to my nose, otherwise I could have told by the smell if it was crude oil or not (From the oil spill?) So far to clean, white sand beaches!

Four **windsurfers** balanced their boards on three-meter-high waves. What were they trying to accomplish: **Riding on the waves of life,** balancing...balancing job, children, old folks, check books, diets; Being thrown off, laid off, told off, written off; being sucked under...by politics, jealous co-workers, ignorant, nearsighted people; trying to get on top of life, top of the class, top of the rat race, top grade, top salary advancement, or simply out of the mud. And during all of these stunts trying to get some fun, satisfaction and excitement out of conquering a wave. Getting up and up again, riding, gliding, losing balance, falling. Never giving up! Playing the game over and over again. One girlfriend was videotaping, but only when he was gliding on top of life. We mostly want to capture the highlights on pictures, but it is the defeats that teach us more: How to get up on the

---

21.   Besides, that's NOT the purpose of Yoga!

surfboard and ride the next wave more elegantly, using the exact momentum of life in motion without resistance and childlike faith.

Watching my **footprints** in the wet sand, asking myself after how many waves they would disappear, I got caught off guard by a long rolling ferocious wave, which swept up my jeans. My footprints were invisible after four waves had smoothened out the sand. We are invisible too, after four waves: Childhood, youth, adult life and Golden Age. Invisible in this world, bodiless. Our spirit goes **home…Home**sick! "**All Sickness is Homesickness**" is the title of a very good book I once read.

From the pink sagging couch...gazing into the night lights of Santander...

Magic word...Gift of love...Grandfather...Kung Fu meditation...Life review...Paradise-if...

I could just store it in my heart, but I don't want to be a pretender, anymore:

PRETENDER

Let down your guards
And send the soldiers
Of your fortification
Home, so that I can see
Your soft and salient soul.

There were two incidents, today that moved me deeply: Around 10 a.m. somebody rang the doorbell. 'To open or not to open' is always the question. The word 'paquete' caught my attention out of a long Spanish sentence. That was the **magic word**, which made me push the button. The mailman brought an over-sized packet, too big for the mailbox, and two letters. I recognized the handwriting of my father-in-law (Opa) on a half-letter-sized envelope, addressed to his son: Prof. Dr. etc. An eighty-three—year old father, in the advanced stages of Alzheimer's, has forged these elegant capital letters. They don't stand as strong and straight anymore as they used to. You can detect the pauses when he gathers strength for the next letter. Sometimes he presses hard not to lose track on the paper. Mother said it took him one hour to complete that envelope. What a **gift of love**! I shall preserve that envelope, because it might very well be the last one...

Around 4 p.m., just when I was having a PrinzMetal spasm[22], an email was forwarded to me by my husband from the first floor to my workplace in the second floor at Santander University, from an old friend of his from Houston, Texas. With great joy he wrote that they had found the Chinese medicine, KUN BOA WAN, for my diffuse menopause symptoms. His wife had checked all the

---

22.   Sudden cramping of the heart arteries

Chinese herb shops in town and none carried it. So they asked a friend in Beijing to get it for me. This colleague, who so deeply cares about other people—and I don't even know him, yet—is a ten-year survivor of liver cancer. I have never heard of anyone who has survived liver cancer for ten years. He says he kept it in check, because his **grandfather** had taught him a special **Kung Fu meditation** when he was little. Just now, he had his second surgery, because the tumor had grown back. Barely recovered from the surgery he already reaches out to other people to help. He has experienced a **life-review**, too. That's when you get a glimpse of the 'other' world and your life rolls by like a movie, and you recognize what is <u>really</u> important in life. I feel deeply moved by his grace, wisdom and compassion. The planet could really be a wonderful place—**a paradise—if** we all learned how to reach out and support each other.

Domingo, 26. Enero

In front of my computer at Santander University...<u>hand</u>writing into my travel script...

Personal travel agent...mischievous...Ambassador of Peace and Understanding...Don't trust computers...Host professors...Universal Thank You's...Co-hosts... Sisterhood...

It is a dreary Sunday, and since there is a holiday[23] tomorrow, St. Thomas of Aquinas, we decided to do some work today, and drive out to the countryside tomorrow. It is a good day to say **Thank You**:

Special Thanks, a hug and a kiss (and other goodies!) go to **my personal travel agent** and companion (traditionally called: husband), Prof. Dr. Hansi, who made it possible with his international scientific relations, for me as a Foreign language teacher, to travel and experience other cultures and languages. On the trip he was my extended memory, my zip drive, when I had forgotten certain localities and expressions. He was my "drive" alright to walk another three miles when my body was about to give up, my driver for the next 200 km, when my spirit flew out the window, and sometimes he drove me sheer nuts with his Hausrat (stuff). But most of the time, we shared all the laughter, joys, pain and memories.

I find it sneakily **mischievous** that the usual acknowledgements do not appear at the beginning of the book. One has to work towards them, like really labor through the text in order to be acknowledged. Once you get <u>here</u>, you really deserve to be recognized, even celebrated as a fan of mine,—or let's put it in more neutral terms—A fan of other cultures and languages, a co-traveler through Inner and Outer Landscapes, an **Ambassador for Peace and Understanding**. You can see that I have a fascination with the word Ambassador, ever since I was a little girl.

A special Thank You and a hug are being sent off to my Superintendent back home, who backed up my travel script[24] on his computer, because I **don't trust**

---

23. Only for the University: What better day could there be to pass out diplomas and doctor titles than to celebrate the great sage Thomas of Aquinas?!
24. Remember: Professional credits for salary advancement...

computers, only people. And sure enough, at one point when I lost it all (Lost it…not only on my blank disc due to the humid climate) he backed me up, so that I could piece it together again. I also thank him for his steady and challenging support in professional matters, since he is retiring now, and wish him the best for the rest (beginning!) of his life!

My heart goes out to our **host professors** and their wives who have built a cozy home away from home for us. I thank them especially for providing a computer workspace for me, answering my 1001 questions, teaching me about language and culture, and nourishing my body and spirit.

Danke to **Guenther** [25] **in Germany!**
Ef caristo to Sokrates and Dionysos in Greece!
Tschoc merci to **Azerbaijan** and Shirkan in Turkey!
Thank you to **Budhi**, Shanti, Siddappa and Narajan in India!
Gracie to **Verdi** and Renato in Italy!
Gracias to **Philipp II** in Spain!

Namaste
—To the Ambassador for nourishing the teacher and writer in me.
—To Wizard for pulling all the strings behind the stage.
—To Divi for his humor and wisdom.
—To my adopted Indian sons, Hemant and Rick, for their driving services and spiritual eye-openers.
—To quiet, observant Ranji to acquaint us with homeopathy.
—To Vijaga to support my Ayurvedic treatments.
—To Bilal, my Egyptian friend in Berlin, and critical analyst of my script.
—To Opa for teaching me about body and spirit and living in the moment.
—To Kobra King for the gift of music.
—To Shanti for the Mt. Abu experience.
—To Siddappa for the healing experience.
—To the Ambassador for the teatimes and his signed novel.
—To Guenther for the espressos and cultural, political chats.
—To Budhi for arranging everything, and sharing spiritual matters.
—To Divi for revealing his warrior nature.
—To Wizard for his cultural eye-opener at the Cricket Club.

---

25.   Primary hosts are underlined.

—To Hemant and Babbarao for getting me places safely with a beautiful smile and gentlemen-like manners.

—To Narajan for clearing up my cultural uncertainties.

—To Scribas for showing us the beauty of the Alps.

—To Shanti for his wonderful grandson.

—To Wolfgang Amadeus, Sigrid, Walter and Annemarie for Gemuetliche Adventszeit (cozy advents time)

—To Sokrates for sacred audiences, Dion, Chalkidike, Tavernas etc.

—To Dionysos for his charming German accent and Pella.

—To Kerim, Zara and Shirkan for all the laughter, jokes and happiness.

—To Bhavin (Rick) for sharing his family life and spiritual matters.

—To Mennem, our favorite house manager, for solving "domestic problems".

—To Dillip, our food manager, who spoiled us with "Kitchen Kontinental".

—To Rajo for his quiet, noble services on the trip to Mt. Abu and in the guest-house of Sadar Patel.

—To my Physio for integrating body, mind and spirit.

—To Philipp II for sharing matters of the Sandwich generation, etc.

To all my **Sisters around the world** who have taught me about womanhood in different cultures:

—To Maria Rojo, the architect, chef cook, and beautiful painter of Alexander The Great.

—To Athena, the Dionysian dinner composer and University teacher.

—To Sigrid, the Dresdner haute couture expert and retired pharmacist.

—To Annemarie, the Ulmer Zuckerbacker im Handumdrehn (Sugar baker in no—time)

—To Madhuri, the Saree expert and Ayurvedic mixer.

—To Chitra, the teacher expert and cultural traveler.

—To Asha for her spiritual revelations.

—To Anita for her lovely dinner.

—To Zara, my Turkish language teacher, fellow-belly dancer and rose garden companion.

—To Evi, the Alzheimer expert and co-hiker.

—To Guenther's wife, Traudel, who helped clean up the mess after the flooding.

—To Sangita, the beautiful mother of Bhavin's son Tilak.

—To Camala, Manisha and her brother, the salva and Indian dinner experts.

—To Oma, the restless caretaker and anchor of a sinking ship.

—To Siddappa's wife for the sacred ceremony and the Ganesha plate.

—To my little sisters (Budhi's daughters) Bryanca and Pranyta for their surprise visit on Diwali.

—To Renate, the Berlin expert and cultural gourmet.

—To Nieves, the administrative expert and soul of the Santander Physics department.

—To my Spanish Carmen for finding this gorgeous apartment, and for sisterly neighborhood.

—To Ana, the daughter of my American Carmen, for her clear and timely lectorship.

Now, YOU can solve the puzzle and match up husbands and wives in order to prove to yourself that you have read the literary travel script attentively.

Maria Rojo, wife of Alexander The Great?

Happy matchmaker!!!

THANK YOU again for having been (or still being) a co-traveler through my Inner and Outer Landscapes! **NAMASTE:** I greet the Godhead in you! I recognize the **ONENESS** and the **SPIRIT** that binds us all together in

PEACE, LOVE, and **HARMONY.**

From my favorite Bahia seat...

Sitting by the window, meditating during the misty morning hours, staring into the milky soup over the Bahia, the Indian temple elephant takes shape in the hazy mist and brings raindrops to my eyes:

TOUCHED BY AN ELEPHANT

Her Majesty—I think it was a She,
Because her trunk was pink
Could stomp me into the ground
And throw me into the air
But ever so gently she touched my hair
And nestled my hand into the end
of her musty trunk.

She let me touch her gray pink skin
And tenderly brushed my Eurindian chin.
It felt like sandpaper and velvet all in one.
A poacher would hunt her down barbarically
And rip out her precious ivory ferociously
While she could pierce his greed to death.

But nonetheless, she would not touch his dignity
Unless her memory cried out in misery
for her diminished family,
You see, Her Majesty, the Elephant,
Is a noble creature
While he, the Poacher displays
Bestialic, animalic features.

potawi

Miercoles, 29. Enero

From the pink, sagging couch...

Flood of Thank you's...Mexican Night...Perro/Pelo...Elections...

Another **flood of Thank** you's emerges, looking out the window into another gray, stormy and rainy Santander day. Prof A. is right: Santander must have more rainy days than England, but when the sun shines here, it is as bright as in Colorado.

CORDIAL THANKS

—To Tante Christine for being a mother, sister and friend, especially since my mother's death in 1987.

—To Elisabeth for the Rheiki treatments and for sharing spiritual matters.

—To Jean Pierre for his refreshing, probing questions. (Yes, Jean Pierre, there was a Lidl in Thessaloniki and there is one in Santander, too)

—To Therese and Gerhard for sharing professional matters.

—To Rosel, Wilhelm, Oliver und Tante Herta for picking us up and dropping us off at Frankfurt Airport which seems to be a 100 times, this year. Especially to Rosel for getting my mind off Alzheimer's every now and then.

—To the Colorado Club for teaming up with us in Dresden.

—To Friedel und Friedoline for their trip to Dresden.

—To our Dresdner Prof Peter and Inge for the dinner reunion.

—To Sigrid for the regular girlfriend reunions in the Bootshaus.

—To the young man at the Acropolis for lifting up my spirits.

—To all the chance encounters that taught me about the national soul.

—To our Thessaloniki house manager, Somna, for sharing her Istanbul-Constantinople-pain.

—To Siddappa's doctor for cementing the Hippocratic Oath into my belief-system.

—To my Ayurvedic sisters for their effective treatments.

—To our Floersheimer house doctor, Fessy, for his insightful and open communication.

—To Schwester Anneliese for looking after the parents.

—To Hannelore for her insights about Alzheimer's and supporting mother.
—To Prof Peng for sending the Chinese medicine from Beijing.

Last Saturday, we **cooked Mexican food** for Philipp II, Prof Ruffy, Prof Pepe and his wife Claire, a French teacher. There we missed a splendid sunny day, but it was all worthwhile: Dieter cooked the best Mexican taco filling ever, because of the freshly ground excellent Spanish beef and his moody combination of spices. Spaniards can't eat that hot, so we kept it on the tangy side. As an appetizer we served Nachos; for the first plato Tacos, as second plato soft tacos with flour tortillas, as third course cheese enchiladas, and for dessert Spanish coffee (Dromedario 50/50[26]) and Black Forest tart from Lidl's. It tasted almost like my homemade. All the Mexican ingredients we got from Courte Inglese. It is hard, though, to obtain English and German reading material. The clientele of the 200.000-inhabitant city of Santander is just not big enough, but we found a few sources of Stern, Spiegel, News Weeks, The Economist, and one bookstore in Corte Inglese that carries English and German books for double the price.

The **Mexican night** was belly-shakingly, muscle-achingly funny, because of all the language jokes Pepe generated himself involuntarily or retold as jokes: A Chinese neighbor who can't produce the Spanish "rrr", and therefore substitutes it with Chinese "LLL" wants to report to the Spanish police that the neighbor's dog is driving him insane with his barking late into the night. Now, **perro** is dog, and **pelo** is hair. What the Chinese neighbor is actually reporting to the police—and I am getting a belly-shaking attack, right now—is that a hair in his a== is bothering him and what he should do about it. The police said: Scratch yourself! That's only one example of this hilarious night. Just watching Ruffy's and Philipp's faces welled up many eruptions of laughter in me.

Now stay with the "LLL" and "rrr" reversal! An American asks a Chinese: Do you also have elections in November? The Chinese answers: No, evely moning! (Don't touch spelling!)

---

26. Which is Philipp II's favorite, because of the darker roast, mine is Dromedario natural

Afternoon 4 p.m.

From my favorite Bahia seat...

**Fontanero...Plumbing problems...Clever Casimiro...
Spanish time...The pulse of a Nation...Churro time...
Spanish health care system...Medical expert...Human
aspect...Security blanket...Competition of curiosity and
fear...Wounded animal...Inadequacy of language...Live!
not talk!...**

I made it up here in 10 minutes, today, from the university to our apartment. That's my athlete, all right. Not too shaggy for an "old" teacher, walking one km steeply uphill. I am waiting for the plumber (**fontanero**). This gorgeous apartment has its little aches and pains. First the kitchen sink wouldn't drain. Then there was a power-outage, because the plug of the combined oven and washing machine connection had burnt through, and now we have discovered the real reason: The decline of the drainage pipes is almost horizontal, instead of 10% downhill. The water from the washing machine is not draining completely, but running down on the plug. As we all know, water and electricity don't mix. Not to mention the poor apartment owner underneath having downy water drip into his cook pot. Would it make the master rooster extra soft? It's an old problem, too, as I discovered water damage lines, lying flat on my belly scanning the cavities with a flashlight. (Thanks, Friedoline! It came in extremely handy!) With my few words of Spanish I probed Casimiro, our house manager, and he confirmed the problemo viaje.

    Communicating plumbing problems is not the easiest topic. We looked up words in the dictionary and pieced it together in writing, but when it comes to speaking, communication goes down the drain. **Clever Casimiro**, however, found a computer science student in portal 1 of our apartment complex who speaks English quite well, because he has studied in Ireland for one year. Ireland is Europe's number one country for computer technology, and has enjoyed an enormous economic upwind.

    I was ten minutes early for the plumbing appointment, of course, and the plumber is still not here at 4:30. Oh well, 4 p.m. **Spanish time**! So just relax, Potawi, and use the time for writing:

Every **nation** has its **pulse**, I discovered. People do things at certain times: When I look out the window at 6 a.m. no lights are on, yet. Spain wakes up, i.e. our neighborhood (Thank you, Wizard!) wakes up between 7 and 8 on workdays. The baker opens at 9 a.m. (in Germany at 6 a.m.). The Spanish rhythm is moved back into the night hours by 2-3 hours. A student wanted to meet with me in the <u>morning</u>. She meant 12 noon, while I was thinking 10 a.m. latest. Between 11 and 12 a.m. it is extremely busy on the streets, because people go grocery shopping almost every day. All the shops are in the vicinity of 200 meters and there is a cafeteria/bar every 20 meters, really. With the shops, underneath the houses in the first floor (Erdgeschoss), Santander is a <u>living</u> city, not like the Frankfurt city center where nobody is actually living. Coffee break is between 11 and 12, lunch break between 2 and 4:30 p.m. when most neighborhood shops are closed. Cafeterias are filling up between 5 and 6 for coffee break and tapas or pinchos (little snacks). Spaniards eat their dinner around 10 p.m., and go to bed around midnight.

Churro time—those are the deep-fried curly "snakes" served with sugar and cinnamon—is Saturday night and Sunday. I heard from Pepe that they have them in Madrid for breakfast Sunday mornings. There is a Churro stand 200 m from our house. Thank God they have only open on Saturdays and Sundays. It is nearly fruitless to want to lose weight here, with the excellent Spanish red wines, the multitude of Spanish cheeses, and the oven warm breads. Manchego is my favorite cheese.

Nutrition and health play an important part in each culture. Recently I got acquainted with the **Spanish healthcare system**, too, as I finally had the guts to make the long overdue appointment at the gynecologist, i.e. Armada M.D. made it for me, since the receptionists did not speak English. I experienced very professional treatment by a well-known senior doctor, and fortunately, his protégée (trainee) Dr. Carmen, a younger doctor, mediated with English. He was the **medical expert**, and Dr. Carmen took care of the warm **human aspect**, which is most important in that vulnerable situation. In the US they would never do a hysteroscopy without local anesthesia (ouch!), but it was my choice of either going to the hospital and have it done there with anesthesia, or pay myself here without—pretty ironic that I paid for my pain—but I did not want to submit myself to "strange" people again. Dr. Carmen was my **security blanket** here, so I stayed, plus I preferably have everything rather done today than tomorrow. It turns out that I need a hysterectomy, because the layer built up to 10mm and doesn't look healthy. So I get to experience Spanish hospitals for three days any time soon. You see my **fear and curiosity** are competing with each other here. It is not exactly what I had dreamt of in Spain, and I am deadly afraid, too, because of the rudimentary language skills, but somehow my deep faith in the goodness of mankind and a Higher Power will carry me through.

I sound pretty faithful now, but you should have seen me after the hysteroscopy walking up the 500 steps of the stairs to our apartment. Of course, my Prof would have picked me up with the car if I had called and he had known, but shocks like that I need to **digest in solitude**. I am very peculiar about that, like a **wounded animal** retreating into the underbrush. Sometimes, I hold in overwhelming experiences for a long time before I am ready to share. And sometimes, they just stay inside and are never shared; sacred experiences for which I have no words to describe accurately, and nobody would understand anyhow. Because of the **inadequacy of the language** they would come out so ridiculously diminished and stripped down to the bare bones that all the essence and awe would get lost. So I keep the treasure in my heart.

<Yes, the plumber is working now and Casimiro joined him, too (5:30). He is drilling the walls open and I see myself cleaning into the night. >

Language covers only a small part of the experience. The emotional body carries all the joys, pains and memories. Therefore we must **live life, not talk** about it. If the plumber (fontanero) hadn't come so late I probably never would have written this chapter. So you see, the outer and inner "plumbing problems" are related, somehow.

Sabado, 1. Febrero

From my favorite Bahia seat...

Mexican Night out...Served Spanish style...Baby pig roast...Master driver...Spanish neighbors...Language toddlers...Imperfectionism...

The sun seems to claim dominion today over the Bahia but a thin layer of clouds is cutting off the tips of the snow-covered Cantabria Mountains. The thermometer fell down to 2^0C, last night on our way to the **Mexican restaurant** *ANTONIO* where Professor Ruffy had reserved a table for eight. When we arrived at ten to ten there was still ample space, but the restaurant filled up rapidly at 10 p.m. In Germany, late at this time, they would have already 'rolled up the pedestrian sidewalk' as the saying goes. (Buergersteig hochklappen) It is interesting to watch how your 'home' culture is served in another country. The food tasted very authentic, but was **served in Spanish style**: Bigger parties love 'raciones', small portions of the same item on a big platter, one for each person. They brought out seven plates in sequence: Tostadas, flour tortillas, corn tortillas with mild and spicy chicken fillings, enchiladas, refried beans—the healthy kind with no lard—rice, chilly rellenos and fajitas. The fajitas were filled with—or rather we filled them with **baby pig roast** pieces, so crunchy and tender, I had never tasted before. At one point, Philipp II and I were desperately waiting for another beer mug to extinguish the burning chilly-relleno fire in our gourmet organ before we could continue the meal.

Our mixed group of Profs, Ph.D.-students, MD and a teacher, laughed and dined for 2 and 1/2 hours straight. At 12:30 a.m. Dieter said: "I can't believe that I am still awake." The meal was topped off with one round of Kaluah[27] with an equal amount of whipped cream on top. (Like the Austrian Schlagobers) And since it tasted so good, young Professor Ruffy, who could be our son, ordered a second round. Before 1 a.m. we departed the Spanish way with a kiss on both cheeks and lots of happy 'noise' in the street in front of the restaurant.[28] **Master driver** Philipp II and Armada who can fit his car into the tiniest parking space,

---

27. Mexican coffee liquor
28. Carmen, Dieter IS being conditioned for our Puerto Rican daughter-in-law!

took us home to our apartment, which is only 50 meters away from theirs. It is a balmy feeling having Spanish neighbors and friends like them.

All the people we deal with here, be it Casimiro, the repairmen, the landlady, the grocery shop owners or the people at the university, are all very patient, helpful and witty. They observe and praise the stumbling Spanish efforts of us little "language-toddlers", setting foot before foot, marching out into this world, stumbling, getting up and trying over and over again. Yesterday, I shouted across the atrium to the administrative ladies in the glass booth "Feliz fin de semana", not noticing that there was a whole row of students sitting on benches, breaking out in laughter. Ruffy said it's normally "Buen fin de semana", and when it was 'feliz' you had an extremely satisfying date over the weekend. One can make a lot of people happy with **imperfectionism!**

Around 4 p.m.

From Café del Mercado at Carrefour's...

**Rebaja...Ode to my three sons...Different gifts...
Alexander...Sven Markus...Manuel...In their own time...
Major Motivation...Trilingual...
Secure and firm boundaries...Full time energy into child
rearing...Full womanhood...Coming from the Light...
Prenatal submarine...Myth of Super Mom...Number One
priority...Continuing Education...**

We are shopping at Carrefour's, today, mainly because they have a variety of olives in barrels, and since we experienced Greece, we are very particular about olives. Many **rebaja tables** attract shoppers with their low prices. I bought two non-matching wine glasses for 55 cents each, because I really prefer wine out of a wine glass instead of a water glass.

I decided to write an **ODE TO MY THREE SONS**, this afternoon, which will end in an educational conclusion. I should write "our" sons but I will continue with "my", to establish an intermediate, direct connection, and not having to speak for both of us. Besides, mothers have this special intuitive relation with their sons that fathers often have with their daughters or granddaughters.

Continued at home

Although physically very much alike—tall, slender, muscular and good-looking (of course that's in the eye of the beholder!)—my three sons have very **different gifts**, which were observable at an early age:

Alexander (33), the oldest, took every toy apart, always needed to get inside of a machine, got up at 5 a.m. on major trash collection days to pick up old bicycles from the Sperrmuell (junk garbage). With the old parts he built 'new' bicycles and sold them for a few bucks.

Sven Markus (32), cried for Jimmy, the ladybug, who had lost a wing and wanted to repair it. When his Tiger cat got run over on S. Mill Ave in Tempe, Arizona, and was lying on the street, his beautiful head separated from his agile body, he wanted to sew him together, again.

Manuel (22), reached out to people wherever we went. As a baby I carried him around in a belly strap. Especially older people made contact with him and told us their stories. When we came into a dead quiet waiting room in a Doctor's office people were starting to warm up within five minutes talking to him and to each other. His nickname 'Manny' sounds exactly like money, and as a little kid he already loved the feel and smell of bills.

Alexander is in charge of Kiowa and Blackhawk maintenance at Ft. Drum, today, and finishing up his B.S. in Liberal Studies.

Sven Markus is training as a doctor with the Air force in Bethesda, Maryland, and little **Manuel** is a 'banker' in Ft. Collins, taking evening classes in business and management. Older, 'difficult' clients line up at Manuel's counter to wait patiently for him although the other lines are shorter.

None of the boys chose the traditional way of studying. They all woke up **in their own time**, realizing that a degree would be useful and necessary for building a comfortable life for their families. Sometimes I wonder how **Mark** does it, raising three sons and passing his medical exams as head of the class. Every graduation I went to, he was honored by his superiors. He is the 'studiosus' (Lat.) while **Alex** learns things best hands-on. A philosophy-ethics course is a major challenge in abstraction for him, yet he maintains a 3.9 GPA. He can take turbines apart and build them together, and get into the inside of any broken machine and fix it. He is Mr. Fixit, all right, and he has a great sense for organization and logistics, too. **Manu** is the community leader. When he goes out and does a fundraiser, people open their pockets. Neighbors love to come over for his garage sales, because it is so much fun to wheel and deal with him.

A **major motivation** in the educational progression of all three boys have been their wives, either by giving them a kick in the butt, or by holding their backs free to study. (Ruecken freihalten). All three of my daughter-in-laws, Frauke, Laurie and Vange, have degrees and come from different cultural backgrounds: German, American Hispanic and American Puerto Rican. All grandkids have a chance to be brought up bilingual or even trilingual, an invaluable gift for life. With English, Spanish and German you can 'conquer' the whole, wild world.

All three boys had very different mothers to raise them: For Alex I was the young, inexperienced mother. Although I was 22 they wouldn't sell me beer in Utah to my husband's amusement, not even with 28. Me, having been influenced by the antiauthoritarian movement, this strong-willed little son of mine didn't feel enough **secure and firm boundaries**. When his brother Sven was born one year later, he rejected his competition and wanted mom all for himself. His babying: being held and carried around, was cut short with his brother's arrival, which manifested as a constant rivalry between the brothers. By then I had learned boundary setting, and that little kids are most happy and safe with a set of familiar rules.

However, with two little, energetic guys, often giving me sleepless nights and a teaching job, I was overwhelmed although we had a nanny in the morning. So I quit my job to devote my **full-time energy** to their upbringing while 'reforming' the world around me, drawing Early Childhood Music Education to my village, adult education, neighborhood help organization, mother-children's groups, baby gym, etc. When Manuel was born, ten years later, I had already come into my full womanhood and experienced a few spiritual encounters, so I named him **'The One coming from the Light'**, after the Russian name 'Krishan' had been rejected by Grandma. I wanted to have her some fun, too, calling the little rascal. He got his intensive cuddling from all the members of the family, and I could already observe the fatherly qualities in my big boys, diapering, feeding and playing with their little baby brother. (And torturing him, too, as Manuel says, quite common among brothers)

When I went **back to school** at 39 to get my MA degree, my boys were my biggest fans and strongest supporters. They always made birthdays and mother days special for me. I remember one birthday especially, when they sent me to bed early. I took my study materials to bed while they roamed around in the kitchen 'till midnight. The three of them had baked the best bund-cake ever. Because they had forgotten the baking powder, and the oven setting was too low also, the cake stayed moist and chewy.

Guys, your little **prenatal submarine** is going to be removed, next week. My little blue planet[29] is as blue as I am. I shall be content, however, because it has carried, rocked and nourished you into three strong, healthy, loving and compassionate young men, husbands and fathers. Love MOM!

The educational conclusion is that kids will develop according to their own time schedule if properly watered and nourished. And another conclusion for all of you who believe in the **myth of Super Mom** is: A woman can do it all, just not at the same time. She has to set priorities, and children should always be her number one priority as a life-giver and preserver of the big blue planet. And a third conclusion is that most parents do their best what they believe to be right at their stage of development. Since the School of Life is a **continuous educational process**, both parent and children have the obligation to develop themselves.

Just in case:

> Manu, Sunny, please finish what I began:
> 200 house copies: to family, friends and all the people mentioned in the "book"
> Binding: royal blue with gold back or safari tiger style or white lacquer with cut out peace dove (see art folder) and velvet azure back, or any design you and Vange will come up with. I know you'll hit exactly Mom's taste!
> Part one opens with rainbow, part 3 and 4 are in revision with Ana in Chicago.
> Bilal is the critical analyst in culturally sensitive matters.
> Thanks, Love MOM (The One who comes from the Light will go into the Light, some day. Until we meet again…)

---

29.   It really looked like that on the ultra sound,

Martes, 4. Febrero

From my favorite Bahia seat...

Universal health insurance...Dentista...Can only happen in Spain...Inner landscapes: rain, rain, rain...Small "c" culture...Emotional capacity of understanding...

Another rainy, foggy day in Santander, Spain. There should be **universal health insurance** around the world that no matter where you go to, you get decent treatment for a reasonable cost. This is our 4th health insurance package since we left the USA, and every time there are exceptions, so-called preexisting conditions, and you end up paying yourself. This is going to be a very expensive sabbatical if we end up paying ourselves for the hysterectomy.

I went to the dentist, this morning, after I finally had dared to make an appointment, yesterday. The receptionist didn't speak a word of English, but conveyed with her warm and friendly body language that we would get it all together. I said something like: "Deseo peder cita con **dentista**", and she wanted to book me in next week. I said that I would have an "operación" soon, then she said: "Mañana, once hora!" So today at 11:00, I had to wait for 20 minutes, 'till it was my turn. The young Argentinean female dentist spoke English quite well. Very skillfully she did an X-ray and an amalgam filling where the crunchy Campesino bread had broken down the previous one. The praxis was modern, state of the art equipment, right across the street from our apartment, and the price was reasonable: 35 €. US HEALTH CARE COST IS # 1 in the world, followed by Switzerland and Germany. When we were tourists in Denmark my husband was treated for free in the hospital.

Today, we have to find out how much the health insurance pays, if at all, and start the preoperative, mandatory check-ups. Tonight at 9 p.m. (That **can only happen in Spain**) I'll have my **EKG**, and the following morning I have to go to another location to have the blood work done. Meanwhile I have to figure out the consent form in Spanish with the help of Armada MD. When all three forms are signed I have to go back to my surgeon, and they will call in for a hospital bed. It's a very modern hospital, I heard, on the route to Bilbao.

My inner landscape looks just like the Santander weather. Having to figure out all the different locations, dealing with a different set of people in Spanish, trying to understand the different cultural mechanisms tires me out, and I just want to go home. But it really wouldn't do justice to all these nice people who try their best to make me feel at home. It's just that you get frustrated as a foreigner, because you don't know the rules of the game. This is what is known as the **small "c" culture**, the inside workings of a society. Imagine how insecure and frightened our Mexican kids must be during their first year in Colorado. No wonder that they stick to each other like glue during lunch break. It is like the Alzheimer's experience: Unless you really have to go through a situation yourself, you are lacking the **emotional capacity of understanding** the problem. You might grasp it intellectually, but that is only part of it.

Miércoles, 5. Febrero

From my bed looking into the night lights of Santander...

Second opinion...Art show...60 % non-verbal...Experts all around the world...Ready to leave?...Gift of Life...Surgeon General...

I am glad things don't move along as rapidly as it looked like in the beginning. That gives me adequate time to be prepared internally. Dieter always likes to build Rome in one day. (German saying) Preferably he has everything done, yesterday, that's why he is flooded as a referee for physics publications, and because of his competence and fair, independent decisions, of course. Armada MD wants to take us along, tomorrow night, to her gyno out there in the countryside to get **a second opinion** and to choose the procedures for how the operation should be done. There is a menu to choose from, just like at Mc Donald's: With eggs or without, sunny side up or through the tunnel (drive-through), with lots of ketchup (conventional cut), or mayonnaise, super-sized (everything out) or regular (just the prenatal submarine).

The heart specialist, Dr. Peña, was a very caring and warm person. I could even initiate a minimal conversation about his surgeon friend, Dr. Millxxx, and about the original art work hanging in his office. He pulled out a brochure to show me who the artist was: Julio de Pablo *Mi Bahia*, a local artist from 1914-1978. I felt right at home in his office with an **art show** all around me. He had a good rapport with my husband, too, who can speak a bit more than I. I am really sure now that **60%** of the communication is done **non-verbally** in situational conversations, not in theoretical ones, though. He spoke with his eyes, his hands and the timbre of his voice. One can feel if somebody's heart is open or closed. He was about my age and the warm fatherly type a woman feels safe with in stressful situations. My EKG was fine. PrinzMetal would not show up with this kind of routine exam. He made a note though for Dr. Millxxx.

At the Diagnostic Center, this morning, I was very impressed with the skillful medical assistant who drew my blood with a baby syringe. My veins are not easy to find and not very thick. In former times many assistants had a hard time drawing the red juice, and some gave up to let the doctor finish it. With an observing eye and a gliding touch of her finger, she found a spot where nobody had inserted a needle before. And she chose her needle carefully among three sizes. There are **experts all around the world** in every country.

Have you ever thought about whether you were **ready to leave** this planet if you were called off your post? Ready in your heart to go towards the Light? Maybe they give you a review and send you back. At this point I am at peace like an old Native American Indian: "It's a good day to die", and then they went up to their mountain or out into the desert. Don't get me wrong: I love life with its mountains and valleys, the sunrises and the sunsets, all the love I receive, all the love I am capable of giving. It was a beautiful life, it <u>is</u> a beautiful life, and I am grateful for the **gift of life**. I would not leave it in desperation, only in aspiration of a higher task.

It's a beautiful planet, but it is in a lot of pain, just like my little blue planet. I am afraid the Big Blue Planet has to undergo surgery, too, in order to heal. Those cuts will be painful for many people, but restorative for the womb of mankind as a whole. When the **Surgeon General** calls I will follow.

Viernes, 7. Febrero

From my favorite Bahia seat...

Protective cocoon...Torrelavega...Misplaced...Warmth and expertise...Human touch...Against HRT[30]...Go, tell your President...Hippocratic oath...More angels than crooks...

It is a beautiful, sunny day over the Bahia, but I don't feel the drive yet to go out into the world. Every time my little Blue Planet is invaded, I feel the need to stay within the **protective cocoon** of my home away from home.

Yesterday, Armada MD drove us out into the countryside to get a second opinion. About 9 km outside of Santander we passed the modern Mombia Clinic (hospital), driving another 30 km or so, until we reached the second largest city of Cantabria: **Torrelavega** (The tower to Vega). The sulfuric stink of the Chemical plant Solveigh hung in the air.

The waiting room of the famous doctor, a colleague of Armada MD, was full of women. "I feel misplaced", said my husband jokingly, and fortunately five minutes later another Marsian[31] entity entered the oxygen-deprived room. The waiting room emptied relatively fast, since many women waited only for their "resultada", while "consultadas" took a lot longer. The waiting time went by swiftly since we were talking with Armada about our experiences in the Spanish culture and listening to her insightful explanations.

When we entered the doctor's office I felt surrounded by **warmth and expertise**. I watched him inquire Armada step by step about the previous happenings, until he got a clear picture of the situation. He tried to cheer me up with a joke as I laid on the examination table—this one had comfortable stirrups, not the cold chromium ones where your legs dangle in the air—but it really didn't feel funny up there at all. While Armada was by my side the doctor frequently reached out to me with a **human touch** to reassure me that everything would be OK. At first, Dieter didn't dare come into the examination room—it would make him too upset, he said—until I urged him to see the polyp, on the monitor, which was causing me all the trouble.

---

30.   Hormone Replacement Therapy
31.   Title of a book: *Men are from Mars, Women are from Venus*

Imbedded in a family community I felt a lot less pain than with the first doctor. Dr. Gomez proceeded logically by taking out a specimen of the tissue to send it to the lab for examination. The other doctor missed doing that, while I had anticipated that step. During the consultation Dr. Carmen said that I must have misunderstood something. It all didn't make sense anymore and we lost trust. Trust, however, is a necessary ingredient for healing. Depending on the lab results Dr. Gomez will proceed with a corresponding operation. He is not the kind of surgeon who will take out everything automatically, only the inflicted parts. He is also **against HRT**. "Me, too", I said, "What good is a stress hormone (Premerin), extracted from the urine of a pregnant mare, for a woman's body, anyhow?!" In America a doctor took 50 minutes of her precious time to try to convince me to take Premerin for the rest of my life. There is money to be made with the Pharma industry, that's why.

While helping me down the table with my legs slightly shaking from the invasive procedure (hysteroscopy) Dr. Gomez said to us: "**Tell your President** to go out for coffee with his wife and not to lead us into another war. Nobody wins in a war." At last he squeezed a smile out of me when he said Good Bye with the charming Spanish phrase: "Renata encantada!"

His office manager took <u>one</u> health insurance check, instead of three, <u>after</u> the procedure and not during, like this other guy who took € 100 on top of it for not sending in the specimen to the lab and making me feel like an idiot. In every culture there are doctors who take the **Hippocratic oath** seriously, and others who look after the money first. It is getting harder and harder to find the first kind.

While we are trying to meander our way through the Spanish health care system, we are getting heart-melting emails from my Dr. Son and from a son of an old friend who is a gynecologist himself to support our decision with sound medical advice. Right beside me, a student working on a geological graph on the computer brought me an art book about Julio de Pablo. You see there are **more angels than crooks** in this world.

Same day, 7. Febrero

From my bed, enjoying the night lights of Santander...

Heart drive...Culturally offensive...Authentic...Cultural biases...Be my Educator...Co-traveler...

What is a writer to do on a Friday night when her husband is snoring on the pink, sagging couch? Write, of course...it is good that he sleep, though. He worries too much about me. I am starting my Spanish spiral and another closing chapter has condensed in my mind. It is like on the computer: We are constantly closing old files and opening new ones. Some precious files we store on our **heart drive**; they can never be erased. That's the advantage of a "human machine".

Dear Reader:

> One friend has advised me to take out all the aches and pains. Well, as I told you: I am not a pretender, anymore. The times of super woman are over. It was a myth. Another friend advised me to take out the "Stolen clothing chapter", because it could be **culturally offensive**. Well, then we would miss the chance to see that things were put right. Besides, then I would have to take out all the negative experiences in each culture. No culture has <u>only</u> gold to offer and my experiences wouldn't be **authentic**, anymore. I might as well send you to the bookstore to get a neutral travel guide.

> So I leave it all in, the good and the bad, in health and in sickness, and hand it over to my intelligent, critical, benevolent readers to make their own discernments, to form their own opinions, to detect the **cultural biases** of the author, and make her aware of it through emails: <u>renaterainbow@web.de</u>, **or: renaterainbow@earthlink.net**

> **Be my educator!** Thank you for having been a host, co-host, **co-traveler** through Outer and Inner Landscapes. Aren't we all in this world?!

At Corte Inglese…Bar de la Plaza Café…

Saturday treat…Guacamole…Listen to the pulse of the ocean…

My poor little Blue Planet is crying. Since that invasion had to be done twice, because of that first moron doctor, I can't walk much. So I am sitting here, watching people and having some churros and café con leche. My husband is shopping at Hipercor. That's not a punishment, that's a **Saturday treat**. I was looking for a ropa del baño earlier, because I might need one in the hospital. They take up a lot of space and I try to avoid it. But if I really need one, I know the location now, the color, the size and the price for my husband to pick it up. Right beside me is a Sureste Asiatico exhibition that makes me a little homesick for India. Maybe we can get that special chilly paste, and then we'll be able to cook that gourmet soup with a yogurt base.

After the Torrelavega outing we had Philipp II and Armada over for **guacamole**, oven-warm pane and red wine. Campo de Viejo is a fine table wine. Philipp II enjoys all kinds of exotic tastes, and one doesn't really need to cook a five-course meal to enjoy the evening with friends. I felt shaky after the invasion of the scalpel, but friends always make you laugh and forget about your aches and pains. When they left around 11:30, however, I collapsed on the pink, sagging couch.

It is a beautiful Saturday, today, and I hope to be able to take the bus from our house down to the Playa later. Then my little prenatal submarine can communicate with the sea and **listen to the pulse of the ocean**. That will be good for her.

Same day, 8. Febrero

From my bed...Recovering...

Mi Bahia...Message of the Sea...Mi Bahia encantada...

In the afternoon I felt strong enough to walk down to Magdalena peninsula, but we had to take the bus back. While Dieter was listening to the Spanish pipe sack players who were practicing in the park, I sat quietly on a bench by the branding sea. *"Mi Bahia"*! I can identify with Julio de Pablo's love for this piece of land on earth: The roaring basses of the incoming rolling waves, then the hissing flageo-lets[32] overtones when they brake against the rocks; Little sailboats dancing on the turquoise waves, seagulls sailing motionless in the upwind, lamenting notes of bag pipes mixed with children's laughter, and then the **message of the sea** comes through: Feel the hole; fill the hole! Feel the hole; fill the hole! Emotion-action, emotion-action, like a rolling wave.

Message to my little Blue Planet

Feel the hole, fill the hole:
Feel the loss, fill it with hope!
Feel the sadness, fill it with joy!
Feel the pain, fill it with healing thoughts!
Feel the darkness, fill it with Light!
Dance like a sailboat,
Sail like a seagull,
Laugh like a kid,
Soar like an eagle!
Mi Bahía encantada!
Forever yours, Renata!

---

32.   French expression used in music when jumping octaves.

Domingo, 9. Febrero, 1 a.m.

From the pink, sagging couch...

Eternal song...Live and love life...

I love those quiet night hours when the soul has no distractions but to listen to her own eternal song. My wedding anniversary is just around the corner, so it is a good time to take inventory:

Potawi's Zwischenbilanz[33]
I am glad I did...

I am glad I nourished my **marriage** for 33 years through "thick and thin"! (Ger. saying)

I am happy I raised three creative, compassionate **sons!**

I am satisfied that I put most of my energy into my **family!**

I am glad I had **mentors** along the way who taught me about life!

I am proud I had a **mother** who carried me to terms, although she was deserted at that time.

I am glad I had a happy **childhood!**

I am grateful that I received a good **education!**

I am proud I went back to school to get my **Masters!**

I am glad my students taught me the art of **teaching!**

I am glad I had the opportunity to **raft** the Colorado River through the Grand Canyon!

I am thrilled I **skied** the Colorado Mountains with my Baby son!

I am glad I get much comfort out of **art, music and writing**!

I am glad my husband took me to the **land of my Forefathers** and through half of the **world!**

I am glad I had **friends and angels** along the way!

I am glad I did **live and love life!**

I just got the message that the father of Philipp II died on Sunday, Feb. 9. So we are all driving out to Cabezón de la Sal, this afternoon, lunes 10. Febrero.

---

33.   In-between checks and balances

Martes, 11. Febrero

From my favorite Bahia seat…

Night lights…Funeral…Village of Cabezon de la Sal…Old Church…Cemetery…Spanish burial…Northern Spaniards…Vigil… Separates and Unites…Tolerance…

There is something comforting about **night-lights**: The feeling of being imbedded in a living organism. Although you don't know these creatures behind their blue TV-tinted windows, their basic human emotions are the same, and it is very likely that you wouldn't be alone in this world if you needed help, on a godforsaken, lonely highway in America for example, or out there in the woods or the desert if you got lost. The ships, entering the narrow water way into the Bahia, follow the beacon of the light tower and the lights of the Lotsen[34] boats every night, night after night. They just follow the Light. They trust in the Light. They are guided by the Light. Our daily physical life is one whole metaphor for the spiritual life, if one is able to see the analogies.

Philipp II wanted to take us out to his village for a happy occasion, but things developed differently: Yesterday, around 4 p.m., the whole department left in private cars of four to five people each to Cabazon de la Sal for Philipp's father's funeral. It is a great privilege when one has the opportunity to participate in baptisms, birthdays, holidays, weddings, funerals, and other festive ceremonies in another culture, because one experiences a great deal about the soul of a nation.

Leaving the coastal area behind us, we drove south up into the High country and reached **Cabezon de la Sal** twenty minutes before five. The Romans harvested salt here in the "Big-Head"—salt mine some 2000 years ago. Cabezon means head of the valley, little hill, and is also an old Roman measurement unit for measuring salt. We parked in front of the church at a side entrance, right in the center of the 8000-inhabitant village. Spaniards lovingly call their hometown **village**, even if it has half a million inhabitants, but this community met the criteria of a village. Right opposite the church was the house of Philipp II's father. It reminded me of houses in Amsterdam, in red and white, six floors high and narrow with lots of bay windows. A huge wreath appeared in the wide open house

---

34. Lotse (Ger.)=guide

door and was carried to the funeral limousine parked by the front entrance of the church.

Since we were early I took a peek into the **old church**, dating back from the 1800's with its mighty walls and moist mildew scent of myrrh. The altar was beautifully ornamented, all coated in gold, and stood in rich contrast to the barren, clear-lined pseudo-Romanic structure. Mourners were gathering around the church in little groups. When the death bell[35] rang in its monotone, arrhythmic, skimpy sound like a fading soul, all visitors entered the sacred halls, which filled up completely, including the side wings by the side altars. The closed coffin was standing in the main hallway, in front of the altar. I got separated from my husband, since he didn't want to squeeze himself by two old ladies who didn't want to scoot up. I missed his warmth and comfort right beside me, until everybody reached out to shake hands right before the communion. The mass was read in Spanish, but certain phrases reminded me a lot of the old Latin mass, because of the common Romanic roots. The priest addressed the family to give comfort—the old family priest was on business in Madrid—and I wished I would have understood the whole sermon. After the mass the family did not line up in the back of the church like in Germany, but went outside to accompany the coffin to the limousine.

About half of the churchgoers drove out to the **cemetery**, which was situated outside the village on a hilly green pasture. Surrounded by a white wall, it also had mighty walls inside with engraved templates of the deceased. While most graves are one by twos in the ground in Germany, Spaniards cement the coffins into the wall, i.e. Spaniards with Roman Catholic background in Northern Spain. After the short ceremony in the cemetery—and I did not observe all of it since we arrived fairly late as non-locals—the mourners expressed their condolences to the family of Philipp II: "¡Lo siente mucho!" "¡Te doy el pésame!" "¡Mis condolencias!" "¡Te doy mis condolencias por la muerte Señor so and so!"

Since we had already hugged Philipp II and Armada in front of the church we did not line up a second time. **Northern Spaniards** are very proud and private people. They mourn quietly inside while in other cultures, or even in parts of Spain where Islam is prevalent, pain is expressed openly through loud lamenting. I felt the pain of Armada and Philipp II in my heart when I held them in my arms. They had spent a lot of time by their father's bed; weekend after weekend, and during the weeks in the hospital. They were looking forward to a "free"

---

35.   Totengloeckchen (Ger.)

weekend as a couple, since his brother came up from Madrid to take care of father.

Now, they were standing guard one last time from Saturday till Monday afternoon. As in many cultures families congregate around the deceased or hold **vigils** all through the night 'till the coffin is closed. Since many souls hang around in disorientation after the separation from their bodies, they find comfort in having their family around. As a young nursing student I always felt the presence of the wandering and wondering soul when we had a death at the station. The vigil or family gatherings also give the ones left behind a chance to connect and to say Good Bye.

At the cemetery we met our landlady who is also from Philipp's village. "It's a strange place to meet, but I am happy to see you", she said in Spanish. I can see now where Philipp's roots come from: Solid like the old church rocks, his love for the mountains, his grounded ness, sensitivity and appreciation for a strong family.

Death **separates and unites** at the same time: It separates the soul from the body, while the first unites with the Light. It separates a father from his son, while he unites with his intimate family and his village family in the spirit of his father. The soul reunites with the spirit of the Father, also. The separation is a short, transitional stage for the eternal soul whose home is certainly not the decaying body of the material world. Cemeteries are great places to be reminded of our short earthly appointments and that our main focus is elsewhere.

Maybe I should study theology, but I don't like dogmas. I believe what I have experienced, and you believe what you have experienced. And if it's congruent we'll be happy like little kids on Christmas. Meanwhile we'll respect each other's "strange" experiences, because nobody knows for sure. India is a great place to learn what **tolerance** is all about.

Finger Meditation

The artist cannot separate herself from her artwork.
Part of her essence went into it.
The writer cannot read his own virgin script objectively,
because he created the storyline.
The musician cannot separate himself from his composition.
The song of his soul is in the music.
The researcher cannot separate himself from his experiment.
His ideas of the set-up and his expectations are contained in the experiment.
The maker cannot separate herself from her creation.
Part of her own essence has gone into her creation.
Since his creations are living organisms,
he gets feedback and impulses for further development.
The Creator "feeds off" his Creation.
The Creator has co-creators, like fingers on the hand.
They cannot move without him (the hand),
but only with him and through him.
So nothing really bad can happen,
because we are (on) in the hands of the Creator
who cares about her creation, who loves his creation.

potawi

Viernes, 14. Febrero, St. Valentine

From my favorite Bahia seat...

Happy Valentine's...Fear versus logic and compassion...50% unnecessary...Soft invasions... Iraq...Dependency on oil...Polyp removal...Ring of Nations...Fulbright exchanges for Presidents...Preventive war medicine...ALL suffer...

Happy Valentine's Day to all of you around the world who celebrate it! Armada said every two weeks they have a native English speaker in class, and he told them about British traditions, today. It is just as commercial as in the USA. After Mother's Day it is the second cash-ringing business day for flower and candy shops. Valentine's arrow hasn't quite reached Spain, yet. It is mildly celebrated here.

A load fell off my shoulders today as I got the lab report. Philipp II brought it to my work place. I skimmed it, and with the combined language skills of Latin and French I found nothing suspicious. Coming home from the University, I asked Armada MD to look it over. She said it was OK. The first doctor wanted to take out everything and operate on the basis of **fear**. The second doctor in Torre-lavega will only take out the polyp. He operates with **logic and compassion**. I have recently read in *Stern* that over **50%** of all hysterectomies are totally **unnecessary**, not to mention what that does to a woman's psyche and hormonal system. And after a hysterectomy it ain't over, yet. Women from the Colorado Club had bladder problems after the uterus removal, because there was no support anymore.

Soft invasions are always better than radical ones, in regard to **Iraq**, too: Only remove the part, which causes trouble, and don't destroy the people and the country. Just like a Totaloperation (Ger.) will affect a woman's body, the destruction of one country will affect the whole world. It is already visible in the stock market. As a world leader, America should take creative, unusual steps: Pooling all the scientific forces together to create a different energy source, and to get away from the **dependency on oil.** Imagine all that defense money flowing into research and education. The defense money is already draining the education budget for the universities and public school system. I would agree with putting Iraq under UNO command just like in Bosnia, after the **polyp removal** (Saddam

Hussein), until it has recovered and built up solid democratic structures. (Like Germany after WWII) The wo/man on the street has no desire for another war. Demonstrations against the war are planned all around Spain tomorrow, Sábado at noon. Maybe we should let our world leaders fight it out in the ring. **The ring of nations**! What a hopeful Olympic sign! We are still not there, on a private level, yes, but not in politics.

Once you get to know and love people from other cultures around the world—even if you don't understand some of their societal conventions—it is unthinkable to ever war against them. Here is an idea: **Fulbright exchange for presidents**! The prerequisite for becoming a president should be that they must spend their civil service years getting to know other cultures, and walking the soil of a nation barefoot. Once you are touched by an elephant you will never be able to shoot her. You will suffer with her if anything happens to her. I call that preventive war medicine. I don't see that the Age of Enlightenment is upon us these days. We <u>must</u> jump the hurdle together into a peaceful world order or we'll **ALL suffer** the consequences.

Domingo, 16. Febrero

From the pink couch…

Sacred Sundays…Novales…Outing in the countryside…Lemon plantation…Indianos…Colonial style…Spanish lunch ritual…Vino blanco…Lottery house…Gift of love…Kiwis1x4…Cocido Montañes…La vaca que rie…Mutter Schnee…Dessert with champagne…Different beat…Colonial cupboard…Family life…

Sacred Sunday mornings! I love the solemn feeling, the sound of the church bells far away, the weekend sailing regattas on the Bahia. The ebb is extremely low, today and it is almost noon. There was a full moon, last night when we stepped out of our friends' house in the countryside.

Yesterday, Sábado, we spent most of the day out in **Novales**, a village nestled in the hilly countryside, still untouched by tourism, while the nearby Comillas is frequented because of its gothic sightseeing attractions. Since the family doesn't mind[36] me using their real names I will proceed in doing so. Around noon, Nieves, an administrative assistant at the university, the "espíritu" of the department as I call her, Adolfo, her husband, and their son Alejandro, a 14-year-old basketball player, picked us up in their spacious VW combi for an all-day **outing in the countryside**.

Novales is situated in-between the two well-known tourist towns of Santillana and Comillas. The family had built a house there eleven years ago when they won the lottery. Although the weather was triste[37] and lousy cold all day, wet-cold, the kind of cold that creeps up your sleeves, the family atmosphere, the hearty food and the open fireplaces warmed us up. The earthy-assy smell of country air lay upon the village as we received a tour through a **lemon plantation** by their friends Loli and Carlos. Situated idyllically along a creek, the estate with the 80-year-old lemon trees had been attended to for three generations. A baby lemon tree, about one meter high, is five years old. It takes the love and nourishment of

---

36.   Usually I don't tell them, but somehow they got wind…
37.   French: sad, used in Ger. also for gray in gray (Spanish for sad as well)☺

several generations 'till a tree can come to full fruition. Carlos takes care of the plantation all by himself. Loli's and Carlos' daughter, Patricia, also a high school German and English teacher, said that her great grandfather, like many Spaniards from that time when Spain was very poor due to their loss of the colonies, went overseas to make money. He operated a splendid maritime department store in a tourist town in Cuba. Those Spaniards, coming back from South America to the village, were called **Indianos**. I remember that there were lots of Spanish guest workers in Germany around 1960, in the so-called economic wonderland, under chancellor Konrad Adenauer and economic minister Ludwig Erhard. These guest workers also live in Novales, nowadays. Spaniards, like the Greek always return home. With their accumulated money they built **Colonial style** houses around 1900 in Novales. While the main house is lovingly maintained in its original style by the family, two side houses were sold off, and one ruin might be rebuilt some day.

Colonial style houses have a rustic feel with mighty beams inside, open fireplaces, a Spanish house bar, solid wood furniture from Spanish walnut, and a lively atmosphere when the whole family is around. The two daughters of the befriended families and their boyfriends joined us later, so that we were a lively party of ten all day plus Alex, who was out with his village friends most of the time. Patricia, the GE teacher, gave us a tour through the chilly Colonial house with its solid stonewalls, which is mostly used during the warmer season and during vacations. Carlos and the respective son-in-laws were building an antique cupboard together, upstairs.

After the tour of the house we huddled around the Dutch oven over a Cherry aperitif to start off the whole **Spanish lunch ritual**. Nieves and Patricia translated back and forth to Loli, and when Loli talked to me directly in Spanish I often got the gist. After the aperitif we all went to a country bar, close by the town hall (ayuntamiento). It is a Spanish tradition to meet up in a bar one hour before lunch for vino blanco and some snacks: pinchos or tapas. I had always wondered why the bars were completely filled with people at certain times. Over vino blanco, fried calamari, Spanish tortilla, and olives the barometer of joy and laughter climbed steadily. An old Cantabrian pan flute and drum player was sitting at our table, who was a well-known musician in that region. I took a picture of him.

After the vino-blanco ceremony in the bar we drove over to Adolfo's and Nieves' **lottery house**, which Adolfo had already warmed up nicely with an open fire. Entering the house Adolfo remarked that this house was basically built with the money he had "supported" the lottery with over decades, and was only a "tax return". The two families and us settled around a large table between the open fireplace and another <My husband just brought me tapas to my bed: Tapas with guacamole, chorizo, Manchego, ajo (garlic), and olives on toothpicks. These are the best tapas I have eaten, yet, because they are fresh and come as a **gift of love** right to my bed. ¡Que aproveche! Gracias! He has an aversion against commercial love-days, but he creates plenty of his own Love and appreciation days.> and another electrical heater to keep us warm on that lousy cold day. Cold is relative, however. It never falls below zero, or they couldn't grow lemons and **kiwis** here. You need **one** male and **four** female plants, I learned yesterday.

A Spanish lunch consists of a first plato, red wine, pane, a second plato, liquor, and coffee. For the primer plato we had Loli's delicious crab cake on crackers. For the segundo plato, Nieves had prepared an authentic cocido montañes in her country house the day before. It was composed of beans, cabbage, black pudding[38] and chorizo. It tasted very hearty and was the ideal dish for this kind of weather. Since Loli was steaming right in front of the fireplace and my back felt ice cold, I traded places with her, sitting right beside Adolfo, now. He talked to me in Spanish as if I had been born in Novales. With his melodious voice he told several jokes, which were translated by the two daughters of the families, but like in any translation the climax is slowed down. I warmed up quickly, un-mantled my leather coat, and sat there with my black and white cow vest over a warm sweater. This time Adolfo needed no translator: When I was laughing hard about another joke he lifted up my cow vest and said: "**La vaca que rie!**"

After the country stew Mother Nieves (Schnee=snow) distributed the dessert, which had been prepared by the daughter of the house, Laura, a law student. The two daughters of the befriended families had set out to study languages together, but after two years Laura changed her mind and decided to become a lawyer. It is always beneficial to have a lawyer in the family, and a doctor, a teacher, a farmer, an engineer, and then a family has fortifications like the old Thessaloniki city walls. The delicious cheesecake was served **with champagne**. I have never had that combination before, but it tasted excellent. After the dessert Adolfo served whiskey, apple, peach, and hazelnut liquor. I tasted a little bit of the latter, before Nieves brought out the Spanish coffee, which is espresso filled up with hot milk. Lively conversations and lots of laughter accompanied the Spanish country lunch.

After lunch Laura gave us a tour of the "lottery house". She became nostalgic when she picked up her childhood doll from her bed. Since she always begged her

---

38. Blood sausage with rice

parents to order a little blue-eyed sister, named Elena, they gave her a cabbage doll for Christmas. The little sister, she longed for with all her heart, arrived many Christmases later and was named Elena, of course. (This is how soul relatives meet again!) In spite of that yaki weather we all took a walk around the village, over to the church dating back to 1800. It looked similar inside like the one in Cabezon de la Sal with its pseudo-Romanic structure. Nieves hinted at the proportions of the towers. They were too short, since the money had run out. It had been built by an Indiano who came back with a lot of money. She said it is a beautiful view at night from their house, seeing the old church illuminated, very peaceful and reassuring.

While walking across the bridge over the murmuring country creek I thought: 'There is a **different beat** in the countryside. It is so solemn and peaceful like a Sunday morning.' I can see why the families frequently leave Santander to rejuvenate in their country retreats. We all rejoiced in Loli's and Carlos' house again, huddled around the Dutch oven with a steaming digestive teacup nestled in our cold hands. Carlos and the prospective son-in-laws finished putting the old **colonial cupboard** together while Adolfo smoked his mandatory peace pipe, which reminded me of grandpa's and put me in a nostalgic mood.

When the cupboard project was finished we said Good bye to the friend's family, to lively Loli, quiet royal Carlos, Patricia, my teacher colleague, and her boyfriend, while the rest: Adolfo, a former National basketball player, Nieves the match-maker[39] and us, the world tramps, went over to her house again to tighten everything up, before we stepped out into a full-moon night to drive home to our Santander apartment again. Although very tired but happy I realized what I had missed for so long: **Family life** with sons and daughters around the dinner table with lots of noise and laughter.

---

39. She matched me up with Carlos' son for an English-Spanish exchange every Thursday and Friday.

Domingo, 23. Febrero

From the sunny balcony looking at the Bahia...

Two-day conference...Internal thermometer...Fur coats...Intensive Spanish class...Learning channels...Served on a golden platter...Jump the benchmark... Underperformance...Spanish NO-NO's...Spanish-English exchange...Iraq war...Conference dinner...

It is a beautiful Sunday noon, and Dieter is resting from his **two-day conference:** *Inhomogeneities in Strongly Correlated Systems*, the intensive Spanish class, and his regular office work. The next best to 'tanking' fresh air and sunshine in the countryside is the balcony. After this cold spell where Spaniards were running around in fur coats, shawls, gloves and hats (plus 2^0C!), I inhale the sunrays voraciously through my pores. I love to bathe in the early spring sun with the cool air around me. Spaniards have a different **internal thermometer** than us. For them plus 2^0C is ice cold. For me, a fur coat would be comfortable in Russia at -20^0C to -40^0C. **Fur coats** are a fashion and status symbol in Santander. In Germany you would rarely find fur coats because of the Germans' strong environmental concerns. Also in Colorado, anti-cruelty leagues and humane societies are very influential, and people would not feel comfortable wearing a fur coat there.

My **intensive Spanish** class leaves me little time for writing, now. Three hours of class time, and two to three hours of homework and study time. The class time is divided into two instructional hours of grammar teaching with some oral applications, and one hour of applied communication. There is constant input, input, input, and I am glad I had a quiet Saturday for myself to process the whole week of instruction on my own, while Dieter and our house guest, Prof Guenther, our host professor from Dresden, were attending the conference.

I am **learning** with <u>all</u> my **channels** evenly: Visually, kinesthetically, auditory. I speak, while I write, while I see, and then I go out and apply it. My students are lucky. I teach to all their learning channels in class. Going through the process of learning another foreign language myself, and 'observing' my language teachers, their methods and didactical lesson structure at the same time, I know I have done a superb job. Our American students get literally everything **served on a golden platter**. Here, as in India and Greece, classroom time is solely devoted to instruction. Testing occurs on students' time. In my opinion, far too much instructional time is wasted with testing and assessing in the US. That takes the responsibility of learning and long-term studying off of the students and shifts it onto the teacher, who in some cases even gets reprimanded for too many F's. In other cultures they have to **jump the benchmark** after the course with at least 60 % in order to pass. It is the student's responsibility to pass the course. American students are babied and pampered, and that leads to **underperformance** and mental laziness. Teachers in other cultures have been complaining about the same things, so one needs to research the causes of underperformance and mental laziness in public education.

My Foreign language teachers at the university are very good teachers as they transmit language contextually and apply every structure to one's personal life. There are only six students in the beginner's class: One Yugoslavian, one Australian, one British, two Americans, and one German-American, who should have taken the advanced beginner's class, because he has already taken the Sp 105 at CSU[40]. Our common language is English. Some of the class time is also used to clear up cultural uncertainties, and to discuss the differences between our respective cultures. It is a **NO-NO** in Spain to ask about weight, money, and age, as in many cultures. While the verb 'coger' (pronounce g=ch!), to catch un autobus, un tren etc. is used all the time in Spain; never use it in Mexico or Argentina. It has a sexual connotation there. They would say: tomar un taxi etc. I haven't used a sauna over here, yet, because I didn't know the phrases and conventions; what to bring, what to wear, what the ritual is etc., but I will try it on a day when I can muster all my courage.

I practiced the dialogue with an engineering student with whom I meet every Thursday and Friday for an hour of a **Spanish—English exchange**. My students get to practice dialogues in class all the time. It is an excellent tool for asking and responding swiftly. My Spanish engineering student, who is the son of Loli and Carlos (lemon plantation), has to pass his level-five exam at the end of the semester. So I threw him the topic: What do you and the Spanish people think of a possible **Iraq war**? Political, philosophical discussions are the most challenging in foreign languages, besides writing and analyzing poetry. If he gives me permission, I will include Marco's writing in this script, because it is of political and cultural relevance.

> *Permission obtained:*
> *"Politically, President Bush is trying to destroy the governments of the countries he doesn't like, especially the countries which have natural resources like Iraq. After*

---

40.   Colorado State University

taking over Iraq the intention of the US is to install a military government there in order to control the oil industries. Also the goal of this war with Iraq is to install a base in the Middle East to control the Arabic countries that collaborate with terrorism.

The position of the European community on the war is very complicated. France, Germany, and Belgium are fully against an immediate attack, but on the other hand, Spain, Italy, and the UK are completely supporting the American position. Experts in the political scene say that a war in Iraq will not solve the problem of terrorism, but it will increase the danger of terrorism all around the world, especially in the US.

91% of the Spanish people are against the war in Iraq. Many of them show their opposition by taking part in crowded demonstrations all around the country in a mostly peaceful atmosphere. The main reason for this opposition against the war is the unconditional support of the Spanish government for the USA and the UK, disregarding all the anti-war sentiments of the Spanish population. All three governments support an attack against Iraq without any convincing reason, if there is any reason at all to start wars. People think that this war will be followed with other wars against 'enemy countries' of the USA to make a better world 'in the name of justice and freedom'.

Another hidden reason is the following: Although almost 70 years have passed since Spain took part in a war, many of the citizens have inherited anti-war feelings from their grandparents when they told their grandkids what happened in this land in the late 30s: They suffered through a three-year war, colloquially called 'A War between Brothers', which resulted in the death of half a million people, the exile of another half million people, a very long post-war period of hunger and misery, forty years of military dictatorship under Franco, and the division of a whole country between left and right wing politics.

That experience left a longing for peace and solidarity in the following generation for countries who were suffering from dictatorship and violence. For that reason, most of the Spanish people want to see a world where even the hardest problems are solved without the use of any weapons and where justice and freedom prevail."

Marcos (2nd semester engineering student) believes that his opinion is pretty much representative of his fellow students.

Last night, we all attended the **conference dinner**, organized by Prof Pepe, at one of the finest hotels in town, the Rhim. It was a six-course meal of excellent quality, plus wine, champagne, liquor and coffee. Since I have written extensively about Spanish meals, I will only mention the novelty (for me!). Before the main course, one scoop of lemon-ginger sherbet was served, which refreshed and cleared up the taste buds in expectation for the main course. After a nice digestive uphill walk through a spring-like night, we arrived back home at 1 a.m., while the Spaniards and Prof Guenther departed at 2 a.m. 'Balkonien'—my father always made it sound like a country—is a nice place to be for writing on a peaceful Sunday afternoon, while waiting for a tired husband to wake up for some action.

28. Febrero
1 a.m.

In the silence of the night by candle light...

Mi abuelo imaginario

Riding into the sunset
On Grandpa's horse
Nestled into his arms
Engulfed by his white
Ceremonial coat
I fear no monsters of the night.
There is strength in
Grandpa's arms
Laughter in his belly
Love in his heart
Direction in his reigns
Foresight in his eyes
Grace in his rhythm
Integrity in his path.
I fear no monsters of the night
When Grandpa is by my side.

Potawi

Sábado, 1. Marzo

From Corte Ingles…

Albornoz…European weeks…Spanish Tortilla…Two desserts…Lively discussions…Cool down…Grandpa how?…Grandma why?…Medico encantado…Three maternities…Protector of life…Sanctity of paternity…Red wine and classical music…Devoted husbands…Special Torrelavega cake…

After the first half of the intensive Spanish course, I don't feel so speechless anymore. I can combine the words and phrases I know, creatively and get my point across—most of the time. I was just shopping for a ropa de baño; a better word is **albornoz**, I just learned from the sales person. The albornoz blanco is from soft frottee with a cuddly hood, and will give me some comfort on March 19 and 20th in the hospital. Maybe I also dare to go to the sauna now, since I have un albornoz.

My husband is shopping at Hipercor, along those endless isles with the same articles over and over again, just different brand names. While he gets hyper in Hipercor, I am content writing here at the Bar de la Plaza Café. I had a Waldorf salad, since they have the **European weeks**, now, after the exhibition Asiatico. You feel really welcome when you see your native homeland flag greeting you at the entrance.

Last night, we were invited to Philipp II and Armada's house, just 50 meters from ours, together with three other people from the department. Armada made the best **Spanish tortilla** I have eaten, yet. Her brother, Luis Catorce explained the composition to me: Cubed potatoes, fried in olive oil over low heat for about 15 minutes. Then the olive oil is drained, and the beaten egg liquid with spices is poured over the potatoes. The tortilla is fried on either side, so that the eggs are cooked just so and not too dry. So, the primer plato consisted of a slice of Spanish tortilla and jamón serrano, a very fine raw ham from this region. As the segundo plato a huge fishplate topped with shrimp in cream sauce was divided among seven people, accompanied by fresh pan y vino tinto. The meal was topped off with two desserts, mousse au chocolate and a flan, extra for Jesus, both homemade, and a Spanish coffee, of course.

The dinner was accompanied by **lively discussions** about American cities, rafting trips, Spanish recipes, cultural peculiarities in Spain, Germany, Japan and the USA, the state of former East Germany, and our daily Spanish life as we experience it here. We departed around 1 a.m., and since I always need one to two hours to **cool down** by myself, I got to bed at 3 a.m. Oma called at 9:30 a.m. just to chat with me, but that's all right. We can sleep later, down the road of life, when we don't have the privilege anymore to talk to our elders. Sometimes I just wish my Grandma and my Grandpa were still around, and I could ask them all the questions about life and our family history. It would be even better if they came back, then I could ask them about death, too: "Grandma, did you hear me talking to you when you were in a coma?" "**Grandpa how** was the transition from life into death?" "**Grandma, why** did you get divorced from Grandpa?" "Grandpa, what was my mother like as a little child?" and so on and so on.

Two days ago, Armada drove me out to Torrelavega again to set up a date for the surgery. Dr. Gomez always starts his office hours with classical music. He has a wide selection of CDs in his office. Surprisingly, we were called in early by the nurse. I had anticipated at least an hour wait with the whole waiting room full of people, again. The doctor greeted us with a hearty handshake and a big smile. While I presented him with a bottle of 99 Beaujolais, Rothschild, from my husband, I returned the greeting I had learned from him; "Por mi **medico encantado!**"

When my eyes were fixed on a modern painting he got up and explained the **three maternities** to me: One original Mother and child from the 18th century, one from Russia, and the modern one in tender purple, pink, and whites, framed in an antique silver frame, therefore generating an intriguing tension between the modern artwork and the old fashioned frame. The oil color was applied with a spatula, and the abstract shapes of mother and child were intimately flowing into each other. He explained all of it in Spanish, of course, and I understood almost every word he said. Through his enthusiastic, tender interpretations of the three maternities I understood even more: That this man is a **protector of life**, that he honors the maternal aspect, that he delivers babies with great joy, and that he attends to the prenatal submarines out of that devotion to the unity of mother and child. I also comprehended the **sanctity of paternity**, which he embodied, the protector of life. *Mi Abuelo* is devoted to all the men, who embody the eternal paternal aspect of life.

I did not understand much of the medical part. Armada had to translate frequently. He is going to operate on me on March 19, on the holiday of St. Jose.

When we departed he said that he hopes to have a quiet weekend without deliveries, so that he can enjoy the **red wine with classical music.**

Later, we met up with our **devoted husbands** in a café, who had driven out to Torrelavega directly after a business lunch with the president and the vice president of UC (University of Cantabria). But since we were called in early by the nurse, they could not participate in the doctor's consultation. But we enjoyed their company at the café, and later, we took a walk to a Confiseria where we ordered a **typical Torrelavega pastel**. Philipp II just brought it to our door, because he had lunch with his parents-in-law, today, in Torrelavega. Gracias! It is a special almond torte, layered with fluffy strudel dough (Blatterteig) and vanilla butter cream. No calories at all-!

The doctor did not even charge us for the visit. He made up for the Shark's triple check, which this first doctor had requested from me. And Dr. Gomez reassured us that the cost for the surgery, which we will have to pay for by ourselves, would not exceed the usual allowance from the health insurance. There are sharks and there are protectors of life. I am in good hands now.

Lunes, 3. Marzo

Wild Pony[41]

Rides <u>against</u> the wind
Across those tough Wyoming highlands.
I couldn't tame you in the classroom.
Although I admired your spirit
I despised your stalling and defiance.
Let your spirit fly, out there in the wilderness!

I hope you find a master
Who can direct the reigns
Who can contain your temperament
Who can unfold your gift,
The brilliance of your mind.

Wild Pony,
Your master
Must be discipline!
For discipline are the reigns
of the mind which give it
direction and purpose.
Your purpose,
Wild Pony,
Is to fly <u>with</u>
the wind!

Potawi

---

41. Wild Pony is an RHS student and a weekend cowboy, trailing cattle into Wyoming.

Miercoles, 5. Marzo

From Suizo Café by the Bahia

Ferry to Plymouth...National tourism...English 1. language...Common World language...Oscar...

This morning, when I walked downhill from our apartment to my masaje (Sp.) appointment by the Bahia, I saw the **ferry to Plymouth** leave the harbor: A mighty sea vessel from steel, triste-gray, only the command post and the upstairs cabins were painted in white. When I see it from our apartment, it looks proportional, but when you are close to it, it looks like a monster.

Now I understand why so few people speak English, here: The **tourism** in Santander is mostly **national**: People coming from Bilbao and Madrid, except the British coming over from Plymouth with the ferry. A lot of Spaniards are married to a British partner. There is a second reason: French used to be the second national language. Recently the government switched over to offering **English** as a **first foreign language**, so this will be the first generation of Cantabrians who will speak English almost fluently in about 15 years. The teachers start introducing words in nursery school, and continue building up the language 'till the students are 18. I will have the opportunity of watching foreign language education in the public and private school system, soon.

I am having a café Vienes and a crêpe flambiado. Wow, they use quite a bit of alcohol, here. I still need to do my Spanish homework for the course, this afternoon. "Alcohol loosens the tongue" is a German saying. This is surely beneficial for the communication part. When the Russians first arrive at the Max-Planck-Institute, they speak broken English; after drinking one glass of Vodka, they speak better English, and after three glasses of Vodka they speak fluently. When I take a refresher-French-weekend in the Rockies (CCFLT Foreign language camp) I speak French easily after the cheese-and—red-wine break. It is good though that we are heading for a **common world language**. That makes life and travel so much easier, but that still doesn't absolve us from learning the host country's language and culture. Only through language can you get deeper into the mindset of a foreign people.

Our Australian language compadre in the course had his birthday, yesterday. **Oscar** turned 20, and I always think of my sons when I look at him. The next best to spoiling a son when you don't have your own kids around is Oscar. So I bought him four Easy Spanish Learners (Kid's books) with little sticker pictures inside for matching vocabulary, story lines and cute pictures. He is the kind of kid who will have fun with this. He is studying graphic design, and his father, who is Spanish-Australian, sent Oscar to his aunt and uncle in Santoñia for a year to learn Spanish.

Now, I better head back to the university to get some work done. Friday morning, we'll leave for Madrid with a department bus for Prof A's initiation into the Academy of Sciences.

11. Marzo

From the pink, sagging couch…

Operation…Weekend in Madrid…Castilia…Downtown Madrid…Alcalá…Colon…Cisneros…Cervantes…Carlos I…Concrete history…No passion…Birth house of Cervantes…Spanish Baroque…Plazas…Real life…Academy of Science…Cocktail party…Gala lunch…Prado…Pepe's Little Village…

You wait and wait, and then it happens all of a sudden: The **operation** will be tomorrow. April was another choice, but that is too late, since I need adequate recovery time for traveling the 2000km back to Frankfurt/Floersheim, and then back home to the US on May 19, hopefully, when everything is arranged for the parents-in law.

According to all my lab reports I should have a super healthy athletic body, but something is sucking the life energy out of me. When we climbed up the High Plateau with the bus, on the way from Santander to Madrid, intense pain was shooting down my left arm. On the way back, journeying down to sea level, it did not occur again. I tire out easily, and sometimes I wish I could go back home to exchange my body. If that low-level-energy condition persists, I need to check into a tropical clinic to find out the reason.

The **weekend in Madrid**, i.e. Friday and Saturday, was short and intense. Friday, March 8, we left the institute around 8:20 a.m. with a comfortable tour bus. There was no toilet on the bus, but the driver made predictable stops every 1 ½ to two hours. Climbing up from sea level onto the High Plateau over two mountain passes (Puerto del Escudo, 1011 m and Puerto de Sumosierra), we left the smaragd (a special green) landscape of Cantabria and entered the rugged, barren, brownish-dry, less populated landscape of **Castilia**, which reminded me a lot of New Mexico. Driving over Burgos SE into the heart of Spain, we got to admire the classicistic, monumental buildings of **downtown Madrid** on Gran Via twice, on the way to Alcalá before lunch, and at night on the way to the Academia of Science, situated in a side street off Gran Via. Madrid is a rich esthetic city with futuristic architecture on the outskirts, and grandiose, turn-of-the-19th-century inner city facades. However, Madrid was not the focus of our excursion, except for Prof A's initiation in downtown Madrid.

Alcalá, Pepe's "village" (200.000!!!), the oldest university town in Spain, dating back to 1499, was our focus of excursion. Downtown **Alcalá** looks indeed like a village, while the high-rising modern buildings are grouped around the village. Alcalá is a convergence point in history. All national aspects of mine were reunited in one day: Karl V., the German Kaiser, was also **Carlos I.**, the King of Spain, at that time, because the Habsburg Empire was comprised of Germany, Austria, Spain, plus the colonies in S. America. Here, in Alcalá, Christopher Columbus (They call him **Colon** here!) talked to the Spanish Queen about venturing out to seek new land. We stayed in the Paradores Hotel, directly within the old historical walls of the nearly 500-year-old Renaissance University. The courtyards felt like a monastery, emanating peace and serenity. Founded by Cardinal **Cisneros** in 1510, the former Colegio de San Jerónimo was a center for classical language studies. Three languages were spoken here: Latin, Greek and Hebrew. Today, it mainly houses the humanities and the administration, while the other faculties are situated outside in modern buildings. On the writers' wall I saw the plaques of Lope de Vegas, Miguel de **Cervantes** (Don Quijote), Borges (more modern), Tirso de Molina, Ignacio de Loyola, Calderon de la Barca and others. Imagine the finest Spanish-speaking writers of five centuries eternalized in stone, side by side. All of a sudden I can pinpoint the great minds to a place and time in history. It's concretely written on **concrete**, and not abstract and boring in a **history** book, presented by a teacher who had no passion for history, like ours at that time, or maybe he had **no passion** for his students. Teachers who have no passion for their subject area and their students should pack up and go home!

The city tour was all conducted in Spanish. The tour guide told a bunch of funny anecdotes, which our graduate students and Nieves tried to translate. Simultaneous translations, however, are the hardest oral transactions in foreign language, and you need to be at home in both languages equally, plus your brain needs to work synchronically all the time. Very few people can do this. But we appreciated the effort. We passed the **birth house of Cervantes** and entered one of the few oval-shaped Spanish baroque structures, the church of St. Bernardas.[42] **Spanish baroque** is reduced and clear-lined, while the German baroque is overloaded and ornamented. The oval structures are hard to maintain

---

42.   Not Bernardos, anymore, because there are NUNS now= Bernardas!

because of the tension it provokes within the vault. They had to hang the new candelabra on a separate iron structure, because of the danger of collapsing.

Typical for Spanish cities are the **Plazas** with a round covered pergola for Sunday concerts in the middle, and shady tree avenues on either side to protect the "villagers" against sun and rain. In former times, those plazas were fenced off for bullfights. Saturday afternoon and Sunday, inner cities are closed down to traffic. The citizens take over the center and meet in the "ancient agora" for playing and chatting, the Spaniards' all-time favorite hobby, as we learned in Spanish class. **Real life** takes place outside the house: In the streets, in bars, in restaurants, discothèques, plazas, promenades, etc.

Friday, after lunch around 5 p.m., we drove into the heart of Madrid again for Prof A's initiation into the **Academy of Science**. Only 20 of the brightest scientists belong to this 'Club', and one has to die before a new member can join. Since the Spanish life expectancy is the highest in Europe, there is not much space for the younger ones. Antonio gave a half-hour academic talk in Spanish, which was acknowledged and answered by an established 'excelentísimo'. The oldest member of the 'Club' had a good snooze, and I had to fight too to keep my eyes open, because I could not follow in Spanish. But I very much enjoyed observing the ritual in these Holy Halls (in diesen Heiligen Hallen! Beethoven) and sharing Antonio's joy. Listening to the rhythm of the language made me realize what a beautiful, powerful, vocal-rich language Spanish is. The a's and o's and the end-of-the-word stresses give it force and emphasis. After the awards ceremony Antonio invited us all back to Alcalá into a historic hotel for a very special **cocktail party**. We departed around midnight, while the young folks danced through the night from bar to bar till 3:30 a.m. Professor Roughy looked very pale during the city tour, Saturday morning from 11 a.m. to 2 p.m. Spaniards don't eat a big breakfast, only café and croissants, or churros con chocolate, or pan, mantequilla and mermelada. After the city tour, we had a festive **Gala lunch** in the University hostel where Prof A. was honored by his colleagues. Pepe had composed a poem for him on a scroll. I would need six years of Spanish to be able to really appreciate it and work with the poetry.

About 40 people headed back home to Santander with the tour bus, while others stayed in Madrid for another day with family and friends. We should definitely see the **Prado** museum in Madrid (next time!), the Royal Theatre, the Royal Palace, Plaza Mayor, Plaza España, and El Retiro Gardens. I love to ride into the sunset through a clear starry night, and after a six-hour ride and two breaks, we reached Santander around 11:30 p.m. Alcalá de Henares (river) left its historical marks in my heart, uniting the German, American and the newly acquired Spanish part of myself. The capital is breathtaking, but it is the '**little villages' of the Pepes**, Fernandos, Carlos, Ignacios, Alfredos, Alfonsos, Adolfos, Luis, Jesus, Antonios, and Rafaelos, which win my heart over and make it an unforgettable trip.

12. Marzo

From my snow-white hospital bed...

Relatives stay...In dreamland...Mompia Clinic...Spring tie...

It is 22:00 p.m. My husband just left to spend the night alone in our 'piso'[43]. Did you know that it is a custom here, especially after surgery, that **relatives stay** over night in the hospital? In some cultures they even prepare food for the loved ones in the hospital. I was fed all right, tonight: Chicken soup (for the soul), Spanish tortilla, and a pear cooked in red wine, plus bread and water; a light meal after full anesthesia. I feel all right, except for that headache, which already developed at home this morning, probably because of the caffeine with-drawl.

Dieter and Armada said that the surgery went fast, barely half an hour. The doctor said I went under immediately.[44] I was annoyed when the anesthetist called me back three times to make sure I would stay awake. I wasn't ready to wake up, yet, because I had such a **beautiful dream**, but I can't recall it now, since I couldn't wake up on my own terms. I was in a wonderful, peaceful place or space. That's all I remember.

The **Mompia Clinic** is a very modern hospital. My room is large with a leather couch, an armchair, TV, telephone, bathroom with all the amenities like a hotel room. The walls are painted in pastel-yellow, the doors are in pink, and the water-color-seascape painting on the wall picks up the colors in the room. The nurses are nice, but it is hard without a common language. By the time I remember the words and the phrases from the 'curso', they are out the door. A leisurely conversation is not possible, yet, because it hasn't sunk into the subconscious. When you start dreaming in the target language, that is a sure indicator that fluent communication is possible.

When Dr. Gomez looked after me in the evening, he challenged me to say something more than 'bien'. "¡Vale", I said "Estoy excelente!" Then I commented on his orange-pink **spring tie**, and he said that this was the latest French fashion

---

43. Piso=larger flat
44. Armada MD was watching the operation on the screen. I did not recognize one person in there with their surgery 'costumes'.

for <u>young</u> people. When he finally saw me laughing about his joke, he was satisfied and wished me a good night.

13. Marzo

Recovering on the pink, sagging couch…

DUI…Young doctor with the orange-pink spring tie…Bien and excelente…Expensive night out…

I was too groggy last night to continue. So I switched on CNN to listen to the UN's voices in regard to the war in Iraq, but I couldn't focus on that either, since I drifted in and out of dreamland: **DUI**=Dreaming under influence of anesthesia. It speeds up the healing process, too, when you totally relax your body. In the recovery room there was a nurse who spoke English and French to me. Her father sent her to a summer camp in England when she was eight years old. That's where she learned English and at fourteen, she went to a summer camp in France. She did not speak the languages perfectly, but on a level 3, where you can maintain conversations back and forth. I wished I had reached that level already in Spanish!

My **'young' doctor with the pink-orange tie** woke me up this morning at 7:30. Isn't it annoying when somebody shows up by your bedside, full of energy, ready to conquer the day, while you can barely open your eyes? He checked up on me and asked how I had slept. I said: "From 12-3 and from 5 till you woke me up." I did not tell him that I was drenched in sweat, probably because of a high fever, firstly because I couldn't express it in Spanish or I didn't want to, and secondly because I wanted to go home. Thirdly, I know that my body sometimes reacts with a high fever at night, and then the next morning I am totally healed. They had given me a whole infusion bottle full of antibiotics after two huge bottles of a sodium liquid. My 'young' surgeon said that if everything was '**bien y excelente**', I could leave after desayuno (breakfast). I tried to snooze a little longer, but my husband came in early, too. While he watched CNN and paid the bills, I got ready in the bathroom and 'desayunoed'. It was an **expensive night out**: 1500 €, the food was just so, and I couldn't even dance. But my 'young' surgeon with the orange-pink tie did a wonderful job and my health is priceless!

Lunes, 17. Marzo

From my bed…recovering…

Pudding…Last day of class…Beyond 30…Outside the house…Social life in the streets…Undies…N0 One tobacco consumption…Franco regime…Spain's young democracy…Pasha husbands…Respect for teachers?…Teachers' salaries…American teachers…Which witch?…Magician…

It is neither beneficial having too little time, nor too much. Now, after the intensive Spanish course, and recovery from the OP I have too much time. In-between the activities I need to lie down, or my prenatal submarine starts to swell and cry. So, I have plenty of time for reflection and not enough energy for action. My legs feel like **pudding**, but that didn't keep me from attending the **last day of class**, last Friday. My husband picked me up with the car, and drove me right in front of the entrance. You can't miss more than four times, or they will not issue the certificate.

The last session was rather interesting as the teacher asked us what puzzled us in this culture. "How can so many people spend their money in cafes, restaurants and bars when the salaries are not that high, and living expenses are not exactly cheap in Santander?" we wanted to know. "First of all", Mina, our communication teacher, said, "Families live together, which lowers the cost of living. It is not unusual that kids live **beyond their 30s** with their parents. Secondly, Spaniards don't invest much in their homes, in general; they spend it outside the house for coffees, wine, liquor and tapas or pinchos to meet up with their friends to chat, the Spaniards' all time favorite hobby."

Invitations into the home are an exception. For Tanja, our Yugoslavian compadre, that was pretty incomprehensible, because in her culture it is the custom to be invited into the home. Our teacher said that when she was 'joven', she ate dry spaghetti in order to have enough money for the bars. **Social life**, she said, takes place **in the streets**. There is hardly any industry in Santander. It is a rich service town, and in the afternoon, you see many older people, especially women, sitting in cafes with their expensive furs and jewelry. In the summer, the Schickeria would be seen on the beaches in matching, highly fashionable beach-outfits, including hats and purses. Spanish women cannot stand the Middle and Northern European swimming trunks (rather bikinis) on men, which look like **'undies'**, according to our Australian compadre, Oscar. In Australia, men also wear longer, loose-fitting shorts like in the US. Also wearing sandals <u>with</u> socks is a NO-NO in Spain. They call it girigiri here when you commit such cultural 'crimes'.

Although Spain is **Numero Uno for tobacco consumption** in Europe, it is not number one in alcohol consumption. I haven't seen ONE drunk person, yet, but many, many smokers, everywhere, especially women. As in any dictatorial regime, women were very repressed during the **Franco regime** from 1939-77. Through an activity where Mina had cut out short newspaper clips about the Franco dictatorship, we learned that contraceptives were forbidden; women could not have their own bank accounts and needed the 'firma' (signature) of their husbands for every transaction. When they wanted to travel they needed an official permit, too. Demonstrations were not allowed, of course, and censorship was executed in regard to publications. **Spain's democracy** is only 26 years old. Now, most women work and raise kids (1,2 on average), but there is not enough support from their **pasha husbands**, said Mina. The development of a democracy takes time, and I am sure the picture will change in favor of the women in Spain, also.

The **respect for teachers** has diminished after the Franco regime. Our group presented both of our language teachers with a box of chocolates. Mina was very moved by that, because usually it doesn't happen here that a teacher is honored. She was fascinated by my stories about Johnstown, Colorado, where teachers get presents and get invited to graduations. Also that the teachers give their students presents for graduation and treats for Halloween, Valentine's, Xmas and birthdays.

The average **teacher's salary** is around 1700 € net, but they receive 14 salaries here, one Xmas bonus and one vacation bonus salary. Teachers teach about 15 to 18 hours[45] a week. They do not want to trade with an American teacher, I have noticed. They objected to the evaluation process, too. "What for?" they said, "We are trained professionals!" **American teachers** receive a little more for double the time in school, not to mention the homework, which adds easily up to a 50-60 hour workweek, the extracurricular happenings, like evening music concerts, theater plays, supervision for dances, clean-ups, awards night, graduation, etc. not included. With my one-hour commuting back and forth, I often spend

---

45.   Master's teach 15 hours.

60-70 hour workweeks. Half a Sunday is usually devoted (sacrificed) for my weekly lesson plan. According to my calculations an American teacher would need to be paid 60.000 € per year to compete with the European market. But the fact is that no European teacher would want the workload, the yearly evaluations, the excessive testing, and the biweekly grade reports of an American teacher.

How come teachers are so modest in their salary requests? Shouldn't it be the nation's highest priority to provide the next generation with the best possible education, with the best-trained and well-paid teachers? Our salaries should be right up there with doctors and lawyers, or at least comparative with other 7-year study tracks for Masters. Is it because teachers don't feel worthy because of inadequate training? Or is it because they constantly have to choose between higher salaries or student supplies? Usually teachers are humanitarians: They rather neglect themselves than cutting their students short. And **which** psychological **witch** set up that artificial choice? The best-equipped classroom is nothing but a museum of dead materials. But a highly trained pedagogue is like a **magician**. S/he does not need all that fancy stuff to ignite the minds of his/her students, given the students come to school to <u>want</u> to learn! After my recovery I will have a closer look into the public school system, here.

20. Marzo

From my bed...because the pink, sagging couch is occupied...

Date in History...Baby 22...Home...FL teaching... Books...Grammar...Chorus...T-guided...Language lab...Speaking...Spanish, not an easy language!...Own language school...

What a **date in history**: One meter of snow, back home in Ft. Collins, Colorado. People are basically snowed in. The snow is so heavy because one third is water content. The roof of the Denver airport has collapsed. War against Iraq has begun, last night. My Baby son, Manuel, has his birthday, and for the first time Mom is not home to bake him a cake, sing him a song, decorate the table festively, ring the cowbell, light the candle, and all the weird family rituals, which have developed over the years. **Baby is 22** and engaged. He is in good hands, and I am sure he had a Happy Birthday. I am just mourning the olden days.

I think I want to redefine what *home* means: Besides being at home within yourself, it is also a place where they speak your language, where you can meet up with your intimate and larger family, not necessarily blood family, but spirit family, where you know the inside workings of the small and big C-culture of a society, where you can discuss, negotiate and participate in the social and political life, where you contribute to society through your job or volunteering, where you grow roots. It is a place where you are rooted, which supports your growth and energy grid, gives you a lot of comfort, happiness and purpose.

I wish to reflect on **Foreign language teaching**, after having played the role of a student and watched two language teachers up close. I am grateful for the gifts I have received during this four-week intensive course, and I do not wish to criticize the teachers' work, just point out what I find beneficial in FL teaching:

>I prefer a **book** to flying pages where I can go home and restudy the chapter or catch up when I missed a day.

>One should not insist on the target language while teaching **grammar**, especially not when a student's face looks like a question mark. It is absolutely necessary that grammar is taught in the home language already, and does not <u>start</u> with FL learning.

>Repeating and precise **chorus** speaking is an art in India. Here it is totally neglected. If you consider that a toddler is learning through constant repetitions and corrections, chorus speaking is an excellent tool to include in FL education, especially when you use it in catchy songs and rhythms (rap for example).

>A clearly organized blackboard with clean printed letters is a must, because a FL learner cannot fill in the gaps like in the mother language.

>**Teacher guided** oral exercises are better for level one than independent partner exercises, because mistakes foster when they are not corrected right away. Students need to hear the correct structure clearly over and over again.

>A **language lab**: video, audio and computerized, would speed up the language acquisition process immensely. Students learn the most through applications and not through being lectured.

>**Speaking** is the most difficult process in FL learning. While you can already read short articles, produce nice, little essays, and understand quite a bit, speaking lags way behind. You've probably heard of toddlers who don't speak a word, and all of a sudden, around three, they produce whole sentences. There is a time barrier, too, which one needs to overcome in a FL. Usually after 2-3 years people can apply and combine the structures, because they are subconsciously and automatically available to them.[46]

Spanish is not an easy language, by all means. German is even harder with all the declinations. The difficulty in Spanish lies with the verbs: All the irregular verbs, tenses and endings. The sentence structure is fairly liberal, but an accumulation of little words, like pronouns combined with prepositions and reflexives throws me off. What is also difficult in audio discrimination are the v's, which sound like b's in Spanish, for example, virgin=birchin, or I live in Spain=vivo en España=bibo en españa.

If I had to live for good in Spain, I would learn Spanish as fast as possible, and then open my **own language school**. Our Johnstown students have everything available to them, but I am sure they don't realize this, because they have no comparison: A brand new book with an integrated video, audio and computer system, and an in-classroom language lab. But all of that modern equipment would be a museum without ME, a native speaker, who teaches to all their learning channels and has a lot of experience with foreign cultures and languages. I think I want to be a Roosevelt student, again. I don't think WE appreciated everything either, all our teachers offered us back then, but now I know better!

---

46.   See Stephen Krashen's language acquisition theory!

Domingo, 23. Marzo

From my bed...(It's either that or the pink couch)

'Dr. Svenush'...Opa's Alzheimer's...Support structures...Saying Good Bye long before...Heartless decision?...Santillana del Mar...Abbey of Santa Juliana...Spanish Sunday-pre-lunch ritual...Altamira caves...Neo-caves...Respect for animal kingdom...Stone Age comes alive...

It was 15⁰C today, spring-type weather, and I was not going to spend another Sunday mostly indoors after surgery. Our Indian host emailed that I am known for risky maneuvers, and that I should take real good care of myself. I think I can be very patient with others, but not with myself. Before heading out to Santillana del Mar, I had a long talk on the phone with **'Dr. Svenush'**, my middle son, who spends his spring break at Oma and Opa's house. **Opa's Alzheimer's** is progressing rapidly, but he still recognizes us by our voices, and his favorite grandson, he recognized immediately, of course! Dr. Svenush=Sven Markus=Max was in Opa and Oma's care for two months when he was a baby, while I prepared for my Second State Examination back in 1971. So, a fundamental bonding took place between the grandparents and the middle grandson.

We phone the parents almost daily, and email Fessy, the house doctor, and the Sozialstation. After an initial resistance on Oma's part[47] the **support structures** started to grip, and now Opa is getting used to being bathed and shaved by nurse Anneliese, who looks after them every day, and supervises the medication take-in. On Tuesdays, Fatima, the cleaning lady (jewel!) cleans and tells Oma to wear a fresh 'Kittel'.[48] On Thursdays the shopping lady picks up the list and brings the groceries home. A neighborly friend brings fresh meat and sausage from the butchery on Fridays, and every morning Oma (80) still goes to the bakery to get fresh rolls for breakfast and the Bild-Zeitung for Opa. He hardly watches TV anymore, doesn't drink much wine either, and switches day and night around. On some nights, Oma hardly gets any sleep. After a night like that she is ready to

---

47.   She would not open the door for the nurse, at first, until we got wind of it and emailed to the Sozialstation.
48.   Typical German housedress of the older generation.

let professional care take over. (Nursing home) It is a difficult decision, however, because Opa might just give up without Oma. With an Alzheimer's patient it is like **saying Good Bye long before** the funeral. On the other hand, he might be better off in professional care. It is a 24-hour job taking care of him. But when you've spent over 60 years of marriage together, it is a hard (**heartless?) decision** to give your partner 'away'. But not even my younger friends were capable of taking care of their Alzheimer's parent in the long run. Both got sick and had to bring the parent into professional care where they adjusted nicely and lived for another 3-5 years. Max has all the maturity, sensitivity and intuition a future doctor needs, plus the brains and the determination. He'll be good medicine for his grandparents, and maybe get some insights for himself on the 'frontline'.

Cont. 24. Marzo

Around noon, we left for **Santillana del Mar**, about 40km to the West, along the Atlantic Ocean, in order to explore the Middle Age town, the old Romanic church, and the Altamira caves. We parked our little blue Opel Corsa outside the old city walls, and walked our way up to the Old Town over the century-old, crooked cobblestone. How some Spanish señoras can walk there with high penny-heels is amazing! Lots and lots of touristy shops were embedded in the 500-800-year-old houses, but they did not disturb the old architecture like in Athens (Plaka). Restaurants and cafeterias were nestled in the romantic backyards in-between the historical walls. It is good to arrive in early spring, before the streams of tourists block the view to the mighty **Abbey of Santa Juliana**, founded at the end of the 11th century. Entering the impressive Romanesque structure from the cloister's solemn courtyard, I was surprised by the spaciousness of the mother ship and its two side ships (naves). Usually Romanesque structures are not that wide. Santa Juliana, the martyr, rested in stone right under the dome. New stained-glass windows let in a soft golden light, and added a little warmth to this cold, nearly millennium old structure. In the back, a baroque organ with playful wooden ornamenting and horizontal bass pipes, reaching out like arms at the spectator, loosened up the otherwise barren, clear-lined Romanesque sanctuary.

Since I needed to give my little prenatal submarine a rest, we decided to experience the **Spanish Sunday pre-lunch ritual** in a bar nearby the church. The structure was built from century-old stones and wooden beams. Ribs were roasting over an open cedar fire. Since it was one hour before Sunday lunch, the bar filled up rapidly. We had a café con leche, white wine with langostinos, and Dieter had a caña (draught beer). Trying to lose weight in Spain, he only had one langostino while he peeled seven more for me. In spite of his horse-breakfast (oats with fruit), and ascetic discipline, he is not losing one pound. Forget about losing weight in Spain! Once, we are showered with professional stress again the pounds will melt like butter in the sun.

After our Sunday lunch-snack we balanced back, over the dangerously uneven, 'gappy' cobblestone into our little blue 'coche' to drive about 8km to the **Altamira caves**. The real ones have been closed off to the general public since 1982 because of conservation problems. Only 8.500 people, mostly scientists, are permitted to enter per year. But in order to make that stone-age experience tangible to the computer and space-age homo sapiens[49], an exact 'Hollywood' replica of the breathtaking cave paintings was reconstructed in the **Museo de Altamira**, a minimalist building, reconciling modern architecture with the nature around it.

Entering the neo-caves with a Spanish-speaking tour guide, I felt right at home in my workshop. The earth tone relieves on the plaster ceiling could be reproduced by me on a leather hide. I work with the same shades; even some of the techniques are similar. I am so inspired by the **15.000-year-old cave artists** (Paleolithic art) that I will devote a whole vegetable-tanned cow hide to the themes of Altamira, as soon as I am back home, after my book is finished. The themes are bison, horses and deer, mostly in their natural sizes, reproduced on the ceiling, utilizing the ceiling relief to support an even deeper three-dimensional appearance of the objects. First, the shape is scratched in stone with a sharp stone-tool. I use a tracer and then a swivel knife on leather. Then the outline is traced with coal. The inside is painted with different shades of ground rock, in ochre, blood-brown, green-gray, all the colors you would identify on an autumn leaf. I did not see <u>one</u> violent scene. Men seemed to **respect and honor the animal kingdom**, back then. Their clothing, tools, beds, nourishment were all derived from the animals, in form of hides, bone-tools, furs, meat, etc. Cave man lived through and with the animals.

With holographic figures the tour guide replayed the life of the cave man back then. The whole museum is furbished with high-tech-state-of-the-art equipment to make the **Stone Age come alive** for the spectators. One could spend days in there to try out every gadget, but I couldn't stand on my feet any longer after five hours of walking. I had to recline in the car, and lay down flat at home to reduce the swelling of my little blue planet. When you see an outside wound heal, the healing process becomes visible and tangible, but an inside wound can only make itself (visible) audible through pain. Therefore, I'll take it easy today, sit on the balcony to write and recline a lot, but next week, I am ready for a new adventure: Neo-woman will not cave in!

---

49. Rather 'homo stupido', see environmental mess-up and wars!

26. Marzo

From the pink…

Shocked…Police presence…# 1 show on TV… Casualties…Victims of aftermath…Until reason wins or love…Power 'with' not 'over'…Contra la Guerra…

Today, when I stepped out of the door from my masaje terapia, I was **shocked** to see two police guards standing in front of my favorite Suizo Café. On the way to Santillana del Mar, last Sunday, I had already noticed the **police presence** on major roundabouts, connecting the state roads with the highway (autopista), but I had not related it to the war situation. It is scary to see how the war is affecting our daily lives, now.

It is theee number One entertainment **show on TV**. Imagine if we used all that time and energy to finding creative solutions, others than destructions, being victims in our own homelands, and despair over the so-called **casualties**. What is casual about it anyhow, and who invented that word? They started calling the **dead** soldiers, the **dead** husbands, the **dead** sons, the **dead** fathers "casualties", because they've become brain-**dead** against the horrors of war.

Nobody wins in a war! Nobody! Even the 'winner' will be a **victim of the aftermath** for a long time. And the irony is that Mrs. Contraguerra is the mother of two military guys. Our oldest could be deployed, because he is in charge of the Apache MedVac operation. And if the war takes longer than anticipated, Dr. Max could be called to the frontlines, as a doctor, to piece all the wounded together. Wouldn't it be better to take care of peace now, instead of piecing all the wounded, the destructed houses, and the economy together, later? What a year in **his**tory, in **her**story!

I am not saying that one should avoid a good fight, or be conflict-shy. We don't throw a bomb at our partner either; we fight it out peacefully, **until reason or love wins**. Why can't we do that on an international scale? Because money is involved, oil, greed, dominance 'over', instead of **power 'with'**. Have we advanced one bit as mankind since WWII, besides in technology? And when I see those violent peace demonstrations on TV, I get even sicker. Violence and peace are mutually exclusive! Hasn't Gandhi taught them anything, or is he not included in the history curriculums?

CONTRA LA GUERRA

Cooperation among nations!
Operation Brotherhood!
Negotiations between opponents!
Treaties not to be broken!
Ratio and respect!
Affirmations and confirmations!

Love
Agape

Gratitude for minor progress!
Utopia is possible!
Enlightenment and excitement!
Reason, no season for war!
Ratifications, no ramifications!
Ambassadors of PEACE!

Mrs. Contraguerra-potawi

Sábado, 29.Marzo

From the South balcony...

Communal living...Noisy in public...Censured TV... Manipulated...Utopia...Democracy...Workaholics...Fear ...Grows like cancer...

It is a beautiful spring day. The Bahía is a little hazy, though. Life is all around me: The trees are budding, young lads are playing fútbol in the courtyard, and families are sitting on benches with their toddlers. These apartment houses are designed for **communal living**. Almost every apartment house has a commons area. Behind our house is a soccer field, a basketball court, at least seven benches I am counting from up here, a car wash, and a lawn area. In front of our house is a park with ten benches on a lawn, with about twenty plantana-trees, giving lots of shade in the summer. Right now they are still dormant, but the Japanese cherry blossoms are budding in pink-rosé, and those white tropical flowers, mantas de la virgin, are framing the commons area. Spaniards prefer **communal living** to lonely country houses. The main difference, we stated in class, between Spanish and American people is that the Spaniards are more social, family and community oriented, and that the Americans are the more individualistic, pioneer type. In our neighborhood alone there are four Internet cafés. They would rather share things here than own it themselves.

The other night, a couple was fighting in the courtyard from midnight till 1:30 a.m., wandering from bench to bench back and forth, arguing with loud voices. Marcos, my English student and Spanish tutor, said that it is quite common for Spanish people to be **noisy in public**. I also had an interesting conversation with Marcos about **"censured TV"**. He saw rather dramatic scenes of the war and of the injured on the Arabic channel. They did not show those on BBC, CNN, and the Spanish network. I said: "If the West 'censures' their TV images, how do you know the Arabic channels don't do the same thing?" He said: "Watch channel five, it's fairly neutral", but we only get one and two here in Spanish. I think every country feeds the images to the general public, which supports the direction of the government. So, the regular folks are always **manipulated**. They never get to know the whole truth and nothing but the truth. I repeat: Everywhere I've been people are the same: Friendly, compassionate, caring...95% of the time. They want to live in peace, economic well being, in a clean environment, and want a hopeful future for their kids. Why are they putting people in power then, who are not supporting their 'Utopia'? My 'better' half is calling for the Corte Ingles, his all-time Saturday hobby…to be continued…

Here I am at Corte Inglés, continuing my **'Utopia'**. In America about 30 to 40% of the people vote, depending on which kind of election and the location. Is it the case that the rest doesn't care?

- Democracy has become an institution. Whatever you have, you get used to; unless you lose it, or have to fight for it, and then you become aware of the <u>real</u> value.

- The masses are being kept happy and dulled by the entertainment industry: TV, film, sports, sex industries.

- The election process has several hurdles: People need to register long before they can vote.

  The language of the ballots is so legally twisted and difficult that even an academically trained person has to read the paragraphs three times, and the newspapers print pages and pages of interpretations. Sometimes you have to deal with double negations that make you wonder which trickster has composed that amendment to evoke the 'right' outcome.

- A fifth factor is resignation and disillusion, like: "What does it matter what **I** think. **My** single vote can't change anything. Well, actually it can: Back in 1776, by <u>one</u> vote, German would have become the national language of America.

- **Fear** is another factor, which keeps Americans working like **workaholics** and doesn't leave them much time for reflection: Fear of losing their jobs and with it their health insurance. The most wanted employee in either culture is the one who has a heavy mortgage, credit card debt and children. This kind of individual is a 'slave' in the hands of the employer, because under no circumstances would s/he want to lose her/his job.

If only one third of the nation cares about the state of affairs, then we don't have a real democracy, do we?! It is an Oligarchy (power of few), which tries to reproduce itself through power-maintaining chess moves. Institutions take on a life of their own, blow themselves up (bureaucracy), **grow like cancer** if not clipped back to the essential and hinterfragt (=questioned beyond the surface).

So, what we need is a thinking, reflecting, and acting population, a well educated one, in order to participate in a democracy. Does that 'Utopia' exist anywhere on the planet?

Lunes, 31. Marzo

From the flowery couch...

Deep hole...Aliva's...Churros con chocolate...Paella lunch...Saddam Hussein's money...Germany has to abstain from any <u>attack-</u>war...Rainbow of Nations...WE, the People...Traditional Spanish Paella...Saffron...Beach walk...Pepe's cover-up...

It is a hazy Monday morning. The Bahía is low, and only smaller ships are floating in and out, right now. The pink, sagging couch has undergone a transformation. After Dieter got up from solving his Stern-Xword puzzle—I was hanging over his shoulders, too, in order to help fill some empty spaces in the crossword puzzle—there was a **deep hole** in the middle of the sofa. This poor, sagging couch couldn't handle 380 German pounds[50]. We started our marriage with 320 pounds, so each of us added less than one pound for each marriage year, what a burden! I won't tell you about the distribution! To fill up the hole in the couch, we bought a huge cushion at Corte Ingles, stuffed it in there, and covered the couch with its original flowery cover. Now every time I look at it, I break out in a laughter, because it looks like a dog is lying under the cover, and I imagine Pepe sitting on top of the couch, telling his perro-pelo joke.

Yesterday, we spent a typical Spanish Sunday with friends. In the morning, we had invited Philipp II and Armada for breakfast at **Aliva's**. We met around ten in front of the house, actually it was only nine according to the previous winter time, and walked down to the old town plaza. The streets were eerily empty, because it was way too early for Spaniards on a Sunday morning, and we wondered if Aliva's was open, yet. Aliva's is situated in a side street off the left hand corner of Plaza Pombo, facing inland, and is famous for its **churros con chocolate**. Philipp II and I are churro experts: We agreed that the ones at the stand 220m away from our houses are just as good, just different. The churros at the stand are finger-thick and crunchier, while Aliva's are double in size and have more substance. These churros are dipped in creamy, melted dark chocolate, and the Spaniards and us love them for breakfast or meriendas, teatime, in the late

---

50.   In America we weigh 10% more, (hahaha!), because one pound has only 450 grams there.

afternoon. Over dipping chocolate, we had lively conversations about women's lib(eration), women's careers, amas de casas (housewives), standards of cleanliness, the medical profession, etc. It is a delight starting the day with friends.

Around 2 p.m., we all drove out to Prof Antonio's little village, just outside of Santander, where we were invited for a **Paella-lunch**. After a hazy, cool morning the sun came out and Antonio started the fire in an outdoor grill, in the midst of a beautiful natural garden environment of rocks, little hills, flowers, bushes and trees. The house had been bought in the 70s. Antonio said that they wouldn't be able to afford it nowadays. It was bought with Saddam Hussein's money, when they came back from Iraq where he had worked as a geologist. As I had noticed earlier, during department coffee breaks, Antonio has a deeper insight into the politics of the Middle East, and when you have lived in a country, you have developed special bonds there with the people. I can imagine that it is especially hard for them seeing all these atrocities on TV. His wife, Ronny, is British, so officially both countries are in alliance with the US, while massive peace demonstrations are going on in many countries around the world. I heard it has become very uncomfortable for German exchange students in the USA, because Germany is officially against an **attack-war**. US Defense Minister Rumsfeld needs to study the history books: It was dictated to Germany after WWII that the nation has to abstain from any attack-war, it could only defend itself. Germans will be forever grateful to their American brothers, but they will not follow blindly.

My love for a country is not based on;—and I hope it will never be influenced by—big politics. It is based on the love and relationships I have formed with the people, on the love for the countryside, and the country's special cultural features. Each country has its own specific character, which I have seen combined in an enneagram, once. Together, we would all form that beautiful **rainbow of nations**, each shining in its own specific color and trademark.

Five nationalities and 17 people were participating in the Sunday Paella-lunch: British, French, Argentinean, Spanish and German. This is the way Antonio grew up. They would always host people of different nationalities in his parents' house, and Antonio and his wife are still upholding that tradition. This is how future leaders, Presidents and CEOs need to be brought up; then they would forget about war as an option for conflict resolution. Isn't it about time that **WE, the People**, issued a mandate for our future leaders?

Standing around the huge table and the fireplace, discussing big and small politics, or just joking back and forth, people had the opportunity to watch how traditional **Spanish paella** is cooked. When the flames of the fire receded, a huge pan, about 80cm in diameter, was put on the grill, filled with 2/3 of a bottle of olive oil, and a huge whole garlic was roasted in it. Then precooked chicken pieces were fried, tomato sauce added, raw rice, vegetable broth, peas and green beans were stirred under, langostinos were placed on top, and the huge pan was covered with a multi-folded tablecloth, so that the rice could soak up all the liquid. Paellas can be combined with a lot of different things, just like pizzas. While the paella was simmering, huge platos of raw ham from beef (cerrano) and from pig (lomo and jamon) were served, plus a fish 'pudding' which is similar in consistency to crab cake. The paella was the best one I have eaten, yet. The first one, which I had tried in 1973 in Estatit, near Barcelona, on vacation, I didn't really like. It was all white and didn't contain one of the major, very expensive ingredients: **Saffron**, which gives the paella a deep yellow-orange color.

After lunch the sun disappeared, and the whole party moved up to the deck, while we drove out to the nearby **beaches** with Nieves and Antonio's grand-daughter to take a walk along the beaches. One beach was pretty rough, facing North, but beautifully nestled into a bay of rocks. The other beach, stretching endlessly southwest, was warmer with fine clean sand and cozy sand dunes. Spain has beautiful beaches, and they are always frequented, especially on the weekends.

When we got back to Antonio's house, the women were sitting on the deck chatting and the men were playing cards inside. Pepe said that the card game was just a **cover-up** for drinking beer together. I believed him, because they all looked a little spaced out. I hope the women drove home! After we kissed the Spanish Goodbyes on both cheeks and thanked the hosts for a wonderful Sunday afternoon, Admiral Adolfo and Mother Nieves took us back home around 8 p.m. You see, every social event, they enjoy at least double as long as in the US.

Lunes, 17. Abril

From the stuffed, flowery couch...

Mexican-German dinner...Long disco-night... Comillas...Gothic ruin...Scene from a mystery novel...Seminario...Neo-gothic Castle of the Marquesas...Lottery-house...Huge smoke signal...Argentinean Barbecue Master

The weather is mellow and overcast. The seagulls are flying low, frequently flapping their wings. When the weather is nice, they fly higher and glide elegantly in circles. The weekend went by like an IC[51] train through a minor city:

Friday night we had five people over for a **Mexican-German dinner**: Mother Nieves, Admiral Adolfo, Ignacio, a graduate student, who will work at CSU in the fall for a couple of months, and Fernando, also a graduate student, and his long hidden girlfriend Ana, a PhD Cambridge post doc. Nobody knew if she really existed, but Fernando always undertook those mysterious trips to Sevilla. We teased him a lot about his 'phantom'-girlfriend. So, finally he brought her out of the closet, and she is a delightful young lady, too.

As a primer plato we had tacos. Although we kept them on the mild side, they were already too hot for Mother Nieves, but everybody else seemed to enjoy them. As a Segundo plato, we served German potato salad and Frankfurter Wuerstchen.[52] For dessert we enjoyed Black Forest tart. The tray of pastels, which the Jóvenes brought from the famous Gomez Pastelería, we savored later. We had started our dinnertime relatively early, at 7:30, and that turned out perfectly for the Jóvenes, because they had planned a long **disco-night** with Prof Roughy after dinner.

Saturday, we drove out to **Comillas**, about 60 km to the West, to inspect the Gothic sight seeing attractions. The original Gothic church was a ruin up on a hill, fairly close by the seaside. A white marble angel, overlooking the cemetery, Comillas and the sea, welcomed us with open wings when we entered the portal of the old Gothic ruin, which was now a cemetery. The whole setting emanated tranquility with the sun shining on the marble and the flower bouquets, but dur-

---

51.   Fast Inter City train
52.   Special beef sausage with a crunchy consistency.

ing a full-moon night the shadows of the **old Gothic ruin**, the white, shiny marble, the imagined spirits of the dead would deliver an eerie backdrop for a scene in a **mystery novel** by Agathe Christy.

Driving further uphill, a huge Neo-gothic structure with a Moran portal appeared before us, which said: **Diocesana Universidad**. We parked the car and walked uphill where we had an unobstructed view over the whole town, the ocean, and over the Neo-gothic castle of the Marquesas de Comillas. The Seminario for priests had been built around 1850, with two more distinct additions and styles added later. It is in the process of being sold, we heard over lunch. Whoever buys it, needs a splendid idea for usage and tons of money to renovate and maintain the old structures.

After a walk through the Diocesan gardens—the building was closed for the general public—we took a tour through the **Neo-gothic castle** of the Marquesas right on the other hill, opposite the Seminario, driving down, and pilgrimating up again. It was a quick ten-minute tour in Spanish, and what I remember are the exquisitely carved wooden ceilings, the beautiful stained-glass windows, and the elegant paintings of the proud Marquesas.

After our cultural intake, we had mejeones[53] in a mason with pan and vino tinto. We wanted to take a beach-walk afterwards, but decided that the Santander beaches were much nicer and drove back home.

Sunday afternoon, we spent in Novales again, in Admiral Adolfo's and Mother Nieve's **Lottery house** with about the same 15 people as last Sunday at Antonio's. This time, Martín, the Argentinean professor barbecued for the whole crowd, while Mother Nieves prepared the salads inside. It was sunny and very windy, and at one point a huge flame shot up burning the dried grass close by the fireplace. Nothing much could have happened though, because the ground was pretty moist, but the scene looked as if stranded Earthlings had sent a huge **smoke signal** to heaven in order to be rescued from the war against Iraq, for example, the load of their taxes, and other earthly plagues.

Martín and Adolfo spoiled us with roasted chicken, beef and sausage (chorizo), grilled eggplants, peppers and onions, all roasted in their skins, peeled and sprinkled with olive oil. Antonio said that **Argentineans are Master barbecuers**, and that he will bring over an Argentinean mason to construct his new barbecue addition. Indeed, Martín grilled everything to perfection in spite of the relative primitive equipment. After the huge Sunday lunch, some señores played MUS again, while others listened to a fútbol game on the radio. The señoras chatted

---

53.   Mussels with a lot of muscles!!!

and took a walk into the village, while others relaxed in recliners in the sun. Walking through the village we noticed that many villagers did the same, namely spending a leisurely Sunday afternoon with family and friends. Around 8 p.m. we drove home over serpentine highland roads—it looked like the Vor-Alpen—in Philipp's and Armanda's car, having some good after-party laughs.

During the many weekend activities I noticed that I have a lot more stamina, now, than before the surgery. Not all my aches and pains are gone, yet, but it is going steadily upwards. Pretty soon I shall be so recovered that I can't wait to start a new school year again. One really needs some hustle, buzz and stress in life and a **real mission**!

Domingo, 13. Abril

From my bed with a gorgeous view...

Small c-culture...Boat tour...British tourism...Real estate...Virgin del Mar...Plaza Pombo...Good Bye party for Martín...Hegemonial language expectations...

I have opened the curtains and the window in my room to fully enjoy the view to the Bahía. It is 8:30 p.m. and still light out, on the verge of dusk. This is the time of day I love best, when things quiet down from a busy day. I have prepared dinner, ready to switch on the oven, but we won't eat before 10 p.m. Living in another country I like to fully immerse in the rhythms and customs. The advantage of living in a place, being a non-tourist, is that you absorb the **small c-culture**, which would pass by you as a tourist, because you'd be focused more on the big C-culture, like sightseeing and landscapes.

This afternoon, we took a **boat tour** on the Bahía, enjoying Santander from the seaside. The sea was a bit rough because of the South winds warming up the North of Spain. Just three days ago it was 12 ^{0}C lower, but today we had a balmy 21 ^{0}C. An old lady got scared on the rocking deck of our tourist boat, and fled under deck. Santander really <u>is</u> a beautiful town, from all angles. Most buildings along the Bahía, erected around the turn of the century, are well maintained and shine brightly in a splendid white coat, while others need a makeover. Always before elections, Armada said, they spiff up the town; one can see many scaffolds around the buildings at this time. On the other side of the Bahía there are green rolling hills, mostly with countryside character and low-rise houses. They have very attractive playas on the other side, in Somo, awaiting the **British tourism** in the summer. When we took a ferry over, two months ago, everything was shut down and boarded up, except some shops, bars and restaurants for the locals.

We looked at **real estate prices**, today. They are pretty hefty in Santander, but still affordable in the countryside. A piso like ours with sea view, three bedrooms, two bathrooms, garage, lift, parks, and a house manager would cost around 180.000 to 200.000 €, while you could get a big house in the countryside for the same or less money. The most expensive area in Santander is Sardinero with its white sand beaches, The Casino, ***** and ****hotels, and attractive modern architecture.

The morning, we spent in **Virgin del Mar**, about 10 miles outside of Santander. On the Monday of Pentecost, many religious people from Santander pilgrimate to this old church, which was erected at the end of the XIV century as a gothic structure, but underwent many changes. This place is dedicated to the Virgin Maria, Jesus' Mom, who has been the declared patron of Santander since 1917. Situated on a rocky peninsula, surrounded by the branding sea, this old church presents the sole focus of the 'pilgrim fathers and mothers' which is to light a candle and to make a vow to the Virgin del Mar, who also watches over the fishermen in this region. The landscape is picturesque, and many of the views I have already enjoyed in the bountiful galleries and frame shops of Santander: Islands of rocks in the foreground, surrounded by the turquoise sea, further out light houses, and green rolling hills in the background, with the snow-covered Cantabria mountains topping off the breathtaking scenery.

Returning from Virgin del Mar, we left the car in the garage, and went down the steep hill to **Plaza Pombo** where a huge tent had aroused our curiosity. There was a festive atmosphere at the main plaza: Kids riding in carousels, folks sitting outdoors in Café Pombo, church goers returning with palms in their hands, because it was Palm Sunday. Inside the tent there was an exhibition of about twenty floats with artistically carved scenes about the dramatic happenings from Green Thursday, Good Friday, Saturday and Easter Sunday. These rolling artistic floats will partake in the Easter procession in Santander. Mostly Catholic Spain is devoted to the Virgin, Mother Mary. Live-sized virgins, beautifully draped in velvet, observe Jesus' sufferings with rolling tears and pain-stricken facial expressions. The Jesus statues had Spanish features, Oberammergauer, and sometimes Middle Eastern physiques.

Sábado afternoon, we spent again in Antonio's and Ronny's house for the Argentinean professor's **Good Bye party**. Antonio grilled sardines and dorados, while Ronny had prepared Greek salad, potato salad, Roman lettuce hearts, quartered and sprinkled with a balsamic dressing, and the traditional raw ham plate (Serrano). For dessert we had little bite-sized tartlets from a confitería, which guests had brought along. Since **Martín** had to head out to Santander airport after the Sunday lunch around 5:30 p.m., we accompanied him to the car to say Good Bye, while a group of men played MUS, and the group of women chatted. They told funny stories about traveling and suitcases getting changed by accident, but I didn't understand much.

There is a **hegemonial expectation** in Spain that people who come to Spain should speak Spanish. Part of that expectation developed from history, I believe, when Spain was a world power in the 15th and 16th century. The other reason is that the Spanish speaking community lives all around the world, and mostly people from South America work here. It is a very powerful community, very close-nit, since the Spanish people bathe in communal being, while most English speaking countries are more reserved and individualistic.[54] Spain has been opening her gates to English, now, and communication with the English-speaking world should be easier in about 10 to 15 years.

This **hegemonial language expectation** seems to be characteristic for 'Islanders' or 'Peninsulaners', like North America, Spain and France. World language and world power goes hand in hand: It was French in the 18th and 19th century, which dominated the educated classes around the world. North Americans, except the French speaking Canadians, don't have that expectation, to speak English, towards visitors in their own country but they do have it when they go out into the world and travel. I was told three times on the phone during soliciting calls: "What? You live in Spain and you don't speak Spanish?" After the third call I started asking: ¿Habla Ingles? >NO ¿Habla Alemán? >NO ¿Habla Francés? >NO ¿Habla Suahili?[55] >NO "Lo siento!"(I am sorry) I said and hung up.

The rain is whipping against the windows, and the wind is shaking the whole building. The weather God has been gracious with us over the weekend. Two more weekends will be full of activities, and the third weekend, we'll be busy packing up. The countdown has already begun.

---

54. Author's observations. Don't take it for granted. Make your own experiences
55. Borrowed from Admiral Adolfo

Lunes, 14. Abril

From the best seat in the house...my bed...

Smaragd...My calling...Back on my post...Character education...Challenging teachers...Positive attitude...My home country...

The Bahía is **smaragd** green, right now. Deep threatening clouds are hanging over the mountains on the opposite side, while the evening sun with its mellow light is projecting the sunrays onto the houses left of me. Seagulls are sailing peacefully through the ozone-rich air. Sometimes, they are really combative and quarrelsome, right before the weather changes. Verdi was attacked by one once, which he fought off with his umbrella. From a safe perspective it is funny and reminds me of a scene in Sherlock Holmes, but I bet it felt life threatening at the time.

All the time I have waited for a sign or a dream to show me the way professionally, if my calling would still be in teaching: Today, it arrived in form of an email that over 30 students from the upper grades alone have signed up for German. That has not occurred in Roosevelt High before. I guess my High Commander in Chief wants me **back on my post**. The counselor can't wait for me to come back, either. Yes, I guess I miss that professionalism, camaraderie and sisterhood. Once my energy level matches that of my teenagers[56] (hahaha), I'll be ready to go back to the Teacher Academy in early August. I am definitely enthusiastic about my subject areas (German, ESL, Multi-cultural education), and kids are different every year. So, I'll pack up and go home: To teach again!

The subject area is only the medium through which a pedagogue educates the whole student: **Character education** is most effectively transmitted by daily example: By being kind, honest, fair, humorous, forgiving, patient, polite, strict, tough, etc. For some kids school is the only 'home'. They lean on a stable, kind adult. A pedagogue needs stamina and the firm belief that what s/he plants will some day bear fruit, even if the adolescent is resisting the teachings at the time. I do not remember my 'easy' teachers. I do remember my challenging, demanding teachers. Those helped me grow most. I guess both types are necessary to keep

---

56. Will it ever?

the balance: The nourishing type and the challenging type. These traits can be combined in one person.

A good 'old' friend of mine wrote that I should keep a **positive attitude**. It's true: I had an attitude problem. As I told you earlier: Germans have an attitude problem. They would rather see the glass half empty than half full. I need to go home to my American Brothers and Sisters again, to the land of my forefathers, to see the glass half full again. It is all a matter of perspective, and mental and physical health.

What do I love most about **my home country**: The 260 and more days of sunshine in Colorado, the Rocky Mountains, the dry climate, the esthetics of my hometown Ft. Collins, a sporty, healthy University town of 120.000 inhabitants plus 30.000 students; The American people with their childlike open hearts, upbeat attitude, generosity and friendly nature. Somebody said recently in a conversation: "The violence in America scares me to death." "Those are the 5% who make the daily headlines", I responded, "Those are not the American people, trust me, I am one of them!"

Pascua Sábado, 19. Abril

From my 80 cm bed...

Celebration of Pascua...Lecture version...Picos de Europa...Church bells...Teleférico...Invigorating mountains...Lemon plantation...Lemonade... Paella...Lemon tart...Albañil...Troubadour...

No wonder my Hispanic kids are not in school on Good Friday. In Spanish speaking countries the **celebration of Pascua** (Easter) has a deep religious character: It starts with Green Thursday, the day when Jesus celebrated the Last Supper with his disciples. Good Friday is a holiday here, when Jesus was nailed to the cross. Saturday, the shops are open, again, and festive Easter Sunday celebrations with processions are taking place all around the country. Germans also celebrate Easter Monday. Public schools and the University have Easter vacation for ten days, from Green Thursday on. Many families headed to the South of Spain, to the sunny beaches on autopistas backed up 22km or more.

Since the weather was triste today, we spent the afternoon working at the University. Right now, I am working on a **lecture version** of my script for educational purposes, cutting out all the events and thoughts, which I do not want to discuss in the classroom. Although Sevilla, in the South of Spain, had been highly recommended to us, we did not want to spend ten hours on overcrowded autopistas with coches moving like worms on a dried-up pavement. We preferred to spend the time in nature, in beautiful smaragd-green Cantabria.

Green Thursday, we headed southwest over Torrelavega, in the direction of Oviedo to the **Picos de Europa**, an older high mountain range of about 1850m. At Fuente Dé, a village situated at the bottom of the Picos (750m), we purchased tickets for the Teleférico to ride to the top. (1850m)

<I just stepped outside on the balcony to acutely take in the sounds of the **church bells**, ringing in name of the resurrection of Christ for Easter Sunday. It is half an hour before midnight. How I miss the sound of church bells in America!>

Overcoming the distance from sea level in Santander to the very top of the Picos is about the same as starting in Ft. Collins (1500m), and climbing to the very top of the Rocky Mountains. The tickets were numbered, and we had to wait one and a half hours for our ride in the **Teleférico**, which could transport

about 25 people in one gondola. We used the time for comida (lunch). By accident I ordered the most boring sandwich I ever ate: A queso sandwich, which is
that white, almost neutral tasting cheese. I should have ordered queso <u>curado</u>,
because that region is famous for its cheeses.

The temperature at the bottom of the Picos, in Fuente Dé, was 15^0C, and
when we reached the top after a steep 10-minute ride, the temperature was still a
pleasant 7^0C. Fortunately the wind was still, but it was overcast. We meandered a
little higher, partly on snow-covered paths, but returned 2km before Aliva's, a
high mountain restaurant and hostel for climbers, since we were not equipped
with snow boots. On the way back to the teleférico station I fully enjoyed the
vista, which reminded me a lot of the Rockies. Whenever I need to revitalize from
schoolwork I drive to the mountains. The same happened at the Picos: The high
mountains were so **invigorating** and energizing for me that I could not fall asleep
until 3 a.m.

Good Friday afternoon we were invited to Royal Carlos' and Jolly Loli's
lemon plantation in Novales. Mother Nieves drove with us in our blue coche to
show us the way, while the 'lonely' Admiral followed a little later in his white VW
Combi. We took our own car, this time, since the families planned on spending
Easter vacation in the countryside. Novales is such a peaceful place, nestled into
the valley, protected by middle mountain ranges all around, generating a micro-
climate conducive to growing lemons, oranges, kiwis, and mandarins. When we
arrived at the yellow gate of the estate, Carlos was raking grass. I don't think he
ever sits around, except for when eating. He had hired a person to mow the lawn
of the huge lemon estate. The trees had been fertilized with cow manure, draped
in a ring around the trees. No, it did not smell at all! Marcos, my Spanish tutor
and English student, his sister Patricia, my German—English colleague, their
grandmother Carmina, and Nieves' and Admiral A<u>d</u>olfos's daughter Laura, the
law student, joined us for lunch, too.

Freshly squeezed lemonade was the overture to a picturesque **paella** lunch. For
the primer plato we had Grandma's famous potato salad: Ensaladilla Rusa,
accompanied by Mother Nieve's noodle-tuna salad with her special salsa rosa: 2
eggs, 1 c. of olive oil, salt, vinegar, ketchup, beaten creamy with a mixer. As a segundo plato Loli placed a huge paella pan for 20! people, beautifully decorated
with marisco (frutti di mare), in the middle of a large, sturdy wooden table, surrounded by 10 people. The paella was glowing in its deep yellow-orange color
and contained many different kinds of seafood. Since I needed to know the diameter of the paella pan, Loli had everybody guess, and then measured it with a tape:

55cm. The hot paella tasted excellent, especially in that nippy weather. Dark clouds were moving in after a sunny Good Friday morning.

After the main composition the lemon theme appeared in the Coda again: Nieves had baked two **lemon tarts**, which were sticking to the bottom of the pan. Carlos doesn't talk much, but he is very aware of his surroundings, and a very attentive, funny host. Since Nieves had problems getting the lemon tart pieces onto the plates, Carlos put a paleta de **albañil** on the table, a tool used for masonry, which looked like an oversized tart shovel. (Torten Heber)

I teased Admiral Adolfo a lot over lunch, basically using all he had taught me in a different context, firing back at him, and he was ready to make peace. After coffee he kneeled at my feet with a lilac weed in his hands, pleading: "I love you!" I sealed the German-US-Spanish alliance with a kiss on both of his cheeks, dramatically taking the lilac to my heart. This **troubadour** scene could only happen in Spain, maybe in Italy, too. The party said I should press the lilac in my book. Right now, I will put it in my ocean arrangement of water, turquoise glass dots, seashells and sea grass. Weeds are beautiful flowers, too! I took a picture just now.

Pascua Domingo, 20.Abril

From my favorite Bahía seat...

Easter Sunday...¡España es diferente!...Procession...KuKluxKlan...Back in the 16th century...Easter address of Joh. Paul II...Courage, facing the whole world...Overcoming evil...

It is **Easter Sunday** and the Bahía was engulfed in a heavy, gray, nebulous soup, this morning. It was pretty dark over breakfast, but now the houses on the opposite countryside are already visible. The birds are singing in expectation of some warming sunrays. They sing at different times here: "**España es diferente!**" our Spanish grammar teacher always used to say. They sing in two different shifts: around 3 a.m., and then around 6 a.m. again, while in Germany they start with the breaking of dawn. I did not fall asleep until 3 a.m., last night, because at 2 a.m. when I was finished with writing and intended to go to bed, all of a sudden, a stream of cars went through the streets like during rush hour. Also a lot of pedestrians were rushing home. I figured they had returned from Easter resurrection mass, since all of Santander's church bells had been ringing at 11:30 p.m. Religious ceremonies play a big part in Spain.

After the paella lunch on the lemon plantation we went to church, too, in order to experience the **procession**. Jolly Loli was all dressed up, and wore a beautiful lipstick, matching her lox rose bush in her front yard. While I had really longed to see that old church from the 16th century, I had not opted for 2 ½ hours of religious ceremonies. Loli had thought that the procession would start at 6 p.m., but it was the Good Friday mass, which started before the procession. From the emporia we had a fantastic view to watch every detail: The church was built in a Romanesque[57] style with a heaven-blue—golden baroque side altar. The main altar was draped with a black cloth. The priest, his assistant, and a layperson read the story from the bible of when Jesus was sentenced to death by Pilatus. The church was completely filled, and groups of different colored '**KuKluxKlan**' were distributed all over church. Nieves said they belonged to different religious groups in the county, and the meaning of hiding the faces under the pointed hoods, is repenting in anonymity.

---

57.   The original Romanesque style was built as early as 800 A.D.

After the communion one of those groups in purple lifted the black drapes, climbed on ladders, and took Jesus off the cross, nail by nail, passing the nails, the INRI[58] sign, and the thorn-crown to a group of young 'repenters' in white. When they had taken off the last nail they presented the dead corpse to Mother Mary, and then laid him into a glass sarcophagus (coffin). Basically, they replayed the scene from the bible when Jesus was taken off the cross, salved, and put into the mighty stone grave of this rich guy, Josef from Arimathea. During the scene the priest could have really woken up the dead corpse with his voice. My purse was vibrating in my hands, and every time he started singing, Loli looked at me, and we couldn't help gasping, like teenagers behaving badly in church. She said that his church is never full because he likes to drag out the ceremonies. It was the way that she said it, which tickled another laugh attack. I really felt the priest's voice resonating in my bones. It was out of this world. After he gave his last blessings to the church community, singing in Gregorian chants with his beautiful **elephant trumpet voice**, the 'KuKluxKlans' got ready to shoulder the floats of the Virgin Mary and the glass coffin with Jesus. Accompanied by drummers the procession moved slowly to a nearby chapel.

Since the dark clouds formatted into a black wall and we all felt chilly, we departed from the procession near the 'Village Inn', and went to a bar to warm up with some hot tea. I did not regret the 2-½ hours of religious ceremonies, because it was fascinating to watch how different cultures give different meanings to rituals and costumes, like the 'KuKluxKlan' outfit. When we were watching the replay of Jesus' burial, Loli said: "Now, we are really back in the 16th century, aren't we?" Dramatic plays like this are intense teachings, and kids will never forget them in their lives. The Easter rituals are deeply ingrained in the hearts of Catholic Spain.

When we arrived home from the Novales' Good Friday ceremonies I watched the Pope on TV. He has the same illness as Cassius Clay (Mohammed Ali) and Michael Fox: Parkinson. Pope Johannes Paul II gave his Easter address to millions of people gathered around the Vatican. Many times his speech got stuck with his oncoming Parkinson shakes, and his forehead skin would fold in sorrow, while at other times his sermon flew rhythmically. During his Gregorian chants he had no problems producing the words. That's why I use music and rhythm in the classroom frequently because they are soul liberators. Watching the frail Pope with his aware mind I thought: 'Now, <u>this</u> is **courage, facing the whole world** with all your human frailty!'

---

58. Jesus of Nazareth, **Rex**...

After the Easter address of the Pope, the Santander night procession was brought right to my living room. The floats I had seen in the exhibition on Plaza Pombo earlier were beautifully decorated with natural flowers and brightly illuminated for the night procession. Twenty carriers shouldered the floats, directed by a ceremonial master who insured their rhythmic and even steps from side to side; otherwise the artistically carved statues would have been in danger of collapsing. Easter is even more intensely celebrated here than Christmas, because with the resurrection of Christ, mankind had been given another lecture in history for **overcoming the evil** in this world.

Same day, 10 p.m.

St. Vicente...

Upon Patricia's recommendation we spent Sunday afternoon in St. Vicente, a fisher town, past Comillas, about 68km from Santander. Since it was Easter Sunday a swarm of tourists were feasting in the seafood restaurants. Easter menus ranged from 20€ to 40€. We saw a native establishment, where it cost 17.50€, but that was completely filled, so we decided to have lunch in Comillas later, after our sightseeing. We walked steeply up the hill along old city walls past a Fort for the old church from the 15th century. It was closed. The vast courtyard looked fortified. In the Middle Ages town folks must have sought refuge up here. The hustle and buzz of the main tourist street below us sounded like irritated bees suffering from pollen deprivation.

The view over the wide river delta, flowing into the sea, was spectacular. An old bridge with at least 20 arches, looking like an old Roman viaduct, spanned across several side arms of the river. The scene looked eerie, though: Because of the ebb and not having enough rainfalls, smaller boats were lying forlorn and distributed all over in the mood. The larger fish drawlers swam on water in the harbor, but ten meters further the oily moody landscape began again. I think the best time to go to St. Vicente would be in the morning when the fish drawlers float in, and the wheeling and dealing over the daily fish prices begins. Then one gets to see the real people and the real character of the town.

Lunes, 21. Abril

From the stuffed, flowery couch…

Interview with Marcos…Spanish youth…School system…Healthcare…
Working mothers…Politics…Economy…Cultural traditions…Trash…
Shit=Good Luck…

This morning, I conducted an **interview with Marcos**, my Spanish tutor and English student, in class:

>What are the **hobbies** of the Spanish youth?

Fútbol, go to the beach, go out on Friday and Saturday night, usually from 10 p.m. to 4 a.m., depending on the age. That's when the bars close. We also meet with friends at home, friends from different countries.

>What do young people like to do **at home**?

Watch TV, play on the Internet, download free music and free movies.

>What about **reading?**

No, we don't like to read.

>What **chores** do young people do at home?

Clean their rooms, clear the table after dinner, and hang up clothes.

>What do young people **care about**?

Their friends and clothes.

>What about **politics**?

Usually not, only when there is something important.

>What type of **music** do they listen to?

Disco, electronic and pop music.

>Which are the **favorite singers**?

Alejandro Sanc, Ricky Martin, and a group from the Basque country: La oreja de Van Gogh. He lost an ear (oreja) and went crazy.

>At what age can Spanish youth **vote, drink and drive**?

Vote at 18, drive also at 18, and drink at 16, although this is not reinforced.

>Can you explain the **school system** to me?

Guarderia starts with the age of 3 to 6.

Colegio primaria from 6 to 12,

Colegio secundaria from 12 to 16, which is mandatory.

Instituto from 16 to 18 (High school)

After 18, if you don't pass the exams, you have to go to a Colegio de adultos.

>Tell me about the **exams**! How many tests do you have?

We have 4 exams: Before Christmas, Easter, in-between, and in June. About 10-20% fail and have to repeat the course.

>What is the **grading system** like?

5-6 sufficiente

6-7 bien

7-9 notable

9-10 sobresaliente

>How are you graded in a course?

Mainly on those four exams.

>How large are the classes?

30 students average

>What is the **healthcare** system like?

It's free and some people, who can afford it, have private insurances. There were some problems with hospital buildings not being properly maintained.

>Under the Franco regime not many mothers worked. How is it today?

There was a law under Franco that women had to take care of their children. They were not allowed to work. Today, over 50% work, usually from 8 to 6 p.m.[59]

>How many people vote in Spain?

60 to 70%.

>What effect did the Euro reform have on Spain?

It was good for the economy. Spain places in the middle of the European Union. Compared to Germany, France and England it is still poor.

>Poverty is relative: Spain looks like a rich, modern country to me. (Women <u>always</u> need to have the last word!)[60]

I learned something else during the interview with Marcos: The Easter processions are not so much an expression of religiosity and deep faith, but more of a long standing **cultural tradition**. The KuKluxKlan probably adopted these costumes with the pointed hoods, because the Spanish traditions go way back to the Middle Ages. He also had a funny explanation when I asked him about the **trash** on the floor of the bars. I said: "Santander is such a clean city, considering that people drop everything on the ground, dog shit everywhere, and the high winds

---

59. Remember there is a longer lunch break!

60. Not really: Sometimes I don't have any words at all!

blow the trash around." Marcos replied: "It creates jobs." Trash is collected every day and heavy city machinery cleans the Plazas and streets in the early morning hours. "**We clean a lot in Spain**!" said Armada MD some time ago. When you step in shit here it means **Good Luck**, as in Germany. I think they invented this to overcome the shit more easily!

Miércoles, 23.Abril

From my 80cm bed, sitting Yoga style...

Writing process...Discipline...Rough draft...Computer draft...Necessary distance...Editor...Student buddies...Electronic editing...Sneak preview...Culturally sensitive matters...Updated/Outdated...Backups...Sick of your script...Doubts...Share your insides?...3rd person singular...Ezekiel...

The countdown began: 10 more days in beautiful Cantabria, then we transition over to Germany to look after Oma and Opa. Since no established writer ever writes about the **writing process**, I thought a Greenhorn like me could allow some insight into the writing discipline. This could also be an eye opener for my students to realize that writing is a craft you need to file constantly, like a piece of wood to smoothen out the bumps and rough spots. You cannot just 'whip' your project together the night before, and expect it to be a piece of artwork. Although some of you are real 'good whippers', that does not apply to the majority of us mortal humans: We need to work really hard at it with a lot of discipline, because not everything in writing is fun.

My **rough draft** is flowing out of my pen into a spiral notebook, which I can carry everywhere I feel comfortable writing: In special places at home, at Cafés, by the ocean, in airplanes, busses, at bus stops (missing the bus), and in airports. I like the early morning hours, or the quiet night hours for listening inside, for deep reflection. But if I have a lot to report on I can also write in busy places, establishing my fantasy island in the midst of branding, chatting waves, honking horns, and howling motors. At home, I light my aroma therapy set, choosing a scent, which corresponds with my mood, and a candle for illumination, do a short invocation that my writing may serve for the higher good, and switch on some soft music.

Writing my virgin draft, I try not to stop the creative flow by censuring myself. Emotions need to be e-moted and flow into the rhythm of the language. After the chapter is produced, I read my creation. That is the most enjoyable part. Next morning, before I go to the University, I read it out aloud to hear if the rhythm flows, and if the words sound too casual, too baroque, or too sophisticated, and I make the first changes.

While I transfer my handwritten script onto the computer, I work predominantly with my logical brain, while at night, all the feelings try to find expressions in words and sentence melodies. During the **computer draft** I edit again. Then I do spell checking, but you still need to read your script attentively after the spell check, since the spell checker does not pick up on words spelled correctly, but make no sense within the sentence structure or context. After spell checking, I go back to the previous chapters to see how the added part connects with the previous part, detecting more rough spots, which need to be smoothened out. If you have something important to send off, never do it the same day: It needs to lay over night, or for a few days, until you get the **necessary distance** from your 'creation' to be able to look at it critically and more objectively. A creator can never separate herself from her creation totally, but at least step back and look at it from a different perspective.

To insure that objectivity, every writer has an **editor**. Especially when you write in a foreign language it is necessary to have a native editor. Nobody can ever write in a foreign language 100% correctly, because patterns in your native language will sneak in, those, which have settled in your brain ten years before you started learning a foreign language. **Student buddies** in school are the best editors, because when they don't understand your writings clearly, you know it is time to 're-vamp' it, to search for other expressions. It is sheer nonsense that students should not 'grade' other students' papers, because we are ALL a Community of Learners. No, they should not give the final grade—that's the teacher's responsibility—but they should be involved in the process of editing and learning from each other.

So, after each part is finished, I send my script off electronically to my editor in Chicago. (☺!!) She edits it electronically, inserts these smiley faces, sends it back and I right click on the changes to either accept or reject them. When the English is cleaned up I send the respective part to our host professor for a **sneak preview** to make sure there are no factual mistakes, or culturally offensive parts—although I would never compromise the truth-, or anything they can't live with. My critical analyst and cultural adviser in Berlin, my Egyptian friend, has been especially helpful, because he is a bicultural kid just like me, and possesses heightened awareness in **culturally sensitive matters**. Sometimes, the advisers contradict each other, or the writer has strong sentiments about a part: Then it is the author's decision to leave it in there, and she has to live with it.

Some close friends and family I have let participate in the 'unclean' computer draft, called Spain etc. **Update**, because it would be **outdated** by the time the 'clean' computer draft is produced. After editing the editor's corrections, one needs to work on the settings, page-breaks, and esthetics, especially the layout of the poems. During all those transactions, revisions, and moving to different 'speaking' computers one needs to make sure to have the necessary **backups**, because discs can go bad, other people can mess with your computer, discs could be confiscated during checks, my backpack could be stolen, as happened here recently to someone else. At this point I would rather have my money stolen than my discs.

Even the 'clean' draft still contains some typos, and whenever I get new insights I go back and change things. In-between the changes you get really **sick of your script**, get **doubts** about the quality and relevance. Then friends pick you up with encouraging remarks to spur you on. Finally, some day it will go into print, because you really want to see your 1000 hours and more in black and white in one clean piece, and give joy to your co-travelers in the form of a hard copy, but there will still be typos and even mistakes in there. (Never trust schoolbooks! They are full of mistakes!) And you just have to live with those mistakes, or hope for the next cleaner edition.

Sometimes, you get doubts about your privacy if you really want to **share your insides** (no spelling mistake here!) with the rest of the world. That's why <u>real</u> writers create characters, so that they can play themselves out in a character and develop a drama or storyline around it. This insures their anonymity, but it really doesn't—not for a trained reader! The writer will always shine through his/her opus, even in the **3rd person singular**. Whenever I get stuck, like now, searching for a closing, because I want to go to bed, I ask my writing guide for help. I had this dream once: His name is **Ezekiel**.[61] I thought I made this up, a creation from both languages: Easy + Kiel (Ger.: old writing feather). But now I saw on the Spanish calendar that this guy really existed, and I remembered that there are Old-Testament writings by him. So, my 1st person singular just says Good night to Ezekiel and my benevolent readers, now, and goes to bed, hoping for an 'Easy Feather', tomorrow.

---

61.   Ezekiel: Whom God makes strong. Prophet of Judah's exile experience.

Viernes, 25. Abril

From the stuffed, flowery couch...

Cabárceno...Nature Zoo...Missing Tiger...Felix...Alpha Wolf...Rhino Aphrodisiac...Mountain Man...Hardest good Byes...Bullet proof vest...A Mother's Heart (poem)...

Yesterday, Juéves afternoon, during Easter break, Philipp II and Armada took us on an excursion to **Parque de la Naturaleza Cabárceno**, 15km outside of Santander. If the mountains opposite the Bahía were made of glass one could see the limestone columns and rock formations of Cantabria's second best sight seeing attraction next to the Picos. This 800-hectar-nature **zoo**, with 27km of roads inside the park, houses many of the endangered species on the earth. Because of its natural environment Cabárzeno's breeding program has been extremely successful in raising elephants, white rhinos, brown bears, and tigers. They need their privacy, too!

Unfortunately, we did not get to see any of the tigers. I am always fascinated by their beauty, strength and majestic movements. The jaguars had beautiful fur markings, and the lions with their royal manes were impressive, too, but nothing compares to the **tiger**. I am a cat person: I love their independence, their moody, unexpected behavior, their intelligence and playfulness, their soft, cuddly touch, and their sometimes-aggressive paws. I missed Felix, our black and white tomcat with a black heart on his left shoulder, a lot this year.

The elephants gave me a flashback to India when I was touched by the temple elephant and the Ganesha ceremony, but those in the park were the African elephants with the huge sailing ears. When we were watching the wolves, I thought of Konrad Lorenz[62]: How much passion and patience one needs to study animal behavior. While most of the pack was playing at the pond, nestled in the corner of their huge playground, one female was keeping guard in the middle. On the left hand was a thinner male wolf that caught my attention, because his tail was totally tucked in between his hind-legs. He was on guard and afraid, but curious enough to watch the playing pack by the pond, moving cautiously back and forth. All of a sudden, the **alpha wolf** raced away from the pack, and chased his

---

62. Konrad Lorenz: Animal behaviorist, discovered that baby geese were 'imprinted' by his mother image when they saw HIM first.

younger rival into an underground cave. 'Was ein Hundeleben!' would the Germans say: What a dog's life, meaning: What a miserable life!

The brown bears blended in with their natural environment of huge yellow-brown, reddish-brown, high-rise "Sedona"-rock formations. One was standing about 2,50m tall, rubbing his back against the limestone, while the cubs and some females played by the pond, and other teenage bears were climbing the rocks. In spite of their body mass, the rhinos were moving agilely behind the strong barrier from steel. One had a green horn from rubbing off the color of the barrier, and Philipp II said the powdered horn would be sold as an aphrodisiac in Asian countries. There was really nothing sexy about those stinking animals with their huge, drooling mouths and their muddy fecal skin.

Armada did not like any of the animals, except the esthetic jaguar, and Philipp II was even more fascinated by the rock formations. He is definitely a **mountain man** and a nature fellow. In this nature animal park, the Romans were mining iron about 2000 years ago; hence, the different shades of red. It must cost a fortune to maintain the park and feed the animals. It was a 'zoo' here on Easter Sunday, said Philipp II. He saw it on TV: Thousands of cars. Fortunately, we could move freely through the terrain, moving in and out of the car, admiring the animals and the landscape of the high, vertically standing 'Redrocks', yellow rocks, and gray rocks with greens sprouting out of every gap. One area was called Rock Gardens.

I will miss the Spanish music, too, which is playing in the background. It is very lamenting and passionate. How many times have I said Good Bye, this year, and every time my heart is lamenting. We'll give a Good Bye party for eight people, tomorrow. Our host professor, Philipp II, needs to go to Barcelona to work on a search committee. "We'd better say Good Bye, tomorrow!" he said, checking in at my workplace. Then it dawned on me that the time was almost up. Hellos are full of curiosity and expectation. Good Byes are full of memories and pain. The **hardest Good Byes are yet to come**: In August, our oldest son will be deployed to Iraq. "I will wear my bullet proof vest at all times", he said—'In August in Iraq', I thought, 'and then the rough winter in December.'

A Mother's heart

A mother's heart is not from steel
Like canons, bombs, and rifles.
They fire into soldiers' hearts
Whose mothers feel the pain
Of dying sons, with softly beating,
Tearing and lamenting hearts.
A mother's heart is not from steel
And has no stars and stripes
Or Union Jacks
Or half moons either.

potawi

One should not indulge in pain for too long, or one could drown. After our Nature Park excursion, we dined in the little Pizzeria, right across from our houses, where they even offered Indian pizza. If Philipp II comes back in time from Barcelona, we'll have one last Churro—outing together, before we hit the road to Floersheim, Germany, for our 2000km return trip in our blue coche.

Lunes, 28. Abril

From the 1. seat in the house...

Lunatic weather...Sledgehammer drilling...Black Forest green...Swabian onion cake...Secret of the Sauerkraut... Japanese Healthcare...Sea and the Mountains...Santoña...

I have opened the curtains and the window to let my thoughts drift with the waves of the Bahía. It is **lunatic weather**; the high-speed south winds are driving people edgy. You can't even write outdoors without the wind grabbing your papers and the dirt blowing in your eyes. I can't sleep very well either, at night when the wind is howling around the building. Sleeping with the window closed is not refreshing for me either. And then the hammering and the drilling go on downstairs for the 4th week now. He and his wife moved out during the reconstruction, and left us with daily nerve-racking dentist noises and **sledgehammer drillings**. They must have taken out whole walls for a totally different layout of the piso. I saw him working on the draft board over Xmas. Now I know what he brewed up back then. For a while I thought permanently living in a piso would be a good idea, but now I am longing for my house. I just want to go home.

Wow, Lightening! Horizontally across my window, which takes up the whole width of the room. Relief is in sight: The weather will change. The Bahía has unusual colors right now: Crocodile green, **Black Forest green**, tender early spring green. Thunder is rolling and the mountains on the opposite side are disappearing behind a misty wall. An airplane is flying in from Barcelona or Bilbao, landing right at the Westside of the Bahía. How comforting: The church bells are ringing harmoniously! It is 10 minutes to 8 p.m.

The Good Bye party on Saturday was light and happy, but my stomach was not. I really enjoyed my own cooking—usually I do a day <u>after</u> the guests are gone—but it was far too heavy for me. One at a time would have been 'vale'—you never say OK in Spain—but all three in combination were fatal: As a primer plato I baked a **Swabian onion cake**, similar to Quiche Lorraine. For the segundo plato we had Sauerkraut, Rippchen and Kartoffelbrei (smoked pork chops and mashed potatoes). And for dessert I had baked a lemon cheese tart, extra for Armada! Philipp II and Armada also brought this typical Torrelavega tart back from their weekly lunch with the parents. Armada's father, who is a very skilled and well-known physician, had read my husband's EKG. And since we knew he loved German food so much, we packed up a portion for him, too. I fare best with light vegetarian food, and occasionally some fish or chicken.

Since Mercedes wanted to know the recipe of the onion cake, and Ronny, Antonio's wife, wanted to know the **secret of the Sauerkraut**, I am going to add a German recipe, too, to my travel collection: Onion cake: Butter kneading dough or yeast dough for a base. Topping: Sauté 10 onions in olive oil, add a little white wine, salt and fried bacon pieces, let cool down, add 6 eggs, one sour cream, one crème fraîche, salt, pepper, Maggi[63], pour on pre-baked dough, and bake for 35 minutes on 180^{0}C (medium high), or until golden brown. The secret of the Sauerkraut is: adding 1-2 tablespoons of brown sugar per can and one apple. Look for Kuehne or Hengstenberg Mildessa at Lidl's. That's <u>mild</u> Sauerkraut.

The conversations were lively and funny, as always. What I remember are Jesus' and Mercedes' medical accounts of their two-months stay in Japan: When Mercedes had **"just" a rash** and wanted some quick medicine, six people, who did not speak English nor Spanish checked her over from head to toe, even putting an infusion into her. "Watch that they don't operate on me!" she said anxiously to her husband. "And next, they would have followed up with a computer tomography and a cat scan", added my husband. Without a language you can't argue. Tough job! I should know! All the guests enjoyed the view from the balcony down on the Bahía. This is probably the only time in my life when I will have the sea and the mountains all together. So, I will enjoy it for the final 6 days.

Sunday, we spent in the little fisher town of **Santoña**, ca. 60km East of here, in Oscar's Spanish hometown. (Remember the Australian guy from the curso) I call it my Little Santander: It is beautifully situated around a Bahía, too, and has nice, white sand beaches, and an old Fort, dating back to 1638, right at the strategic gate of the Bahía. *I just did a Google search and read the most horrible English translation on the web page about Santoña: Archeological findings date back to the Romans, and around 800, it was a religious and political power center. In the 17th century it was called "The Gibraltar of the North", because of its strategic importance in the Spanish wars with Dutch, France and England. Santoña was called PORT of SANTOÑA. The rest you can read yourself in a travel guide or on the web.* It was our last Sunday outing in Spain, and I got a little mellow over caña and rabas (draft beer and calamari). Although it is time to go home, I will miss the people and the special customs of beautiful Cantabria.

---

63.   The German's all time favorite liquid spice in a cute bottle. (see Lidl's)

This is a good place to say my **last Thank yous:**
To Philipp II for my computer workplace, our hilarious outings, the bureaucratic errands, and the friendship.
To Armada for her medical guardianship and sisterhood.
To Mother Nieves for adding so much warmth, comfort and joy to our stay.
To Admiral Adolfo for teaching me the basics, including his name!
To Royal Carlos for his hospitality.
To Jolly Loli for all the happiness and laughter.
To Marcos for his insights into the Spanish youth, culture and politics.
To his sister, Patricia, for taking me to school.
To Pepe and Claire for his nut-cracking jokes and sharing his 'village' Alcalá.
To Antonio and Ronny for their international hospitality, and the Madrid/Alcalá excursion.
To Jesus and Mercedes for sharing their funny cultural experiences.
To Ignacio for the relaxing coffee breaks and his computer assistance.
To Prof Roughy and Almudena for the memorable nights in and out.
To José Ramon (Chair) and his wife for organizing the Xmas party and the Madrid excursion.

I still plan on going to school (Colegio secundaria), this week, so stay tuned for another entry. I am looking at the reflection of my Crabby Diem T-shirt in the window. Dieter sneaked in the other day and shot an ugly?, but typical picture of the travel-reporter.

Martes, 30. Abril

From the panorama seat...

Pre-conference...Private school...School uniforms...Santa Maria Micaela...

I just got back from a **pre-observation conference** (we would call it in America) with my German-English colleague, Patricia, the daughter of Royal Carlos and Jolly Loli, and the sister of Marcos. Patricia[64] picked me up by the bus station in front of the City Hospital in order to show me her school, so that I could find the way tomorrow.

It is the only **private school** in a young neighborhood of high-rise apartment buildings, which grew from a village into a subdivision within the last ten years. Educated people prefer private schools to public schools. Since school is compulsory up to the age of 16, they don't even have to pay for private school, and the teachers' salaries are paid by the state also. A private teacher's salary is less, however. Why? I haven't found out, yet. Perhaps they have to deal with less discipline problems and can't be bought with money. Pupils have to wear school uniforms. Only for the last two years in school, are teenagers allowed to wear their own fashion. Teenagers are very self-conscious about clothing, and parents complain that they have to spend a lot of money on clothing and would rather have them wear uniforms.

Santa Maria Micaela used to be run by nuns, but there is only one nun teaching still among a young teaching staff of 30 teachers. Students have homework every day for six subject areas, and sometimes they complain. Lessons are from 9—1 p.m. with a 25-minute break and from 3:30-5:30 p.m. In the morning the sessions are 50 min. long, and in the afternoon 60 minutes. Students up to the age of 12 go home for lunch and teachers also. Patricia takes a 15-minute nap after lunch. I told her that I hit the couch, too, for a half-hour nap after my 8 to 9-hour school day (homework not included). Patricia said that English is the primary foreign language now, then French and German. Since the European Union, German has become more and more popular. They want to offer it to the 12-year olds, next year.

While we were sitting in this noisy, smoky Bar/Café (Patricia's favorite was closed), discussing tomorrow's chapter about German schools, grades and sched-

---

64. Spanish c= English th

ules, Nieves appeared all of a sudden in front of the window. She and her sister were going to have an afternoon coffee, too. (At 7:30 p.m.!) In the Bar she was greeted by another fellow. As the Germans say: 'Bekannt wie ein bunter Hund!'…'Popular like a colorful dog!' Half of Santander seems to know her. I am looking forward to diving into school life, tomorrow!

Jueves, 1. Mayo

From my Bahía seat...

Unions...School life...English class...No tolerance for...Nos concentramos!...LA...Bustamante...Uniforms... English at 3...German class...Roosevelt...Spanish Literature class...Federico Garcia Lorca...3 poems...Lunch room...Specific Questions...See you in Colorado!...

This is MY month of the year, my birth month. We'll celebrate in Floersheim on the 6th of May, but we may have to deal with less pleasant things first. Today is a holiday here, also in Germany: Day of the German Worker. It is a day for **Union** proclamations and demonstrations. While the Unions were very necessary to liberate the workers from inhuman conditions during the Industrial Age, nowadays, they sometimes go overboard and stay in the way of reasonable changes. The Bahía is hazy, today, but many little fisher boats are out there catching the fish of the day: I am counting at least 20 in my section. We will not travel today. We are done with sightseeing. One gets tired of that, too! Later, we'll go the University, because a) there are only 2 days left to finish up and b) Prof Roughy has invited us for lunch in the neighborhood.

I dove into **school life**, alright, yesterday. I even taught one hour of German. Since it was raining cats and dogs yesterday morning and I was running late, I took a taxi. No, it is not affordable: I paid 4,50 € versus 45 cents with the bus. When I arrived 5 to ten, all the primary kids with neat uniforms were waiting under the covered entry hall for the doors to open. Private tour busses brought them directly to the front steps. Patricia fetched me, before the crowd moved in, and introduced me to the headmaster, who was on her way to music class with a boom box in her hands.

My first observation hour from 10-10:50 I spent with an English colleague in a light-flooded classroom with a great vista to the mountains, but I had no time for dreaming. Her lesson was tightly structured with fast transitions, and she had no **tolerance for inattentive students**. "We have no time for this!" she said, when a student was repeating the same question as the one asked before. The topics of the lesson were adjectives, comparative, superlative[65] and the near future

---

65.   She did NOT have to explain the grammar expressions first!

form, the continuum like 'I am going to'. This particular lesson was grammar based and teacher-guided with many student applications.

A longer listening exercise about LA followed, which was well prepared with pre-guided questions, presenting the whole piece first, and then analyzing sentence by sentence. I especially liked her "**Nos concentramos!**" and the still atmosphere, before she hit the button on the boom box. She had them point out the continuous forms and frequently asked for translations. In the listening piece two teenagers were taking a sightseeing tour in **LA (Los Angeles)**, visiting Hollywood, the Jurassic Park, downtown Pueblo, the oldest part of town, and the Laker's Stadium. Interesting information was transmitted in a style tailored for teenagers. The teacher in her 30s was also dressed like a teenager: Modern, bell-bottom-hip jeans with a black belt and a black silk blouse. All the teachers of the young staff were dressed pretty casually.

The students were in their sixth year of English, British English! It was a full classroom with 30 students: 1/3 boys and 2/3 girls. I asked about the ratio: They ALL have to take English. There are 200 students in the upper grades (12y-16y) in this Colegio secundaria, half boys and half girls. It used to be an all-girls school in former times, when it was run by nuns. All the classrooms, I visited, were decorated with the crucifix over the blackboard and a picture or poster of Mother Mary. Student displays were hanging on the walls, and the classrooms had a personal-living-room ambiance: It is the home of the class, who stays together all day, except for lab hours and PE. The teachers move around to the classrooms like in Germany, also.

After the lesson I was surrounded by students, who were eager to try out their English on me. They asked me all kinds of questions about the purpose of my stay and the countries I had visited. They recommended two popular singers to me for my teens back home: **Bustamante** and Bisbal. When I said I liked their **uniforms**, they were all protesting and said that they were looking forward to next year when they could wear their own fashion. We took a nice group picture, and then Patricia picked me up for the 25-minute break. We went down to the basement to visit the nursery school with the 3-6 years olds. On the way, while eating her sandwich, Patricia said that the teachers start teaching English now from the age of three on. The little ones looked rico y guapo (cute and handsome) in their little 'Kittel' and immediately got me involved in a colored number game. I could have spent all day there.

After break, from 11:15-12:05 Patricia put me to work in her **German classroom**. What a difference in discipline! I attribute the noise level partly to the uniforms, which they don't have to wear anymore in 9th and 10th grade, partly to the two combined classes, and partly to the different developmental stage. These were 10th graders, I believe. They were in their first year of German, but with only 2 hours per week. Patricia gave a short introduction in Spanish about me and today's topics. After they had exhausted all the basic German-level-one questions on me like: What is your name? Where do you come from? Do you have brothers and sisters? How old are you?, Etc., I taught them structures for asking questions in their subject areas on specific days and basic time telling.

During the last 5 minutes I did 'Show and Tell' with my black **Roosevelt** Field and Track-shirt, talking about my school and my students, and then handed the 'sweaty' T-shirt over to Patricia: "It's like on the football field", I said, kissing her the Spanish way on both cheeks. "You have to wash it first. I got the idea this morning!" Then I said Good Bye to the students and the Math teacher, who also participates in this classroom on a regular basis in order to learn German. There is a zest for learning foreign languages among the educated. Next year, Patricia said, they are going to increase the foreign language hours: 4 hours for English and 3 hours for German. **With** homework, that's just as effective as a 5-hour course. Math and foreign languages are considered the most important in the curriculum.

Following my German lesson, Patricia handed me over to a German speaking **Spanish literature** teacher. From 12:10-1:00 p.m. I learned about Federico Garcia Lorca (1898) in Spanish as much as I could understand. The whole class wore spunky sweat suits, because they had sports that day. The kids were attentive and quiet. I think the "German" lady would not tolerate it any other way! First, the teacher gave an introduction about the "Romancero Gitano", **Federico Garcia Lorca**, about his 'obra poetica' and his two distinct phases: primera etapa and segunda etapa, covering the following movements: Futurismo, Cubismo, Expressionismo, Dadaísmo, and Surrealismo. Then she had students read the information in the literature book. While she re-read the paragraphs, she prompted the students to underline the important information. I asked for a book, too, because seeing the written Spanish, I can derive from Latin and French, and understand a whole lot more than just following orally.

I would have sponged up this lesson voraciously with a Spanish-level 5 ability, because they were dealing with **three poems** of Lorca: One about mothers in pain, which reminded me of my last poem, one about El Toro, celebrating the intelligence and strength of the Spanish bull, and the last romantic one: Romance de la Luna. I soaked up as much as I could with my level-one capabilities, but I also had the advantage of understanding poetry intuitively. The teacher tried to get the students to read the pieces like poetry and not like prose, but many had no antenna for this. I would have loved to over-dramatize the romantic reading about La Luna to invoke more response from the students, but I did not want to interfere with the lesson. However, they did a good analysis of that last poem together. Displaying feelings and passion is not for teenagers. They need to <u>play</u> it cool, and a rational analysis is a safe place to stay. There were 18 literature students in the class, a comfortable number to work with. All the students were used to sitting frontally. I did not see any group or partner work, or independent projects in these particular lessons. **Teenagers are the same everywhere**: A bit noisy, a bit rambunctious, cool, but curious, refreshingly open and energizing, and also energy depleting on some days.

After my observations Patricia and I went down to the basement to watch the lunch ritual of the day-care students, while most of the students went home for lunch. In this huge, noisy **lunchroom** with tables for 8, mostly the little ones ate lunch here, but there was also one table with older students, who raised their hands with the victory sign when I took a picture. Now I saw what role the nuns played in this institution: They ran the lunchroom with whistles and discipline. It looked like a family meal around the dinner table. Two nuns work in administration and one teaches religion, which is a subject area in most European schools. You can take ethics instead if you don't belong to any particular denomination.

After the lunchroom inspection we went to the teachers' lounge where I asked some **specific questions**:

>Now, what are the school hours for the older students exactly?

Mo, We, Fr 8-2 p.m. with a 25 min. break and 50-min. sessions

Tue and Th 9-1 p.m. and 3:30–5:30 p.m. with 60-min. sessions

>They have 30 instructional hours per week then, right?

Yes!

>What do you think is the reason private teachers earn a lower salary?

You have to pass a lot of state examinations for public school teaching, and it is a secure job, while we have yearly contracts.

>How many hours do you teach?

25 hours, and in public school they teach 15-18 hours. The higher degree you have, the fewer hours you have to teach. ('What a dream job: 15 teaching hours for me times 50-minute sessions!')

>What are those 2 years called from 16-18 years of age, after the compulsory schooling?

Bachillerato!

>Do they also have something like the German Abitur?[66]

It's called Selectividad, but you only have to take it when you continue with University. Can I take you home now?

>Not necessary! I'll take the bus to my massage-therapy appointment, and later I'll have a salad at Suizo Café. Thank you so much, sister! See you in Colorado, some day!

---

66. Difficult Final exam, state mandated, after 13 years of schooling. Counts for 36 credits in the USA!!!

Viernes, 2.Mayo

From the best seat of the house...

Last coffee break...Henkersmahlzeit...Not in the mood for...Lazy boy...Erasing my 'heart drive'?...Religio...

Today, we had our **last coffee break** with the people from the department around 1:10 p.m. Ignacio, who is my adopted Spanish son, will come back to the US in September for two months to live with us and do graduate work at CSU. We promised to stay in touch with the people and encouraged them to stop by in Ft. Collins.

At 2 p.m., Mother Nieves picked us up for one last meal in her piso. It is called '**Henkersmahlzeit**' in German, the meal=Mahl, before you are 'hanged'=Henker. The whole family was gathered around the dinner table for comida; At night it is called cena: Admiral Adolfo, Alejandro (16), the quiet, dreamy basket ball player, Elena (17), the sister with the blue eyes and dark hair that vivid Laura (26), the law student, had prayed for for so long. The older brother didn't live in the piso anymore. Everybody shared a room—well, Alex was the king, now—and one could observe that they were team players and children, who were mothered and fathered very well. It was very pleasant eating lunch in that harmonious family atmosphere.

Since Nieves was concerned about my frequent food allergies, she had cooked a very light meal: A creamy squash soup, oven-baked salmon, and fresas con nata (strawberries with whipped cream). Admiral Adolfo poured a light red wine from the South of Spain. We were **not in the mood for** teasing, but the children kept the Good Bye light, promising to show up some day. The piso had a beautiful layout, with two balconies overlooking the Bahia, the Light tower, and Magdalena Island, a spacey living room with two ocean-blue leather love seats, and a **Lazy Boy** for the Admiral to watch his German war movies and to smoke his pipo. Elena said that her father knew a lot of history, but that she had problems, tying all the historical facts together. She was going to study for a history test at the neighbor's later. The family and the neighbor had developed a long-standing tradition that the Admiral's kids could come over for studying to escape the beehive of little brothers and sisters. Later, Laura's boyfriend Ruben joined us for an after-lunch coffee, too, and the whole family and us had lively talks around the coffee table. They showed us pictures from their communion and when Nieves was a teenager. She looked like Elena.

Around 5 p.m., the Admiral and former basketball champ, took his son to basketball practice, and Mother Nieves brought us back to the University where we finished erasing our **hard drives**, while she was checking email. Half an hour later, she stopped by to say Good Bye, and handed me a sticker with their telephone number and address. We hugged and smiled, but on the way back to our piso, climbing up the hill, tears were rolling down my face. Maybe one should never say Good Bye, only Hello i.e. Hola!

What is it that hurts so much in a Good Bye? It is attachment, it is '**religio**': the bindings one has developed to another person. Buddhism preaches detachment. But when I am detached, I am not involved emotionally. If I am not involved emotionally, I don't feel deeply; I am just an observer. Then it seems to me that I don't really live life. Isn't that the purpose of our life here on earth to actually feel all the emotions, because those are also powerful motivators for personal development and artistic expressions in art, music and poetry? I think I take in the pain and am content with an earthly life for now: I would rather have deep 'religio' than be a detached 'saint'.

Sabado, 3. Mayo

From the sunken flowery couch...

Stuff...A gorgeous Good-Bye show...Back in time...Viva España!...

Two sections of the couch gave up now: I am sitting in the left hand corner of the couch, stuffed with cushions. It is all cleaned around me, no **stuff** anymore. The stuff is stuffed in our little blue 'coche' up to the max, waiting to leave tomorrow morning. It seems that clothing doubles in volume when you want to repack it again.

It is reflectively quiet now, after the fireworks over the Bahia, in commemoration of the French-Spanish war, ended with ten mark-trembling cannon shots. From 11:00-11:15 p.m., I watched the most breath-taking fireworks from the balcony: Fountains of stars in all colors were lightening up in the dark-blue night sky. Most of all, I loved the white star rain, floating towards me like the Milky Way from a space ship. It was a **gorgeous Good-Bye show**. Philipp II came **back in time**, one hour ago. We all sat around the dinner table, drinking our last two beers together and eating olives. Philipp had had a tough week in Barcelona, because five almost equally good candidates were competing, and the jury had to go through the process steps five times.

Since there were many leftovers, unopened jars and packages from the Doc's in-home-grocery shop, we had packed them all up for Armada and Philipp II for a take-out. Each one of us carried 2-3 bags over to their piso, and then it was time to say Good Bye. We hope to see them in Colorado, some day, because Dieter is really sick of traveling, now. He does not want to go anywhere for a long while: Adios! Hasta luego!

Viva España!

Vivamos en España!
Viviamos en España!
Nosotros revolveramos otres dias!

End of part 5: Spain

PART VI

Alzheimer's, Germany, Homecoming

From the upstairs kitchen table...

In a cage...Nervous breakdown...Panic look...Angel-like...German oak...Colorado blue spruce...55th birthday...Utterly alone...Golgotha... Letting go...

Back in Floersheim, in my husband's father's house: I am the keeper of the house, right now. I brought my mother-in-law (Oma), who lives **in a cage** because of her husband's (Opa) Alzheimer's, to the hairdresser. Once she looks like a lady, and not like a ten-year old mop, she'll feel a lot better. She told me to watch the bean soup that she cooked at 6 a.m. From 4 a.m. to 6 a.m. she ironed a load of laundry. She is eighty and ready to let go: Let go of her partner of 60 years of marriage, who needs around the clock care now. She already diapered him twice, this morning. My husband got him dressed and helped him with breakfast while I drove Oma to the beauty salon. Opa has deteriorated rapidly since my doctor son Sven visited him during spring break. It seems that he gathered all his strength to see his favorite grandson one more time. Now, he is resting next door in the living room in his armchair. His son is recovering downstairs from another nervous breakdown attack.

Tomorrow, he has to do the hardest chore in his life: Bring his father to the Landesklinik to get him medically adjusted for an Elder home. It can't be done at home anymore. Last week he fell and hurt his head badly. Yesterday, he fell twice, almost soundlessly onto the carpet. Since Alzheimer's patients not only lose their motor functions, but also their olfactory capabilities, he eats very little now. He moves with tiny little steps while holding onto both of my hands, as I pull him from the front. He has no muscle control over his bowl functions, and sometimes loses bladder control, too. During his restless phases he has that **panic look** on his face, moving aimlessly from his armchair to his chair at the kitchen table, back and forth, and back and forth until exhaustion sets in. Sitting in his armchair, he shivers and trembles like a Parkinson's patient. I put a blanket over him and caress his hands, his forehead and his heart. "Don't leave me!" he pleads in fear. "Don't worry! I'll stay till you rest." Finally, the horrific features of panic and crucifixion relax into an **angel-like** ascension face, and he dozes off for sometime, until the next attack comes.

During Opa's relaxation phases his son is overcome by the same symptoms, since his father's energies are out there looking for attachment between heaven and earth. When it started during the last ten days in Santander, I had a certain suspicion that it might have to do with his father's energies. But now it is experimental science: I calm down his father upstairs: he dozes off; I go downstairs and the same attacks start happening with his son: The same panic look, the same disaccorded movements, the racing heart, the heavy breathing, the cold sweat, the muscle twitching. You have to see it to believe it. At one time, when Dieter was holding his father's hand, the father said to his son: "Don't let me fall asleep. Keep me awake!" Did he know on a subconscious level, perhaps that his son was troubled with the same symptoms when he fell asleep?

Have you ever seen a **German oak** fall? That is how it feels for me right now. It was the saddest birthday ever. But I do not have time for tears. That may come later. I must stand strong like a **Colorado blue spruce**, grounded and flexible. Sharing joy is easy and light. Sharing pain shakes your inner core, your faith, and tests the strength of your own roots.

And in the midst all this human frailty and disorientation Opa congratulated me for my **55th birthday**, yesterday, when all my three sons called and he got 'wind' of it. They are my strongest pillars right now, but in the end everybody has to live through their own purgatory or hell utterly alone, even when there is a compassionate partner around.

Nurse Anneliese from the Sozialstation just left. She looks after the parents every day. She reassured us that tomorrow's '**Golgotha**' is a necessary step to everybody's recovery. She looks at the situation from a compassionate, professional standpoint, but the fact is that emotions are a lot stronger than the logical brain. Even if people wish for a certain outcome, the emotions rule the body, especially when the brain is rendered ill for some reason. One can only turn it over to a higher power then and mumble humbly: "Not My will, but Thy will I intend to fulfill."

Letting go is the secret to inner peace. The easier one can let go, the smoother the transition from life into death, from wake into sleep. Indians can sleep everywhere; they have peace of mind. In America, over 50 % of the population suffer from sleep disorders: They cannot find peace of mind. They cannot let go of fear and worries. They live in a constant stage of combat, fighting life itself. Life has to be lived from hour to hour, in the moment, from day to day. It has to flow like a river: easily, joyfully, sometimes smoothly, sometimes roughly. If the mind is concerned with worries about the future, one misses living in the moment. If the mind mourns the happenings of the past, one does not live in the present tense singular. If one does not live fully in the present, one will not have precious memories of that particular phase. Life is going by then like a landscape by an ICE train.

Thursday, May 8
End of WWII

From the balcony at Oma's…

Hardest ride…Opa…As long as the brain…Gorgeous flower bouquet from my three princes…Empty pockets…Manmade illusions…Absolute truth?…

It is 8:30 p.m. and a balmy 22°C, after a summery spring day in May. Birds are singing their evening songs, and pain-stricken souls are quieting down now, after a stressful morning: Opa has been brought into psychiatric care for four weeks, to St. Valentinushaus of the Landesklinik in Kiedrich. It was the **hardest ride** ever for his son to bring his father into 24-hour care. The psychiatric station for dementia patients has electronically locked doors on either end of the hallway, but within the station patients have free range of motion. His two-person bedroom is light-flooded and spacey with a large shower bathroom. The doctors and staff are compassionate, and have listening skills. Patients do not look drugged; they are encouraged to manage chores by themselves. Opa took his first lunch in the dining room, together with the patients from the floor. We watched him from the hallway: Sitting in a wheelchair with a "seat belt" on, because he would get up 20 times during a meal, he ate his bowl of soup with great appetite by himself. Then the nurse fed him three spoons of the main course and he was done, but his pudding he finished all by himself. That was more than what he had eaten at home, lately. After lunch we brought him to bed for a nap and promised to visit tomorrow.

At 2:30 p.m., foot care was already scheduled for him and physiotherapy for 4:30 p.m. to make his walking apparatus more mobile. But this will only be successful **as long as the brain** doesn't block those functions. They will get lost sooner or later, but meanwhile he needs to train and maintain the little functions that he has. He will have a hard time adjusting during the first week. Dieter felt his panic, his restlessness and his resistance during his nervous breakdowns. The energies of father and son are tightly connected at this point, and I hope both of them find peace and rest, soon.

Last night, a friend from our Colorado Club brought a gorgeous flower bouquet from my three sons with roses, gerbera, and mantas de la virgin, those white exotic flowers, which look like an upside-down mantle of Mother Mary. We talked about the state of affairs in "poor" Germany. "People <u>do</u> have money", he said, "but they sit on it tightly. They are scared because of the high number of unemployed people and the low economic growth rate. Officially, Germany's **pockets are empty** because huge amounts of money have flown into the reconstruction of the former East, into reparation for the so-called Russlandheimkehrer, Germans returning from their war exiles in Russia, and the big scandals of politicians stuffing their own pockets with public money. Spain thinks Germany is rich and the Germans themselves are seeing the half glass empty again.

I think it is all man-made: The stock market, the media hype, and how the psyche of a nation is manipulated into believing **manmade illusions**. Every creation is an illusion, because it can be created differently. It has nothing to do with the **absolute truth**. What is it that remains absolutely true? I think the power of love, compassion, light, patience, and also the power of fear, darkness and despair. Those exist as twin pairs within our dualistic earth experience. Without the darkness we would not know what light is. The darkness is a motivator then to bring more light into this world. Fear is a motivator for bringing more peace onto this planet. When there is peace of mind, there is no fear. When there is compassion, there is no hatred. When there is love, there is light and joy.

Saturday, May 10

Another CD[1]

Dark monstery shadows
Fill the brain with
Manmade illusions,
With walls of hopelessness
With cul-de-sacs of self-elimination.
Dark monstery voices tell you:
I am a failure.
I can't do it anymore.
I am lost.
There is no hope.
I must go.
I must die.

The heart races
The muscles twitch
The body curls into a fetal position
Arms and legs perform spastic rap
The colors of the eyes fade into a hopeless gray
And stare wildly and haunted into the ceiling
The attack lasts thirty minutes
Then the body is relieved by exhaustion
The mind gets a break
Until the next wave of fear builds up to drown the patient
Down into the muddy grounds of the soul.
What is it that has been depressed for so long?
That it explodes from the depth of the being,
Inducing a shortage, causing a power outage?
No energy left. It is all eaten up
By the monster of fear:

---

1.   CD=Clinical Depress

Self-accusations, self-beatings, self-destruction.
How does one switch on the Light again?

Potawi

Monday, May 12

From my fluffy down-bed...

Angels along the way...Hugs from a strange lady...Russian doctor...Gerontological research...Home away from home...Age pyramid...

How does one switch on the light again, I asked two days ago. Well, there are always **angels along the way**. Her name is Gudrun, and she is a light-worker at Mt. Abu. She helped me jumpstart the patient in Frankfurt, today, during a Raji meditation. She happened to be in Frankfurt because of her father's illness. We got to know her at Mt. Abu in India. It was a rather brief encounter, which developed into an email friendship between the Angel and the patient. Tonight, our "hero"[2] could even study a doctorate paper of a PhD candidate. It will be an 8 to 12-months healing process with ups and downs, but at least the self-healing process has been started, today. This illness is a self-defeating hell: Hugh Downs from 20/20 suffered from it, too, and many other close friends have confessed their clinical depressions to us, also. We will overcome!!!

Opa is doing better in the Landesklinik than at home. He gained a little weight, and his walking apparatus is steadier, because they trained him in physiotherapy to take bigger steps. He recognizes us and there is an emotional bond, but he hardly makes sense in his utterances. In spite of the sad situation, he made us all laugh: When we took a stroll with him in his wheelchair through the clinic's beautiful gardens, a young 'deranged' woman patient walked towards him, hugged him and said: "I need to give you love. What is your name?" Opa, not being used to getting **hugs from strange ladies**, said to me: "Get me out of here fast!" The emotional body responds acutely, but the logical brain is immobilized.

Opa lives together with a nice roommate: An eighty-year old teacher, who still reads a lot of books, even if he forgets the contents of the previous page. Therapeutic talks between his family and us ease the pain of leaving a loved one in professional care. The hospital's staff is remarkable: On a bright Sunday afternoon, a **Russian woman doctor** took the time to diagnose and medicate my "hero's" breakdown during a long therapeutic talk. Illnesses of the body are widely

---

2.   Coined by our Indian host professor

accepted, but illnesses of the mind and soul are still stigmatized by society. All ill-nesses originate on the soul-level, and then manifest into the three-dimensional physical body. Also Opa's progressive illness and aging process are frightening for most people, who try to avoid any confrontation with the topic "death and dying", but the fact is that we all have to go through the final stages of surrender-ing and letting go. So, during his illness, he is teaching us to be better prepared for the finishing round. Even the simple acts of diapering, washing, feeding and dressing are lessons in human dignity and humbleness for the caregiver. He needed to go to the bathroom five times while we were there. At first I called the nurse, but then I did it by myself.

Not only is the Landesklinik, but also the elder homes are conducted accord-ing to modern gerontological research, nowadays: Free range of motion as much as possible; daytime activities, such as dance, music, movement, arts and crafts; common meals in the dining room; light-flooded, homey-looking rooms deco-rated with personal items; communal living room with TV and stereo; all-day vis-itation and trained, compassionate staff. We inspected different institutions in Frankfurt, Ruesselsheim and Floersheim. All of these were pleasant **homes away from home**. The average age in a nursing home is 85, and the director said: "You'd better put yourself on a waiting list when you are 60, if you need the space later or not, because the **age pyramid** will reverse." From my observations, there is a life in nursing homes, just a different one. Nobody can give adequate care 24 hours a day, especially not with an Alzheimer's patient. It could be done with a large family living near by, but not with 80-year old Oma and us living in America. It was the right decision!

Tue3sday, May 13

From the down-stair's living room...

Apathetic...Water steam...Sucking life energy...Anchor of peace...

What a change from the Spanish rhythm! This house, and the whole neighborhood, quiet down very early. I am the only one up at 10 p.m., sitting yoga-style on the carpet after a short Raji meditation. Oma and I drove to the hospital by ourselves, today, because my warrior needed rest. Opa was very **apathetic**, today, drifting in and out of 'dreamland', but his gaze was relaxed. There was no panic in his eyes. At first, he thought we were in a restaurant, because he asked if we had paid already. He used to ask this about 20 times when he still was able to go out. That was his greatest worry: Leaving the restaurant without having paid. Many of his utterances got stuck half way through the sentence, then he lost track of what he was going to say. However, one utterance of his aroused my attention: "What is this **water steam**, which is coming from your neck?" he asked Oma. Obviously he is seeing auras during his unfocused, relaxed gaze.

I had to chuckle, lately when I read through the side effects of a specific medicine: Seeing spheres around objects was classified as **hallucination**. Well, the truth is, they do exist. I don't see them all the time around people and objects, but I have seen them often enough during alpha-brain-wave states in meditation, that I do know they are real. Maybe, we really should listen and learn more from the children and those living beyond 'real' life. Children sometimes have memories of former lives and tell stories about it, but the adults dismiss those as children's fantasies. But I guess one has to experience those phenomena first hand, or they will stay intangible.

An Alzheimer's patient is not able to describe the illness for you, but a clinically depressed person can tell you exactly what happens during the attacks: dark insurmountable walls, deep black holes of hopelessness, tempting voices to eliminate yourself. Both illnesses suck the **life energy** out of people: Their eyes look frightened, staring, sometimes lifeless and 'dead'. Even if I experience it second hand, I will never comprehend the full scope of it, unless I have to live through it myself. It must be hell. Meanwhile, I try to be an **anchor of peace** during all those turbulences in-between Oma's outbreaks of hopelessness, her son's dark attacks, and Opa's disorientation. I long for the Colorado sun and my son! Home, sweet home!

Saturday, May 17

From my fluffy down-bed…

Heart pain…Kidney failure…Coffin-cold…Warrior home…Escapes from reality…On the road to recovery… Boat to Helgoland…Go towards the sun…Make love to you own heart…

My **heart pain** has returned through seeing and feeling all the suffering around me. We have two turbulent days behind us. Thursday, we got a call from St. Valentinushaus that Opa needed to be transferred to St. Josef's in Ruedesheim to the Urological clinic because of a bladder infection. The irony is that I reported that urological problem three days ago to the nurse, because Opa needed to go to the bathroom every 10 minutes. Next time, I will do it in writing and have it signed by the Oberarzt[3]; then I'll get their attention. It wasn't just a bladder infection either; it was already a kidney failure. I saw the diagnosis on the chart, yesterday, although I had already figured this out, seeing the malt-beer-brown urine in the plastic bag coming from his catheter. The man was already in the grave with one leg. The left side of his body was **coffin-cold** from his foot to his hand; his face had a pale yellow, waxy complexion, typical for dying patients. His breath smelled like the sweet urine of kids, and his breathing was heavy and achy. Fortunately, the blood pressure was steady: 156/65, so he did recover overnight with bottles of antibiotics in intensive care at St. Josef's. We had already alarmed the family, and our two older boys will be flying in on a military plane to Ramstein, today. I just heard on the phone that they didn't make it out of Maryland, last night, because the plane only had 42 seats and lots of cargo. They hope to arrive tomorrow. Our boys will take over for a while, driving Oma to the hospital, which is 70km away from Floersheim, and Dr. Max will watch over Opa from a medical perspective, also. I need to bring my **Warrior home**, because he is running on his last burner.

Oma is holding up as much as possible, but once in a while she is drowning her sorrows in a water glass of cognac and then the lamenter begins: She is either seeing the world as one big pile of cow manure, or with her pink glasses on. I guess that's how she **escapes reality**, because with Alzheimer's, there is no road to

---

3. Overseeing doctor

recovery. Her daughter, who lives in Texas, will fly in on June 1, and take care for two weeks. Then Dr. Max will fly in with his family again, so that she gets to know her great-grandkids, Tommy and Nikolaus. After the family visitations, Oma has to learn to live by herself and start to nourish 'Elli' again. We installed an in-home-emergency call for her, and also gave the key to the house to the neighbors. The cleaning and shopping service is still arranged and nurse Anneliese will look after her several times a week. We hope that she will discover life again, join her club of former classmates, take day trips, and undertake all the pleasant things she used to do five years ago. We hope that Opa will be transferred to the nursing home in Floersheim after the 4-6-week stationary at St. Valentines, so that Oma can easily visit whenever she feels like it.

We just returned from the hospital. Opa is on the **road to recovery**. He has opened his beautiful, blue shiny eyes to greet us. He even made me laugh again: I asked him: "Did you take your boat to Helgoland, last night?" "What would I do in Helgoland?" he asked back. "I thought that was the island where Dieter was 'made'. "No, that was Sylt[4]", said Oma. That night, when he was on the brink of death, Dieter and I used several mantras while rubbing his third eye, and holding his hand and feet to jumpstart his energy again, or to give him comfort to cross over. One of my mantras was: "Go towards the sun!" because he was ice-cold. And then I remembered that he loved the sea, because he had been in the Navy: "Take your boat to Helgoland!" I suggested, but I had forgotten it was the island of Sylt. It is hard to expand your energy in-between an 80-year old lady with an after-combat syndrome[5], a husband with a nervous breakdown, and an almost dying patient in the hospital. Sometimes, my legs are so weak that I feel shaky and depleted. That's when I need to take care of myself through meditation and prayer, music and writing. One can only nourish others if one gives enough **love to one's own heart**. And through all those processes I have learned that it is my calling to be a teacher—not only in the classroom.

---

4. Sylt and Helgoland are two vacation islands in the North Sea. Opa was stationed on Sylt during WWII.

5. The stress level of taking care of an Alzheimer's patient is comparable to a soldier on the front lines.

Sunday, May 18

From my favorite window seat in the down-stair's kitchen...

Stuff...Transformation...The Ultimate light...Self-evaluation...Teaching process...Healing process...

It is a peaceful Sunday morning; well, as peaceful as it can get in this house under these circumstances. My Warrior is packing, shaking his head every 5 minutes about the amount of **stuff** he has to pack. Oma is cooking in the upstairs kitchen. I vacuumed and mopped upstairs and downstairs. Then I 'mopped' myself, and now I feel some equilibrium again.

Last night, when I was about to fall asleep past midnight, I found myself looking directly into Opa's eyes. He has undergone a remarkable **transformation**. The eyes of old, sick people look dull with a thick opaque film, and sometimes 'death shadows' appear in the outer iris. That's how his eyes looked before the kidney failure. But yesterday, they were clear and blue-gray with lots of light shining through from the inside. He could not keep them open for very long, because he was deathly tired, having returned from the graveyard. Actually what I think has happened is that he returned from the **Ultimate Light**; that he had a life-review where his whole life was shown to him in 'fast-forward', and he had to do his own **self-evaluation**. There is no condemnation, maybe in severe cases: Only trial and error. Learning takes place, if not in this life then in the next life. He had been filled with light and peace by the Ultimate Light, and sent back to be of further use in the **teaching process** for others. His former dull, pain-stricken eyes underwent a transformation, and if he had a memory, he could tell us what happened that night when his body went grave-cold. I think the oxygen therapy also helped clear a bit of his dementia, but I do not have time anymore to observe this. It is our last day here; then our sons, Alex and Sven, and Opa and Oma's daughter Gabi, my sister-in-law, will take over. We need our life back and my "Hero" needs to start his own healing process.

Monday, May 19

On the plane from Frankfurt to Denver...

Flying...

Flying above white clouds
With the sunshine on my face
I imagine that I will always
Fall into soft cotton clouds
That angels will pick me up
Should my wings get stuck
That I will fly towards the Sun
and never run dry
Nor shy away
To conquer the Dark.
I am a Warrior of Light:
I will fight for the Light
On my flight to my soul's
Original homeland.

Potawi

Friday, May 23

E.T. home...From my front deck...

Columbines...Dark attacks...Opa back in Floersheim...Healing process...Homecoming...Love and caring...

Columbines, the state flowers of Colorado, are blooming all around me in our yard, and puppy seeds and bachelor buttons in their complimentary orange and blue colors are surrounding me. It is pleasantly warm at 7:30 p.m. My youngest son, Manuel, who lives in Ft. Collins with his fiancé, Vange, drove my Warrior to the hardware store to get some plumbing parts for the leaking sprinkler system. Handy-work will calm down his overloaded nerve circuit. He has several dark attacks during the day, but I get him out of bed again and again. He was diagnosed with 'Chemical imbalances in the brain', and we utilize allopathic and alternative healing methods combined. Doctors say it will be a yearlong process to get back to normal. Right now, I coach him through the day, but in group and individual therapy, or by himself, he will learn how to offset these attacks.

Opa has been **transferred** to the hospital in Floersheim, which is only 100 meters away from Oma's house, so that she can look after him several times a day. He was bedded on an air mattress immediately to get relief from his bedsores. Since he doesn't eat, they have put him on infusions. He responds to Oma briefly and clearly, but drifts away fast. Oma sounds a lot better over the phone now, and I told her she could contribute to her son's **healing process** and to her own one by thinking positive thoughts.

Although I brought a sick warrior home, our **homecoming** was beautiful: Our kids, Vange and Manuel, had decorated the house with flower bouquets and note cards. Kay and Bruce, neighborhood friends, had put a colorful flowerpot by the entrance door, and brought us lunch in a picnic basket the next day. At night, the former chairman and his wife, Jim and Elaine, dropped by to bring us supper from the farmer's market. They left their cell phone number too, in case I needed help. People are beautiful all around the world. What binds us all together is **love and caring**.

Monday, May 26, 2003

From my front porch...

Memorial Day...Rainbow...Fighting for his life...Spiritual healing...

Raindrops are tapping on the roof. The warm summer rain is leaving a refreshing ozone smell in the air. We have returned from barbecuing at our son and daughter-in-law's condo (=piso) This **Memorial Day** will stay in my memory forever, because Dieter had several attacks, this morning, and when it was getting too intense, I called Manuel and Vange over to help 'snap him out of it'.

<There is a beautiful rainbow appearing right in front of me, the **rainbow** of hope, the alliance between heaven and earth>

Lying in the midst the loving circle of his family, the convulsions diminished gradually, then his body collapsed into a phase of exhaustion and peace. I wish I could present you with a happy ending, but the Hero is **fighting for his life**, right now. And besides, the Ambassador's second hero[6] died from a gunshot, and that's when his novel ended. When Dieter has overcome these dark forces, he'll be a real hero, because they fight love of life itself.

Manuel smudged the whole house with sage afterwards to clear the energies. That is an old Native American cleansing ritual. It is not a matter of medicine solely; it is mainly a matter of **spiritual healing**. Now, that the physical journey of his sabbatical is finished, I will accompany my Hero on his healing path. May your prayers be with us!

Go back to page 205 of part 5 and read the Thank you and Good byes! After that, email any enlightening comments to renaterainbow@web.de., Or email to: renaterainbow@earthlink.net

Auf Wiedersehn
Hasta luego
Good bye
Thanks for having been my co-traveler and back-up on this outer and inner journey. With love and gratitude: Potawi

---

6.   See end of part 3: India

Finally, I can dismiss you on a positive note:
June 4, 2003: Dieter's father died at 6 p.m. German time, today, and for the first time, his son slept through the night again which has not happened for 7 weeks. May the Light bless both of them and give them peace!
On August 6, 2003, Oma followed her husband. They could not stay apart.

End of book

0-595-75098-2

Printed in the United Kingdom
by Lightning Source UK Ltd.
107575UKS00002B/76